KT-910-736

A Matter of People

OTHER BOOKS BY DOM MORAES

Prose:

Gone Away (1960)
My Son's Father (1968)
The Tempest Within (1970)
The People Time Forgot (1972)

Poetry:

A Beginning (1957)
Poems (1960)
Collected Poems, 1955–1965 (1966)
John Nobody (1968)

Translation:

The Brass Serpent (translated from Hebrew, 1964)

A Matter of People

DOM MORAES

ANDRE DEUTSCH

First published 1974 by
André Deutsch Limited
105 Great Russell Street London WC1

Copyright © 1974 by United Nations Fund for Population Activities
All rights reserved

Printed in Great Britain by
Lowe & Brydone (Printers) Ltd,
Thetford, Norfolk

Hardback ISBN 0 233 96578 5
Paperback ISBN 0 233 96579 3

To Leela

The views expressed in this book are those of the author and do not necessarily reflect the policies or directions of the United Nations or any of its member states.

Preface

When, in February 1973, the U.N. Fund for Population Activities asked me to write a personal book about world population problems, I was delighted and flattered. I was also utterly mystified, since I knew nothing about population. Why me? I wondered. Since this is something the reader may also be wondering, I had better elucidate the point. The UNFPA said that they wanted the book to be read by the literate layman, who knew as little about population as I did. The reader would share my experiences as I traveled from country to country, see what I saw, hear what I heard, learn what I learned. And as for why me in particular, I was born in Asia and worked there for some years, and I was educated in Europe and worked there for many years: I had a foot in each continent. It was a huge assignment, involving intensive travel and writing over a period of six months, but I was happy to accept it. My wife, Leela, who is also my secretary and my extra pair of eyes and ears, packed our cases and we set off.

Now it is over, I wonder how we did it. There was plane after plane, country after country, endless drives through strange terrain, interviews, a series of hotel rooms in which I sat and wrote. But it *is* over, and I have learned a lot, though I don't know if the reader will. When I started this trip I thought the whole problem lay in what is called "the population explosion." Now I think it is purely a matter of people.

I owe so much to so many organizations and individuals all over the world that were I to list them all it would take up the next few pages. So I would simply like to thank everyone who helped and befriended us, everywhere we went.

New York City   Dom Moraes
October 1973

A Matter of People

CHAPTER ONE

"Better to have one leopard than ten jackals."

The hawk stood on the wind, freckled wings widespread and immobile, for an endless second. Then it took a short step and dropped down the wind's escalator to earth. Its claws stretched forward, its wings pulled back, and it braked itself on the crumbled brown peak of the village rubbish heap. The scrawny dogs that sniffed around the bottom of the rubbish heap did not even look up. They had scaly, hairless skins, covered in sores.

The main thoroughfare of the village, Dayalpur, went past the rubbish heap. It was a narrow, unmade lane. A gutter ran down the middle of it, full of black water and human and animal excrement. It was difficult to walk down the lane, since unattended buffaloes constantly blundered by, but presently we turned into a small doorway set in a mud wall. Beyond it was a courtyard, with a low mud house off to one side. "In this house," said the auxiliary nurse, a stout woman in a *sari*, "lives a woman who practices family planning. But she is very poor. *Tcha*, she is very ignorant. If you want to ask her questions, ask, ask. But I do not know exactly what she will answer."

The woman sat on an unsteady rope bed on the porch in front of her small house. She had the look of a frightened hare. She was thirty years old, she said, and her husband was a year older. They had three daughters, the eldest of whom was at school. She wanted another child in about three years' time; meanwhile, her husband used condoms. "I get weak if I have children one after the other," she said in a small hoarse voice. "Also my husband

3

is a landless laborer, so how can we afford to feed and clothe many children?" I asked her why, in that case, she wanted to have a fourth child. When the question had been translated, a look of utter terror came to the woman's face.

"Why are you asking me these questions? Are you a doctor? Have you come to operate on me and make me sterile? How can you be so heartless? I told you that as yet I have no son. Please wait till I have a son." We tried to soothe her, but she was ruffled and suspicious now, and eventually we left and walked back, avoiding collisions with cattle, past the huge, smelly rubbish heap scuffled over by scavenging birds, to the Rural Health Center. In the gutter, children floated chips of wood that would never reach a sea. Around Dayalpur the brown plain stretched out to the horizon, laden with fields, haystacks, buffalo wallows, and people—a nameless number without end.

India has 560 million people: Every seventh person in the world is an Indian. Though it is a huge country, sprawling southward from the chilly edge of Central Asia into the tropics, and though large tracts of it are barren and uninhabitable, the population density in 1971 was 168 per square kilometer. Some Indians, a very small number, are extremely wealthy: business tycoons, film stars, and the former princes, many of whom tend to increase their income by tax defalcations. But the mass of the people are poor, unimaginably so to a Western eye. To clothe and feed their children adequately has always been very nearly impossible for the countless families who live on the edge of disaster.

Yet children have always continued to arrive—in enormous numbers. The more mouths there were to feed, the less there was to feed them with. Until 1921 epidemics, famines, and chronic malnutrition yearly killed off nearly as many people as were born. After that year, with the introduction of modern techniques of medicine, the death rate began to fall and the population to soar. The British, who had come to India in the sixteenth century as traders, and who remained as rulers until 1947, seem to have been dimly aware of the problems that would ensue if people continued to multiply at such a pace, but they do not seem to have done very much about it.

The growth rate of population in a country is obtained by sub-

tracting the death rate from the birth rate. In the ten years between 1911 and 1921, the birth rate per 1,000 of the population
was 48.1, and the death rate 47.2. That meant that the growth
rate was minimal. The average life expectancy for an Indian ten
years later, in 1931, was twenty-seven years, which admittedly
cannot be called high, but while the birth rate over the years
between 1921 and 1931 had stayed fairly steady, at 46.4 per 1,000,
the death rate had dropped to 36.3 per 1,000. That meant an increase of 28 million people over ten years, and some people began
to see portents in the sky.

As early as 1925, a Maharashtrian doctor, R. D. Karve, started
a birth control clinic in Bombay, and in the 1930s the voice of
Margaret Sanger, that early prophet of family planning, was heard
in the land. She acquired a number of disciples, mainly society
women anxious to prove that they had the problems of the country at heart. She might have acquired more had Mahatma Gandhi
chosen to lend the movement his support—he thought it was
unnatural, and didn't. Between 1931 and 1941 38 million more
people were added to the Indian landscape. By 1951 there were
44 million more, and the population of India stood at 361 million.

Since in 1901 the population had been 238 million, this meant
that 123 million more people lived in the country than had lived
in it fifty years before. The first Health Minister, a Kashmiri
princess, Raj Kumari Amrit Kaur, added a family planning department to her office. After her, other health ministers came and
went. They were efficient in that the death rate continued to
drop, from 27.4 per 1,000 in 1951 to 22.8 in 1961. Because of this,
the growth rate over these ten years rose steeply: By 1961 another
78 million had been added to the population, which by now stood
at 439.2 million. The government budget for family planning was
increased.

Between 1961 and 1971, the growth rate rose further. The birth
rate in 1971 was estimated to be around 39 per 1,000, but the
death rate had come down still more, so that 110 million people
had been added to the total population in the previous ten years.
The government had been able to make the country more viable,
agriculturally, than it had been for centuries. Industry had increased. But when it came to birth control, the gestures of the
government seemed to be as futile as those of Canute fighting

the rising tide. By 1973 it was accepted that 12 million people were being annually added to the population, steadily and inexorably.

What this means is that by the turn of the century, at the present growth rate, the population of India will have doubled itself, and a billion people will inhabit, or try to inhabit, the country.

The successive ministers of Health and Family Planning have made increasingly desperate efforts to stem the flood. Some of the solutions they have come up with have been slightly comic. Raj Kumari Amrit Kaur called in an American expert, Dr. Abraham Stone, who dreamed up a way of propagating the rhythm method —that is, the method whereby intercourse is practiced only at safe periods—through ornaments, dear to the hearts of Indian women. Bead necklaces were issued to women who wanted to practice this method: some beads were green, representing a dangerous period; some red, signifying a safe one. The women, by shifting the beads around, were supposed to calculate what their safe and dangerous periods were—a simple method, it was thought, for the illiterate. "The beads were of no value," Ashish Bose, the economist, told me in Delhi. "So the women didn't want to wear them. They would give them to their children as toys. I've seen it myself. The children, of course, would shift all the beads around." The upshot was that of every hundred women who received these necklaces, fifty became pregnant.

The Government of India, in the late 1960s, acquired an elephant whose function was to amble around the rural areas near Delhi, carrying condoms, which it distributed, free, to the supposedly eager populace. Several years back, in 1969, I saw the animal in action: It clearly preferred children to adults and scattered its cargo freely amidst the toddlers of every village it visited. The toddlers instantly saw the practical value of the rubbers, blew them up into small balloons, and tied them to sticks. A slogan in family planning is that your children should be happy. In that sense I suppose the campaign succeeded—these children most certainly were.

There have been other little absurdities. The government of Maharashtra state offered a free transistor radio, some years back, to any man willing to be sterilized. Transistors were expensive;

hence to distribute them on any really large scale, the government had to have cheap ones manufactured. This enabled it to afford to hand out transistors, but it also enabled a poor man to buy a transistor without having to be sterilized. All these measures now seem funny, because they failed. Had they succeeded, they would probably be praised as instances of imaginative improvisation in the face of an insoluble problem, which in a way they were.

The publicity campaign for family planning operates on a huge scale. The radio talks about it; so does the television, though the range of the latter is limited. Advertisements for Nirodh condoms appear on buses, trains, and every handy wall. So do the posters depicting parents beaming over two radiant childish faces, with the slogan *Do Ya Teen Bacche Bas*, that is, "two or three children are enough." The inverted red triangle, the family planning symbol, has become a feature of the landscape: not only can it be seen on every city wall, but in the countryside it is painted or pasted on rocks and trees in the most unlikely spots.

How far all this has registered on the ordinary Indian is difficult to ascertain. The Rural Health Center at Dayalpur, a collection of whitewashed houses at the edge of the village, is one of a chain of clinics and subcenters whose headquarters are at Ballabhgarh. This is a small town, a village until it was recently trodden on by the heavy foot of light industry. The Ballabhgarh operation, run by the central government, covers an area of 368 square kilometers in Harayana state near Delhi. There are 94,000 people in this area, and they inhabit ninety-two villages of varying sizes. I was told by field workers that 95 per cent of the people had heard of family planning.

But only 18 per cent of the eligible couples (couples of procreative age with more than two children) practiced it, the field workers said. At lunch in Dayalpur, we encountered six young interns who had been sent to the Ballabhgarh area by the Indian Medical Institute to obtain experience in rural conditions. They were bright young people, and I asked them what they had done during their stay. One laughed bitterly and said, "Nothing. We go into a remote village to vaccinate people, and nobody will come near us. They think we have been sent by the government to sterilize them. They don't trust us. They don't know what we are trying to do."

The Ballabhgarh Health Center was shady and pleasant, an escape from the huge sun overhead. The patients lay on iron beds in the wards; a couple of the women had recently had tubectomies. In a tree-lined courtyard the outpatients squatted awaiting their turn with the doctor. "We treat people for stomach trouble, eye complaints, fevers," said Dr. Lalit Nath, who is in charge of the whole Ballabhgarh operation. "But the be-all and end-all isn't simply the patient's recovery. We also want to know why they fell ill, what to do in the future, and so on, a research sort of thing, you know. And we train young interns like the ones you met at Dayalpur."

Dr. Nath is a spry, dapper man who was trained, and indeed practiced for a while, in the United States. "Part of our health care," he said, "is family planning. It's always seemed to me that those government posters that say 'Two or three children are enough' place too much emphasis on family limitation. What we try and say here is that the family with a healthy mother is a happy family, that a well-nourished child is a happy child. We try and emphasize the area where family planning and nutrition overlap." He led us down a cool corridor to a small room where a woman in her middle years worked at a desk. "She's the family planning adviser to patients."

The woman folded her hands in the traditional Indian *namaste*. She had a very sweet smile. "I have been doing posters, you see," she said, pointing to the rubble of papers in the room. "Sometimes I paint them myself, sometimes I cut pictures out of magazines and paste them on the posters, and I make up slogans that will appeal to our people. See this one." She held up a poster adorned with cutouts of wild animals. "The slogan says, 'Better to have one leopard than ten jackals.' It is a local proverb, and the people understand it. The posters are displayed at all the centers in our district." She smiled and folded her hands once more, in farewell.

This emphasis on what is locally acceptable seemed to me admirable. The various centers in the district employ a number of auxiliary nurses who are also midwives, like the one who had taken us round at Dayalpur, and a number of field workers, who are drawn as far as possible from the local population. They speak the dialect of the district and have contacts with the people.

Those that I met were sturdy, down-to-earth, dedicated women with children of their own. "Some people send out young educated women as field workers," Dr. Nath said. "But firstly the villagers can't understand them, and secondly they're usually unmarried, you see. That's a disadvantage." What he meant was that village women, when lectured about childbirth by an unmarried girl, tend to tell her to marry and have children before she talks about them. It was through discussions with the local field workers and with the doctors at Ballabhgarh and Dayalpur that I began for the first time to understand the diverse and complex difficulties of introducing family planning to rural India.

The economic advance of India has been slowed by the inert mass of people who depend on it; more additions to the mass may well bring the economic advance to a standstill. Time is desperately short, but in this short time the family planners have to shift an entire tradition.

For centuries the Indian peasant has lived by the maxim that the more children he has, the more help he will have, not only in the fields, but in the occasional village feuds. He particularly wants to have sons, as an insurance for his later years. The joint family system is still common in India, even among the educated: The parents, when old, are looked after by and live with a son. The daughters, once married, are, so to speak, out of the family proper. The peasant therefore aspires to have a son—preferably more than one.

The reason for this is twofold. A son may turn out badly. He may quarrel with his parents or prove to be shiftless or a drunkard. It's better, therefore, to have a couple of sons, so that you can fall back on one if the other shows no traces of filial piety. Secondly, about 170 out of every 1,000 children born in India die in the first year, through congenital diseases or infections. Though the peasant may not know the exact figures, he knows from experience that babies are apt to die. He wants to be sure that if one son dies there will be a replacement. In the Ballabhgarh district, Dr. Nath said, most couples wanted between four and five children.

In Ballabhgarh, as in many other parts of India, Hindus and Muslims live in the same areas. The priests of the two creeds do not, Dr. Nath told me, oppose family planning, but some of the villagers, both Hindu and Muslim, remember the bloody communal killings in 1947, and each side feels that to allow the size of its community to diminish would be an open invitation to mayhem by the other side. This mutual distrust, at least in this particular part of north India, is traditional. Traditions are the hardest of all windmills to tilt at: They aren't solid; they are not only in the blood but in earth and rock and wind, an invisible essence of all.

There is a totally fundamental level on which Indian tradition is opposed to the concept of family planning. For thousands of years the *lingam*, or phallus, has been worshiped all over India: In a small village temple, shaded by scented trees, a visitor can see a statue of a *lingam* and often a *yoni*, the female sex organ. The prayers and blessings at a Hindu marriage are all to do with the desirability of procreation. Similarly, a villager may curse someone by wishing him to be infertile. Tradition stresses that to be philoprogenitive is a virtue. Most young Indian men feel insecure about sex, because so much emphasis is placed upon the virtues of virility—and because premarital sex is rare in India.

The difficulties of a village couple who want to practice birth control are real. And they are physical as well as mental. In the villages of Harayana, though the state is one of the most prosperous in India, most joint families sleep in a sort of communal bedroom. There is little space in which to store anything, and it is impossible to keep what you possess a secret from the rest of the family. Hence, supplies of condoms and oral contraceptives are soon discovered by the elders, who are bound to disapprove. Moreover, the difficulties of arising at night in an unlit and crowded room to find a condom are considerable. The same applies to the diaphragm. What's more, most young couples find it inhibiting and embarrassing, naturally enough I would think, to make love in a bedroom occupied by up to a dozen other people. The best opportunity for sexual activity is in the fields, where it often occurs spontaneously, and neither husband nor wife, however much they may want to practice family planning, has had any chance of preparing for it.

It is against all these odds that the doctors, the auxiliary nurses, and the fieldworkers, plodding for miles through dusty fields in summer and torrential rain in the monsoon to bring an unwanted message, labor.

Dr. Nath has ten doctors in his district: Six of them are hospital doctors. The other four cover a population of nearly 100,000 to administer direct services. Each doctor has, potentially, to cover 25,000 patients. Though the dimensions of the work are titanic, Dr. Nath is unquelled. Around the lawns of the Ballabhgarh Health Center are plots of vegetables. "I'm trying to get the local people to grow these vegetables," he said. You know, I don't think most vegetarians in India would eat only vegetables by choice if they could afford it, but here the people don't eat them at all, as a rule. They grow them, but usually only for sale.

"But no population could last, by definition, unless it had a balanced diet, and obviously the ancestors of these people had one. If you ask a villager what he would like to eat if he could afford it, he will tell you meat, milk, fruit, eggs, though not vegetables. Still, fruit gives you what vegetables give you: It's a balanced diet, probably what his ancestors, a long time ago, were eating. If we could lower the infant mortality rate, so that the villager didn't have to store up children like a squirrel storing up nuts for winter, the birth rate would, I think, fall. We could lower the infant mortality rate if the villagers ate a balanced diet, but . . ."

Dr. Nath shrugged, a small, wry, civilized shrug. "The corollary, lowering the birth rate, is difficult, too. I told you the drawbacks of the pill and the condom and the diaphragm. The loop hasn't been too successful, either, because sometimes the woman bleeds a lot, and her periods become heavier, and also, because there's a foreign body in her, she feels uncomfortable. In the villages, talk about this is passed on from woman to woman, and so there's resistance. Vasectomy for men, tubectomy for women, yes, perhaps, but the villagers resist this as well. It's a castration fear with men, and women are afraid of the unknown."

We were sitting in his office at Ballabhgarh, a cool room, though the afternoon sun glared off the grass outside. Dr. Nath looked a little tired; his sport coat had acquired unintended creases since I had first met him that morning. "It must be a hell of a job," I said, "this," and he laughed. "You know," he said, "I used to be a consultant in America. I made a lot of money there. I made several times my present salary. But you can't stay hidden away from the place you are needed in forever. I knew I had to come back." He looked out of the window at the neat vegetable plots. "It's a hell of a job," he said after a long pause. "But I'm glad I came back."

Delhi in March was cool, mainly—only now and then a belch of hot wind from the desert country west of the city rushed down the embroidered avenues, raising embarrassed *saris* and a cloud of yellow dust. The trees stood in tidy lines, and the domes of ancient Muslim monuments rose beyond them, nippled with long spires and steady in their stone. The changing colors of the stippled earth, between dawn and dusk, charted the heavy descent of the sun. Occasionally, driving around, we saw sardonic camels shamble past the monolithic bulk of the Red Fort. Shaggy, tame bears panted along on chains tugged by their owners.

The bears would dance, for a few cents. It was disconcerting, in a way, to watch their slow, capering activity: They were so much like the young socialites in the discotheques, only tremendously removed, their dance done in dust, not on a wax floor. In some respects they were as removed from the young socialites as were the dusty villagers outside Delhi, though the names of the bears and the socialites ("Bubbles" and "Tootoo" and "Binky") often were the same. Enormous dichotomies built up like cumulus in my head as I traversed the treadmill of the Delhi cocktail circuit—and questions with no answer. I think this happens to any reasonably intelligent person in the Indian capital.

There are the diplomats, and the clever witty Indians, and the ministers. Not all are likeable people. R. K. Khadilkar, the Minister of Health and Family Planning, was small and sweet. "I am new to this work," he said, when we met him in Delhi, in a small study cluttered with files in a large ministerial house cluttered with furniture. "I am a labor organizer, really," he added. "But my missus is a GP. I get most of my ideas from her." He spread his hands widely. "What contraceptive to adopt?" he asked me. Since I didn't reply, he said, "Most have failed. We must devise something easily and cheaply available, purchasable in Post Offices."

He didn't, however, seem to know exactly what this would be. He had only been in office for two months, as he explained, and I expect it was unfair to feel that he should know. Eventually he said, "As yet we have no compulsory sterilization after two or three children. If I suggest it in Parliament, all the parties in India will shout me down. But this matter has to come out." He twiddled a red-taped file between finger and thumb. "If sterilization is practiced by choice, the man offered a vasectomy has fears of impotence, and if his wife is offered a tubectomy"—a delicate, an Indian hesitation—"he fears she may go astray, since she can no longer conceive. It is really," he said, "a big problem."

"What do you think the people's reaction would be," I asked, "if compulsory sterilization was introduced after two or three children?" Khadilkar didn't reply. Soon afterward he had to leave. Leela, my wife, who takes my notes during interviews, had put my notebook on his desk, and I scooped it up, shook hands with the minister, and departed. Shortly thereafter, Leela noticed that in picking up my notebook I had also accidentally appropriated a file that lay under it, marked "Top Secret." We sent it back to Khadilkar's house, with profuse apologies, and I must add that though deeply tempted, I did not read it.

That afternoon I lay on our cool white bed and thought a little. Our bed was in the house of the old friends with whom we were staying: Sri Mulgaokar, a noted Indian newspaper editor, and his wife Krishna. Krishna dabbled daily amidst the flowerbeds that flanked the lawn and in the garden hedge, full of flowers. At evening the strong scent of these flowers, mixed with the smell of dust off the road, drifted into the house as guests arrived for drinks or dinner. It was a gentle and complete life, and nobody bothered too much about problems of population. Nobody who lives reasonably well nowadays does very much, and why should they, I thought as the ceiling fan clicked overhead. Neither did I, until I was asked to.

Apart from the government programs, there are a number of voluntary organizations in India that preach family planning and offer services to those who will accept them. The most important of these is the Family Planning Association of India, or the FPAI, which has twenty-seven branches throughout the country.

One of the main ones operates out of Delhi, and though concerned to a certain extent with rural areas, the body of its program
is dedicated to urban slums and industrial areas. Its workers fan
out over these areas, recruit local help, and try to make people in
each place accept family planning. This is not exactly birth control: It is a context for birth control, really.

Family planning, when it started, was a means of ensuring the
health of mother and child, and thence, one supposes, the mental
peace and economic stability of the father. Its main purpose was
health care, and this included the spacing of children, for the sake
of the parents and the child, which was where contraceptives came
in. What the FPAI were still doing in Delhi was, with one exception, exactly this. Family planning started up in the peaceful days,
peaceful in terms of population, before World War II—days in
which European nations said, like Lear, "Let copulation thrive!"
in case there was a shortage of people. In 1973, embattled amidst
the Indian multitudes, the FPAI are trying to persuade people to
limit rather than space their families.

Anand Prabhat (the name means "dawn of happiness" and is a
definite misnomer) is a slum area in Old Delhi, where the FPAI
has been busy. We reached it, with two FPAI male workers,
down savagely narrow and crowded streets, rivers of people, stray
dogs, and cattle; and when we reached it, the area proved surprisingly clean. The paved streets, which tilted down a slope from
a cluttered main road, were scrubbed spotless and flanked by little
plaster houses with little wooden doors. One of these doors led
into a small room, donated by the local community, which was
festooned with family planning posters and charts; it was filled
with a number of earnest men talking to the workers.

"Some want vasectomy for themselves," said one of my com-
panions. "Some want their wives to have tubectomies. They are
requesting advices, you see. *Now* the people trust our workers like
anything; at first they were *very* much objectionable. The reason
they are finding out their mistake is, as urban dwellers they are
seeing that it is not possible in economic terms to having more
children. No housing space, no money to feed and clothe unfor-
tunate offsprings, that is it. Also they are seeing their health conditions are improving since we have come to the area only. I

would be saying about 22 per cent of eligible couples here are practicing contraceptive methods."

Further down the tilted lane was a small house with a court-yard. In a room within were a number of women, mostly young, many with babies in their arms or small children more or less at heel, squatting on the mud floor while an FPAI worker, female this time, addressed them in a firm and capable voice. When I appeared, the women drew their *saris* around their faces and shrank back into themselves, as though I were some foreign mercenary intent on mass rape. The worker told me that they had brought their children to be vaccinated. "I always tell them," she said, "about birth control." She felt that many of them listened to her; many of them practiced birth control.

"In fact," she said, "the husbands often want their wives to have a tubectomy, or the loop, or a supply of condoms." The women whispered behind their hands and looked at me in a rather suspicious way, so I left fairly rapidly. Anand Prabhat, though it is in the city of Old Delhi, is run as Indian villages are run, by a *panchayat*, or local council. I met the *sarpanch*, or headman, in his house, which was very like a village house, with an inner courtyard and rooms around, through which one could hear the shaky moan of Delhi traffic. He was gentle and hospitable, like almost all Indians, and pressed carbonated drinks on me and told me how much his people loved birth control.

On the way back one of the workers told me that Anand Prabhat was a showplace. He said, proudly, "There are 60,000 people in the area I showed you. There are few places in India like this." I looked at him sharply, but he was serious.

There were converging lines of cyclists on the roads into New Delhi, thousands of somnambulistic pedestrians and cattle and cars, cycle scooters, bullock carts, motorcycles. Delhi is not, by Indian standards, a crowded city, but the dust and the afternoon heat and the shrill cries around pressed an ache into my temples. Tomorrow we would be on our way. I looked out of the window at a rubbish heap. A freckled hawk spiraled upward from it, uttering a sharp cry.

CHAPTER TWO

"One nick of the knife, and it's done!"

We dropped out of the sky to the parched dun earth of Bombay. The rains had not come in 1972, and in common with much of the rest of India, the sweltering city was short of water. The public taps on the pavements, which serve many tenement dwellers as well as the thousands who sleep on the streets, ran dry through most of the day. Driving in from the airport, through the hot anonymous white suburbs, we saw the patient queues of the poor squatting before the brass taps on the pavements, as subservient and hopeful as devotees of an unrelenting deity. There were power cuts in the city as well: Air conditioners couldn't function; fans turned very slowly.

Leela and I were both born in Bombay, and we had known each other and the city as children, towards the end of World War II. Then it was a spacious city of parks and colonial houses set on sprawling lawns. This was in the city proper; the satanic chimneys of industry already smoked dolefully in the suburbs. After 1947 and freedom for the country, industry spread. Cheap unskilled labor was needed, and from all over India people flocked to Bombay as to the promised land. Now, like some fuming toad, the city squats in the reclaimed tidal swamps of the seven islands on which it was built. The population has risen to an estimated 6 million people.

A million of these people have no settled homes. They inhabit pavement shanties, or rickety improvised shacks put in the tidal creeks. The police frequently force them to up sticks and move,

and they do, a little way, and then set up their snail-shell dwell-
ings somewhere else. Ironically, huge blocks of expensive flats have
simultaneously sprouted in the city. Rents rise daily, food prices
rise, available space shrinks, and more and more babies are born,
and more and more poor and hopeful people arrive in search of
work. Bombay today is verging on disaster. The conversation of
most residents, I found, was centered on the feared future.

Solutions have been proposed: One is that a satellite city should
be built on a sparsely populated headland across the teeming
harbor. But creating a city is a slow process, though filling it when
it is created will be a quick one. The basic problem of Bombay
is the basic problem of India: how to limit the population to a
size that can be properly cared for. The government of Maharashtra, the state of which Bombay is the capital, has been one of the
most successful Indian states in terms of its health services, which
include family planning. I talked to the state minister of health in
his palatial house on Cumballa Hill, an echo of the old Bombay.

Dr. Rafiq Zakaria, the minister, is a stocky, lively, bespectacled
Muslim. He took up his portfolio in 1967. "Maharashtra," he
said, "has always led India in literacy, education, and social reforms. The first family planning clinic in India was set up here
in 1925. But between 1957 and 1967 only 35,000 vasectomies were
performed in the state. I looked on vasectomy as the most desirable method of family limitation, since it was terminal. I changed
the whole basis of the program. Seven thousand vasectomies were
performed in my first six months in office. Now Maharashtra leads
the country in terms of acceptors." He beamed: he was pleased
with himself.

But down the hill from his house, under the strong noonday
sun, the crowds swarmed through the mill areas and the slums,
on foot and on bicycle, their million feet and wheels mixing the
dust. The dead had their replacements already: Every ninety
seconds an Indian baby left the dark secrecy of the womb and
came weeping into a world that could not afford it. When I
thought about it, the immensity of the task faced by the family
planners of India stunned me. If faith can move mountains, Dr.
Zakaria and others like him throughout India have plenty of it,
but in this day and time and in these circumstances, I doubted
that faith could.

The Government of India says that there are over 300 voluntary organizations in the country that deal with family planning, but they count all the branches of any given organization, and some organizations share the growth pattern of the mushroom and die fast. The largest voluntary organization in India is the Family Planning Association, which is partially financed by the International Planned Parenthood Foundation. Its chairman is Avabai Wadia, a bright lady in her middle years who was once a barrister. She helped found the FPAI in 1949: "It was the second such body to be founded in Asia. It now spreads its wings over India."

I had, of course, seen the Delhi branch in action. The Bombay branch operates in the same way, running educational programs on family planning in factories and rural areas and running clinics all over the city. Mrs. Wadia sent me out, with a field worker, Mrs. Thakur, to look at a slum clinic. Following this I was supposed to attend a rural program: Family planning films were to be shown to the villagers of Bhayandar, outside Bombay. "Family planning," Mrs. Wadia informed me sternly the day before I set forth on this odyssey, "is a human affair. People aren't statistics. We don't only try and limit families: We try and help infertile people too."

The FPAI's Suratnagar clinic at Chembur was certainly a very human affair. It was held in a small dispensary loaned by a local doctor. All around were dingy blocks of government flats: The people who inhabited these flats were industrial workers; the plain, worried women who waited in the outer room of the dispensary (the doctor worked in a second, even smaller room beyond) were their wives. This tiny clinic operated once a week and served 10,000 women. Each of the five field workers, all of them female, who were present at the clinic, simple women who smelt of soap and clean linen, had to cover and motivate 20,000 wives. "It takes a year."

During this year the workers plod around the industrial flats where there are tired women and too many births, trying to tell all the prospective acceptors how family planning will benefit their health and those of their children. The husbands often protest; the women themselves feel embarrassed if their neighbors know that they accept family planning. Though many women come to the clinic for health care, comparatively few do so to obtain contraceptive devices. The average number of children for a family in the area was four. The patients who sat on the wooden benches in the outer room were surrounded by small children.

One of these women had had two daughters and a son. "But the son is ill. I want to wait three years, using the loop, then have another child. If it is another daughter, I will leave it to my husband to decide whether or not we will try again for a son." Another patient had been disowned by her Hindu parents because she had married a Christian. She had been on the pill but had used it rather inefficiently and was now pregnant. The husband was unemployed, and no help was forthcoming from the parents. She was to be sent to a hospital for an abortion. After that, she would be fitted out with a loop. The field workers shrugged tolerantly and smiled.

We drove from the clinic into the countryside, the earth burnt dry on either side of the unwinding ribbon of road. My guide, Mrs. Thakur, who was graying and comfortably plump, sat at the back and murmured cryptic information, like a dove. "We must be going by foot only," she said, "to these faraway villages. In the summer it is very much hot, and when it rains then we are becoming wet. But in Bhayandar, where we are proceeding, there is too much cooperation. There are eight villages in Bhayandar district, and 55 per cent of the eligible couples have been sterilized. This is very encouraging to us. When we come to Bhayandar we feel it is worthwhile."

We turned off the main road, and bumped down a stony track towards the sunset. Off the road ricks of hay stood on stilts; puffs of dust rose from the dry fields. We passed wells where village women in brilliantly colored, tattered *saris* drew water in brass pots. They paused and looked up as we passed, their skimpy bodies immobile and sculptured for a moment, their eyes and teeth white in their dark faces. We were not far from the sea: we came through an area where lunar pyramids of salt stood white in the dusty fields. Beyond it the road was blocked. We took to the fields, the car plowing and wallowing through enveloping clouds of dust.

It cleared, and we regained the road and eventually reached the village of Raie, a village of narrow lanes between mud houses, with a stagnant pond in the middle, gulls sailing above the scummed water in which women and children bathed and washed their clothes. Strangers were obviously a rarity, for we were immediately surrounded by curious partially clad infants. Presently the members of the village council, the *panchayat*, appeared, and welcomed us with a mild sort of dignity. We sat on the verandah of the small Hanuman temple, and darkness fell quickly and thoroughly: pricked out in patterns upon it were the lights of the neighboring villages.

Mrs. Thakur was distressed: She cracked her knuckles together. She clicked her tongue. The mobile van carrying the family planning films had not arrived. Outside the temple, the villagers waited patiently. For them, as Mrs. Thakur explained, the showing of any sort of film was a considerable event. The icy chips of the stars and a horned moon came clear in the dark sky, and Leela and I decided to return to the city: We had a long way to drive, and it was late. Before the villagers let us leave, they took us to the house of one of the *panchayat*, a raftered house with an attic above, and gently plied us with tea and carbonated drinks and betel nut.

This gentleness and hospitality are typical of an Indian village, at least in most parts of the country. But as the pressures of shortages—shortages of land, of food, of water, of education—increase with the population, these qualities must die. In terms of family planning, Bhayandar was a progressive district, since the people were near enough to the city to see that there were other desirable things in life beside children, and since the FPAI has devoted a lot of time and trouble to the area. But around it there were districts where no concept of life had changed and where the chief recreation of the people was still tired and mainly loveless sex.

Shortly before I went to Suratnagar and Bhayandar with Mrs. Thakur, I talked to Dr. S. N. Aggarwala, who heads the International Institute of Population Growth, a little way outside Bombay city. Dr. Aggarwala is a short, quiet man with a surprisingly loud and nervous laugh. "The success of family planning depends on the administration of the state," he said. "Where the administration is efficient all the way down to the lower echelons, the program thrives; where the administration is inefficient, it fails.

Hence in states like Maharashtra and Tamilnadu, family planning works; in states like Uttar Pradesh and West Bengal or Bihar, it doesn't. That's quite obvious."

He felt that the rise of population in India could not be halted, only slowed. "We have to work out how best to look after such numbers of people. One way might be to split the existing states up into smaller units. That would make administrative control more easy. We must plan for the future now. You see, according to our calculations, if the family planning program is as successful as the government hopes it will be, the population will still double itself to over a billion by the year 2001. Then, given the comparative growth rates, India will be more populous than China. If the program fails, this will have happened by the year 1991."

"Ah," said Dr. D. Pai, "so you are the wonderful Dom Moraes," a remark that I confess predisposed me towards him. He sprawled out on a chair behind his desk puffing in abrupt bursts at a cigarette held between middle finger and thumb. He is not a large man but has a massive quality about him. His heavy, handsome head is perpetually lowered between bulky shoulders, like that of a bull about to spill into the arena. "I am like a writer," he said. "I am very egotistical, but I am humble also. So you want me to talk about myself. That I will gladly do." He threw back his head, laughed loudly, and dropped his cigarette on the floor.

After, with an irritated click of the tongue, he had retrieved it, he started to talk. He sawed the air with his hands as he spoke or spread them widely in a charade of innocence. He also threw himself around in his chair with such vehemence that he once nearly fell off. He was excellent value, in fact, and also sympathetic. "We have a lot of time for everything in India," he said, "everything except family planning. The experts here are narrow fellows. Each one rides his own hobbyhorse. At a conference, nobody comes to share opinions, only to express his own opinion. I call such events SBS conferences. That stands for Same Bloody Shit."

In 1964 a severe epidemic of stomach trouble broke out in Bombay. Dr. Pai was then Professor of Social Medicine at the King George Hospital. "I've always liked to tinker with society." He, among others, was called to a municipal meeting to decide what should be done. "The essence of such matters is to reach the people. I told the chairman to commandeer twenty buses for me and issue me a permit for the drugs I required." He then had the seats pulled out of the buses and loudspeakers installed, recruited a work force of young interns from his hospital, and by the afternoon of the same day was out in the most crowded area of Bombay with his team.

"Everyone took it for granted that the people knew all about the dangers of gastric infection. The truth is that people do not know unless you tell them. I spoke to them on the loudspeakers. I told them. They came in thousands to be vaccinated. In seventeen days I immunized more than a million people. People don't come to you; you have to seek them out. I did that, and I beat the epidemic. So I got the name of a troubleshooter." In 1966 the Bombay municipality remembered him and summoned him once more. The vasectomies performed in Maharashtra as a whole had exceeded the state target; those performed in Bombay fell far below the mark.

"They said to me, 'Pai, we want you to insert 100,000 loops,' as though all I had to do was lift 100,000 skirts and push them in." Dr. Pai roared with laughter. "Anyway, I organized a big exhibition on family planning. The idea was that people should become aware of what it was. Do you know where those fools mounted the exhibition? In the city museum. In fifteen days less than 2,000 people went there. So I thought, where to put this damn thing so that people will see it? It must be in an area where crowds collect. But which are the places in the city where the largest crowds collect? The answer came to me in a flash: the railway stations."

The suburban trains in Bombay, at rush hours, are packed with commuters—packed so densely that many passengers, unable to crush their way into a compartment, hang like dark fruit from the door frames and windows. Every week some fall off and are killed, but this does not act as a deterrent. The congestion and cost of the city has driven people out to the farther suburbs, and some commuters live as much as forty miles from their work. At the main railway stations, Pai was thus assured of an inexhaustible supply of potential converts. He started at Churchgate station, where one of the main suburban lines discharges thousands of commuters daily into the city.

He swished the red tape to one side, browbeat the station master into acceptance, and took over an ice cream stall, where he set up his exhibition. The exhibition was staffed by his interns, who acted as motivators. Every day thousands of people who were awaiting a train or had recently descended from one visited the stall in order to kill time. The interns tried to convince the men who already had three or four children to visit a hospital for a vasectomy. This was not very successful, at first, until Pai found out why. He talked one day to a mill worker with four children, told him that vasectomy was simple and painless, and advised him to have the operation.

"I told him to report to the hospital next day. He said he would and walked off. Suddenly, I had the feeling he would not come. So I called him back and said, 'Swear on your children that you will come.' He would not swear. He said, 'Sir, when a government officer asks an ordinary man like me to do something, it's best if you seem to agree. But if this operation is as simple and painless as you say, why do I have to have it in a hospital? A hospital is a place you leave feet first.' With that I suddenly knew what I must do. I told him, 'Come back to the station tomorrow. I will do the operation here, and in a few minutes you will be able to walk away.'"

The mill hand came back next day. Pai put up screens and vasectomized him. "After that I obtained small rooms in several stations as clinics. The motivators move around on the platforms and outside the station and bring people in. The doctor does the operation in a few minutes. It is beautiful to watch. So economical, so clean. One nick, and it's done! Now we do vasectomies in several railway stations. We also do them in our mobile vans. And of course I recruited the leaders of various slum areas. The people are afraid of the leaders and do as they advise. To organize all this in the slums, man, I have risked a knife in my back time after time."

All over India, cash incentives are offered to those who are vasectomized. The sums vary from about sixty rupees in the north to twenty-three rupees in Bombay. Some industrial concerns pay

additional sums of up to two hundred rupees to any of their workers who volunteers for vasectomy. The government emphasizes
that this is not a bribe. The sum paid is intended, it says, as
compensation for any workdays the volunteer may lose. However,
the motivator who brings a man in to be vasectomized also receives payment per head: ten rupees per man in Bombay. Quite
obviously, the motivators want to produce as many men as possible. The system has been under heavy critical fire since it started.

The motivators have been accused of bringing in illiterate men
who do not fully understand what is being done to them, of bringing in unmarried men and men who are virtually senile, of bringing in men who have been vasectomized and men who have
been coerced in some way. Some of these accusations are probably
true. "But there is no time," said Pai very seriously, when I
brought the matter up. "There is really no time. Such a huge
problem and so little time. I think we should now have compulsory sterilization after three children, but others disagree. It may
still come to that. But so far as possible, we try and check on the
patient when he comes."

I inquired whether a railway station was the most sanitary place
in which to perform an operation. He snorted. "The surround-
ings, the room itself, are clean. The other main necessities are that
the instruments are clean and the patient's skin is clean. The
instruments are carefully sterilized by our doctors, the area to be
operated on is carefully cleaned beforehand. We have plenty of
experience. Each of my doctors has done over 6,000 vasectomies.
We have done 320,000 in all: The complications have been less
than 1 per cent." Like a bull teased by flies, he tossed back a
brusque head. "Why do we sit here and talk, man? Come and
see the station clinics."

He swept me into his car and drove it, in an irresistible and
brutally direct style, through the tangle of the traffic towards the
city. Every few seconds he slapped his horn into life. He muttered Marathi oaths whenever anyone impeded our progress, and
yet I felt perfectly safe in his vehemently propelled machine. His
office is in a downtown hospital in the most crowded part of
Bombay, some distance from the center, but we reached our destination in a remarkably short amount of time. It was a suburban
railway station, and over a doorway next to the entrance was a

family planning sign. The doorway led into a small room that smelled of disinfectant.

There was a desk in the room, where two government workers sat, and a bench, which was occupied by two men, prospective clients, who looked utterly terrified. Pai opened a door on the far side of the room, and I found myself in a cubicle watching a man being vasectomized. I had previously indicated to Pai that I had no desire to watch such an operation, however beautiful a spectacle he himself might think it. It was somehow endearingly typical of him to precipitate me into a situation from which I could not now retire, since he had locked the door behind us. A faceless man was strapped to a backward tilted table. He was covered to the waist, his shiny brown testicles tethered and exposed.

The doctor was in white. He held a long curved steel instrument in his hand. He approached his patient. I shut my eyes. "See, see," said Pai. "One nick and it is done! How beautiful! How delicate!" When I next opened my eyes we were in his car, proceeding at speed to another station. He took me onto the platform and showed me a yellow tin stand on which Nirodh condoms were displayed. A government worker watched over them. "There is one on every station," Pai said. "We distribute about 35,000 a day. A fellow may feel shy to buy them in a shop, but on a railway platform he is anonymous." He handed me a packet. "On the house," he said, and laughed a lot.

He also introduced me to one of his motivators, a young man of extremely sinister appearance, in a fluorescent shirt. "In four years," Pai said, "he has earned 30,000 rupees as a motivator. He has not kept a penny. That is because he is of the riff raffs." He pronounced this as two distinct words. "But then the people we are trying to reach are of the riff raffs. No use to send an Oxford scholar to talk to them. My motivators are rascals. I must keep an eye on them always, but they do their work. You know, in the various railway stations, we do anything from 75 to 150 vasectomies every day." He grinned at the motivator. "Sometimes I have to beat these fellows."

The motivator smiled queasily: The jovial ferocity of Pai seemed to disquiet him somewhat. "It is a long time since I was drunk on duty, Doctor *sahib*," he said in a conciliatory fashion, "and I spent my 30,000 rupees on a small business." Once more

Pai showed all his teeth in a smile. "I know that small business," he said. "It is owned by a Muslim fellow who sells country liquor, and for the last four years you have been buying up his stock." The motivator winced. "No," he said, "Doctor *sahib*." Pai smiled fiercely at him; he shuffled off. "My God," Pai said, "the problems they cause me! But I must be using the tools that are ready to hand, isn't it?"

Outside this station, Victoria Terminus, a mobile van was parked. A quiet doctor and a checking officer sat inside. Outside, three villainous motivators were trying to force pamphlets advocating vasectomy on the men who passed by. Most of these men pushed the motivators and their pamphlets aside; out of several hundred, perhaps a dozen actually accepted the pamphlets, and only one braved the interior of the van. He appeared, from his attire, to be destitute and was turned away. "For every ten we operate on," Pai said, "ten are turned away. The checking officers decide whether they are really eligible." He sighed, thinking of the fish that slipped his net.

We said goodbye outside the station. Considering the problems Pai faced, I thought the way he faced them was admirable: the indomitable charge of a brave bull, aimed at a definite target. Pai was as unsentimental as a charging bull, yet very human. Sentimentality is no proof of humanity. Indeed, I had started to feel that the sentimental approach was the main obstacle to any solution of the population problem in India. For all his surface bluster, Pai's mind was hawklike, poised above an abyss that it studied with a chilly, intelligent eye. Such minds could anneal the abyss perhaps—only perhaps: The function of hawks is necessary but unpopular.

CHAPTER THREE

"Fertility has a direct correlation, you see, with insecurity."

Bombay is a kind of halfway house between north and south India. The Indians of the north are tall, fair, and reasonably hedonistic. The Indians of the south are small, dark, austere in their habits, and in the main not only literate but intelligent. Because there have been, and still are, societies in the south that were basically matriarchal, women are more nearly equal there than they are in the north (even though Indira Gandhi comes from the north). In Ernakulam, in the rivery emerald state of Kerala, where people are more literate than anywhere else in India, the first mass vasectomy camp had been held in 1971.

Over 60,000 men came to it. They were given food as well as the normal cash incentive; they were offered film shows and entertainment programs, and for them it was like a holiday. The camp was a success on the whole, but there were drawbacks as well. Since motivators are paid for each man they produce, a number of the men who came to the camp were ineligible. It was also impossible to do a proper follow-up and to check on complications arising from the operation, because many of the volunteers had come from a long way off, and many, through embarrassment, had given false names and addresses. Nevertheless, this was the first of many such camps.

They still flourish in the south, but they have not been all that successful north of Maharashtra. In the south, the diet is mainly vegetarian, and the bedding supplied to the patients need be no more than a mat, since the weather is hot. The north is cooler, and people eat meat there to a greater extent than in the south.

To feed a campful of men is therefore expensive, and the organizers have, moreover, to bed them down in proper cots with blankets and pillows, under roofs that are not composed of stars. This costs money, and though the Indian Government is now spending large sums on population control, the camps in the north cost too much to run, or so I was told.

An extraordinary fact, actually, is that the number of members of Parliament in the central *Lok Sabha*, or House of Commons, from each state, and the central government subsidies handed over to each state, depend on the state population. The larger the population of a state, the higher the number of members of Parliament, and the higher the subsidy. This may make common sense, in fact it does, but the point is that in a way it offers the state governments no incentive to pursue a population control program. Indeed, it offers them an incentive not to pursue such a program. It is noteworthy that the state administrations in the literate and populous south have continued to pursue it.

From Bombay we flew south, to Coimbatore, where a car awaited us. The earth and trees, under a sun even more burning than that of Bombay, looked and smelled different from anywhere else we had been in India. On the horizon, around the small white provincial town, stood high clouded hills: They are called mountains, the Nilgiris or Blue Mountains, and on their slopes coffee and tea of fair quality are produced in profusion. We drove rapidly towards these hills through hot, flat country where fields of paddy and sugar cane, wilted by the interminable drought, flanked the road. There were haystacks in the fields, but the rivers had dried up sadly into pebbly earth.

Amidst these fields we passed an old man in white robes, carrying a staff. Leela, who knows more about India than I do, told me he was a man who had renounced family life and become a wanderer for religious reasons. He fitted in with the landscape of dry fields and huddled cactus. So did the slow peasant women, black but comely, carrying loads of hay on their heads. So did the bullocks with painted horns, pulling carts down the endless road between the villages. We rose through incredible plantations of areca nut palms, standing in orderly lines, very tall, with a feathery frizz of leaves at the top. They exuded a rich powdery smell and a sound like wind.

Then the road started to climb higher, past eucalyptus and
pine. Jacaranda nodded purple heads on the slopes, and waterfalls
dropped steeply past them into the valleys we were leaving. There
were monkeys in the trees by the roadside; the trees, and the
rocks, were painted with the inverted red triangle that means family planning. Presently, 6,000 feet up in tart chill air, we came to
Coonoor, a small town built up a slope, a little below the larger
resort town of Ootacamund. On the slopes all round Coonoor
were round, plump tea bushes, packed together, a source of local
income. There are also occasional round, plump schoolgirls from
the rather bad convent schools that abound in the area.

These schools are another source of local income, but they have
little reality to connect them with the lives of the people who
work in the Coonoor plantations and in the town itself. The organizations concerned with the lives of these people are the health
officers of the central and state governments, the FPAI, and
UPASI, an extraordinary body operated by the United Planters'
Association of South India. On the first, purple, cool evening
we were in Coonoor we had dinner with Marie Buck, who runs
the FPAI in the Nilgiris, and with B. Sivaram, one of the UPASI
officers. The dinner was in Sivaram's house and was presided over
by the stern servitor who had cooked it.

Mrs. Buck, who was described to me by Sivaram as "the oldest
American east of Suez," was leaf-light, fluttery, and haloed in
white hair. She has been in India for more than fifty years and,
after her husband died in 1943, devoted herself to social work.
She has lived for twenty-five years in the Nilgiris. "The aborigine
tribes in the hills, around this area," she said breathlessly, fluttering her surprisingly beautiful eyelashes, "they've practiced population control for years . . . some say by casual infanticide . . .
I don't believe it . . . They do it by herbs and roots and spells
. . . The balance between male and female population is equal . . .
they control it, you see."

The FPAI run a clinic in Coonoor for prenatal and postnatal
care. "Women are most receptive to family planning," said Mrs.
Buck, "immediately after they've had a child . . . Oh, you should
see! We send a bus for the expectant mothers; they come to our
clinic . . . They have good food, hot baths, a bed to sleep in,
someone to comb their hair. . . They're used to looking after

their families, it's the first time anyone has ever looked after them
. . . Maybe it's the first hot bath they've ever had, the first bed
they've ever slept in . . . They have hot water bottles, blankets,
diapers for the babies . . . They take these things back to their
villages . . . It's wonderful, really."

Next day we visited the clinic, where the dark women lay with
huge eyes under yellow blankets, their babies beside them. They
seemed pleased to be there, and they had accepted family planning methods, but there were only ten beds in the clinic. They
could be stretched, at a pinch, to fifteen. It seemed a pitiful number, but it works. The clinic doctor said he had performed a
thousand tubectomies over the previous year, twice the target of
the state government. The FPAI workers have been busy in thirteen outlying villages, where local family planning committees
have now been set up. Mrs. Buck produced two tall, sober men
from a village called Kanthala.

They had the white powder left over from their morning worship still plain on their foreheads. The village is Hindu and
orthodox—no outsider can sell food or settle in it—but it has
accepted family planning completely. "We don't entirely understand it," Mrs. Buck said. "Where the mother used to have twelve
children, the daughter now has two." The grave, tall village leaders said it was because they had become aware of the economic
necessity for family limitation: They were keen that the children
of their people should be educated. There was no opposition in
the village, they said, even from the elder women: They all
understood.

In Coonoor itself, a town of 30,000 people, there are nineteen
wards or boroughs. The FPAI operates in them all. There are two
particular wards, I was told, where the people were equally poor
and illiterate. One had a high percentage of family planning and
the other a very low one. "We've discovered," said Mrs. Buck in
a quivery flood of words, "that the good ward is exposed to educated people, the inhabitants work in town . . . They see the
homes of educated people, the facilities . . . The other ward is
cut off, they don't really come into contact with educated people . . . They don't know what they could have from life." She
paused, breathless. "Does that make a little sense?"

It was pleasant to walk with her and her workers through the sunlight and shade and the wind off the forested blue hills. The workers included an orthodox caste Hindu and a Muslim, who work as a team, Christians, men and women. Apart from the town of Coonoor and the thirteen villages that now have their own programs, they go, often on foot, into twenty-six other out-lying villages to which they try to bring family planning. There was a lady doctor who wrote plays about population problems for children and then produced them in village schools. "We have had some success," she said. "You've had a lot of success," Mrs. Buck said, smiling, flustered, pleased.

From the hill we looked down over acre upon acre of tea plan-tations, with neat rows of houses in amidst the plump bushes. "Yes," V. Chacko said thoughtfully. "Here we have a captive audience." He runs UPASI, which is financed by a chain of plan-tation owners. He is a square, dark, confident man in his fifties, full of an energy more contained than it had been in Pai, he doodled rapidly on a scratch pad as he talked. The experiment he is conducting in the Nilgiris is one of the most interesting in India. The inspiration came from an American, Dr. Ronald Ridker, who visited the area a few years back and talked to the plantation workers.

Ridker had felt that family limitation could be introduced to the workers in terms of the health and future of each individual family unit. A scheme was set up in which any eligible woman between eighteen and forty-five could enroll. The women nor-mally work, picking tea, at a salary of about ninety rupees per month. To this the scheme adds five rupees a month for each of the first two children born. The bonus continues if the third child is spaced, but it stops after that. In the plantations where the UPASI experiment is being conducted, the scheme has been an unqualified success. This is mainly due to Chacko, who is a man with a deep and searching intelligence.

"Here," he said, "we have a ready-made organization in a con-trolled setup. In each plantation, we discovered that in opinion-making, the manager was influential. It wasn't always easy to motivate these chaps, but once we had, we plumbed the other levels of opinion-makers—the estate doctors, the trade union leaders. Eventually, however, if the workers were to be involved, they themselves had to be concerned. We approached the women and said, 'You've too many children, your body can't take it.' The women said, 'We bear children in the same way as all the other women we know.' So we said 'Your husbands have to work too hard to support them.'

"That usually brought a flood of imprecations from the women: They'd say their husbands were shiftless and irresponsible and drank all the money away. But if we then talked of the health of the children rather than the health of the parents, the father and mother would both become concerned and involved. The message they got from the government, from the red triangle posters, was 'Don't do this, don't do that.' They were all aware of family planning already, they simply weren't involved. But what we said was, 'It's a joy to have children, but only if they are healthy and happy.' However illiterate the workers are, that message reaches them."

Chacko is concerned with family planning in the true sense. He has set up nurseries on the estates, where the children are cared for while the parents work. "The children are made aware of movements and colors, sounds, and smells. We keep an individual record of their progress, and a nutritional record. The mothers are hugely impressed. Its a gold mine for us, an idea transfer made backwards, brought by the child to its parents. Often such parents come to us for sterilization. We tell them to think it over before they decide. We continue with the children. Their individual records will be sent with them to primary school, showing their aptitudes and preferences.

"Then they can be trained for a craft. Our aim is to instill self-reliance into these children without their having to have degrees." Chacko paused and looked out of his window at the slopes beyond. "Everything's important: yes, education, but nutrition, too. I managed to bring out some dairy cattle from Sweden. They came last week. Their pasture's on that hill there. They'll give the children good milk." The odor of cattle had, in fact, been drifting upwind for some time: They certainly smelled rich and ripe. "All this," said Chacko, "is a means of providing the people with security. Fertility has a direct correlation, you see, with insecurity."

He strolled with us around the flowered lawns of his offices, looking down from above, with a cool and steady eye, at the protected valleys. "Security isn't like a lollipop," he said. "It's brought in by strengthening long-term fixtures. Because insecurity results in an inability to plan ahead. When we offer them security"—he waved down at the workers' houses, neatly roofed in tin—"in return for their acceptance of family planning, they are willing. But we aren't sure yet that the deferred incentive of security we offer is the most compelling force that motivates them. After all, they will have to wait a long while for their security to come.

"The most *immediately* compelling force is the fact that so many of the women in the estates accept family planning methods. We are only dealing, in the experiment, with a population of 6,000 people, and the women know each other, they live in the same lines, they see one another at the nurseries and the clinics. So if one woman doesn't accept family planning, or if she slips up, the other women all know. That is the most *immediately* compelling force that makes them not only accept family planning but try and practice it properly, and we capitalize on that fact. Of course, our success here is tied up with the fact that we operate on a limited scale.

"But the government has allotted me some money. I'm trying to spread the experiment over six districts that contain a million and a half people around this area. There we'll be trying out locational organizations for situations that are quite uncontrolled, unlike this one. We'll use what we've learned here, but the deferred incentives will be in terms of assistance on the farms. It should work." He cast an eye over the valleys once more. "It works here, so it should work in the six nearby districts. If it works there, there's no reason why it shouldn't work all over the country." His hands were alert and restless by his sides, like those of Dr. Pai.

We had the next morning to kill. By this time we were in Madras, and our plane to Madurai did not leave till the afternoon. So we hired a car driven by a sturdy young Christian called Fernandes and wheeled our way through the hot sedate city whose colonial houses and stately government offices sat by a steely blue sea. Fernandes, a man of little discretion, told us about his entire life during the first few minutes of the trip. He had eight children. It seemed to me surprising in one so young, and I said so. A few minutes of not unwelcome silence followed. Fernandes appeared to cogitate over the wheel.

He then mentioned his family once more. He now had five children, and one, he said, was not his but his unemployed brother's, whom he supported out of the kindness of his heart. On a brown hill, helmeted with a church, above the city, where Thomas the Apostle was alleged to have been stoned to death, I thought about Fernandes and about India. Fernandes had the impression that I was a person of superior status, so when I appeared to be surprised at the number of his progeny, he had lowered the number, because he thought that this was what I wanted to hear. One of the main drawbacks to family planning motivation in India is surely this tendency.

In a remote village, a government officer is godlike. When the government officer tells a villager that he should have fewer children, the villager says, yes, indeed, he has always thought so himself. The government officer departs; he will not return for a long while. Meanwhile, the condoms he has generously distributed shrivel on a dusty shelf or are bequeathed to the children as balloons. In a country so vast, with so few trained personnel, it is difficult to follow up what happens in rural areas to people who answer questions with what they do not consider to be lies but are, in effect. Personnel must be trained to cope with all this.

They are trained at Gandhigram, a center about fifty miles outside Madurai. We abandoned Madras and our driver, who at one point averred that our 2-hour ride around the city had cost the equivalent of fifty pounds, which he wished to be paid in foreign currency, and arrived in Madurai after dark. Next day we left early, by car, for Gandhigram. After our time in Coonoor, it was horribly hot in the plains. The red earth smoked up dust, but it was studded with green trees and fields, despite the drought. The horizon was hills, dry and studded with rocks. There were haystacks around, and in the fields peasants drove primitive wooden plows pulled by bullocks.

At the wells, where the women collected, screeching like peacocks in their bright *saris*, the water was raised by wooden pulleys, operated by an ankleted black foot. In the villages we passed, parboiled rice had been spread out in the roadside sun to dry. It

seemed a silly place to put it, since all passing vehicles, which included mobile tubectomy vans, ran through it. But the villagers
smiled politely as our tires scattered the rice in all directions. In a
final spray of cereal and dust, we came to Gandhigram, where a
collection of yellow research institutes stood off the main road.
We sought out the one we wanted and went in to find the
director.

Dr. K. A. Pisharoti, the director, sat in a cool room off the
front porch. He unrolled a number of diagrams to show us exactly
what was being done at Gandhigram. The first priority was family
planning research. This included follow-ups on sterilization cases,
discovery of decision-makers in a village, motivational aspects, and
educational procedures. People were trained as researchers at Gandhigram, and they had recently perfected a cheap health food
made of easily available local products: a cereal, a pulse, oilcake,
and raw sugar. I tasted some and it was horrible, but apparently
people like it because it reminds them of some popular local
comestible.

"We are a unique organization," Dr. Pisharoti said, "because
we are the only ones who integrate training, field services, and
research. There is no point in research unless you try it on the
ground, and this is what we do. We are the center of the family
planning program for four states. Part of our finance comes from
the Ford Foundation." He rolled up his charts and put away his
pointer. "I was at Gandhigram when the Family Planning Organization started, in 1960," he said. "At that time this was all barren
land." It wasn't now: The yellow buildings stretched neatly back
towards the hills, adorned with plots for vegetables, and occasional
flowers.

We toured around, to the media research unit, full of colored
slides and cutouts, through courtyards full of concrete lavatories
("We are trying to bring them to the villages. Our people build
them themselves.") There are thirty-five senior staff at the Gandhigram center, and over a hundred field staff and interviewers. He
has five senior women staff workers. "But I think," he said, "whatever we do here, the facilities countrywide are inadequate. Follow-ups, for example—they're essential.

"Now the supervision of acceptors is largely in the hands of
the paramedics. If we had adequate supplies of drugs, transpor-

tation facilities, the ability to dispatch medical officers into remote areas every so often, more acceptors would come forward
and the original acceptors wouldn't drop out. A good infrastructure is our basic need. Even if a new type of contraceptive, cheap
and easy and reliable, were to be produced, the motivation problem would still exist. The people would become suspicious: Why
had we changed our methods, they would want to know. It's
partly the fault of the planners; they've shifted around their aims
and tactics so much, it's bewildering."

Dr. Pisharoti balanced the seat of his trousers on the edge of
his desk and produced a condemnation of the past and a vision
of the future. "In 1962," he said, "the government was bent on
building up a solid infrastructure for the program. In 1966 all this
was forgotten. There was a concentration on publicizing the program through the mass media. The failure of the loop wasn't
followed up. Now there's a concentration on sterilization. After
two or three years it may be something else. If we had good
autonomous bodies, well financed, to run the program, we could
achieve a spread of family planning methods all over the country
in fifteen years. We must accept that our population will double
within that time.

"We need to plan for a generation, rather than try short-term
measures over the next four or five years. Look at India's agricultural problems. It took a generation for us to turn the corner. The
same with family planning. We can feed more people: Our acre
yield is still only a quarter of that in the United States. But we
have to plan ahead. The trouble with the government program
is that it is staffed by bureaucrats: They are guided not by a service interest but by job regulations. There should be, as I say,
autonomous bodies run by experts to make policies and guide the
government." Dr. Pisharoti paused, and his fingers drummed on
a sunlit corner of his desk.

"Compulsory sterilization after two or three children is a mad
solution. I think it would wreck the mental health of the population; it would ruin individual families and also the social climate
of the country. It would create group support in opposition to the
program, which doesn't now exist. We must plan, not coerce people." He shrugged a little and smiled and said, "Why don't you
take a drive out into the area where Gandhigram workers operate?

You'll see what we are trying to do?" We left him in his office, climbed back into the car, and with one of his program officers, drove out through the parched fields, the red dust swirling up around us.

The small dark villagers cultivated tomatoes and onions, sugar cane and paddy. Hobbled donkeys stood patiently by the road-side, or, unshackled, plodded townward under loads of produce. There were scraggy sheep in the fields. Bullocks with their painted horns (their dignity has to suffer) pulled cartfuls of hay down the roads. A man stood by a bush burdened with flamelike flowers, a torch in his hand, smoking the wild bees out to collect their honey. Among the women by the road were some who went blouseless, the bared dark figs of their breasts partially concealed by their *saris:* widows. The villages were composed of white-washed houses with roofs of red tile or brown thatch.

In one of these villages, about ten miles from Gandhigram, we drew up at a small tiled house by an old temple. The house consisted of a cool, cluttered main room full of children who were being looked after while their mothers were at work. The room also contained a number of workers trained at Gandhigram: four young women and a man, who stood rigidly to attention, backs pressed to the chipped white wall, and answered my questions with an air of being prepared to do their duty whatever the cost. Their nervous, coltish youth touched me—also the fact that they worked so hard. They started at dawn, six days a week, bicycling or walking into remote areas.

Here, with small exercise books clutched to their chests, they went from family to family. They made notes of the most recent births and deaths. They tried to convert eligible couples to family planning. They were not always well received; the village women sometimes swore at them. But they not only looked for acceptors but supervised the health problems of the villagers, particularly the health of mothers and children. In the end, people came to accept them, they said: They had had some success in promoting family planning. The three midwives, the lady health visitor, and the young male health inspector covered 20,000 people in all. It was hard work.

Still, they said, they had had 894 sterilization acceptors in the last year. And there were many other fields in which they had been of some use; for example, a number of people in the area suffered from leprosy. They knew about it. Not only had they been trained at Gandhigram, but most came from nearby.

The death of ambition comes hard in a person and rarely of natural causes. But in these young people it seemed to have died naturally and been replaced by a desire to be of service to others. I reflected that there were thousands like them in India, setting off each day in cheap, clean *saris* or frayed shirts and trousers to the work lying across the dry fields.

Last time we had been in Calcutta, in 1971, the Naxalites, or militant Communists, had been busy at arson and murder in the huge, filthy city that sits where the holy Ganges empties itself reluctantly into the sea. They had finally been stamped out by 1973, but the city had the air of having been stamped out too. We took a taxi from the airport, a taxi whose seats had burst open as though their plastic skins had been corroded by disease and whose outer shell was cracked and scarred. Leela, who is terrified of traffic, asked the driver, who appeared to be about fourteen years old, to go slowly. "Don't worry," he said sadly. "This car can't go faster than ten miles per hour."

As we crawled towards the city in this tortoise taxi, which, because the steering did not work properly, swung very slowly from side to side of the road, under the bows of oncoming buses and the shark snouts and fins of better-furbished cars, it struck me that Calcutta had become a disaster area. It seemed as though a war had hit it and ricocheted temporarily away: The buses had huge holes in their sides and smashed, unmended windows. The buildings we passed, swarmed through by people, had a gutted and abandoned look. In the bar of our reasonably smart hotel, once we had, after some considerable while, reached it, a huge, grey sewer rat scuttered around the floor.

The reason for all this was not only the efforts of the Naxalites, but the fact that the city is coming apart at the seams. Some 8 million people now inhabit it, and few of them live what could be described as a reasonable life. Every night an uncounted, uncountable number of people lie down on the sweaty pavements to try and sleep; and every morning it is discovered that many of them have succeeded beyond all their expectations and are dead.

The public services appear to be on the point of collapse: The endemic water shortages and power cuts of India when we were there occurred more erratically and drastically in Calcutta than anywhere else we had been.

Mother Teresa is a Catholic nun who was born in Albania but has lived in Calcutta for much of her adult life. She has devoted her time to working for the poor: Her nuns and she, for many years, scooped the grasshopper skeletons of the dying off the streets and took them to a place where they could complete the short, dreadful cycle of their lives on clean beds, with food available, and kind people around them. She and her nuns also helped lepers and abandoned children and fed the needy insofar as they could. Mother Teresa was then discovered by the mass media: Television films were made about her for the West. Malcolm Muggeridge wrote a book about her.

Her integrity, through all this, remained inviolate. She received donations, awards, and funds from ordinary people and world bodies, and she funneled it back into her charitable works. One of these is a house called *Nirmal Hriday*, which means "pure heart," where the dying are brought off the streets. When I visited the place, with Leela and a svelte young socialite, Mrs. Rita Dev Verma, who is a disciple of Mother Teresa's, there were seventy-four men and eighty-one women there. They lay huddled together, on austere but clean bedding, silent, perhaps too tired to speak, exuding the sweetish, stale smell of approaching death. "I come here every week," Mrs. Verma said.

The dying entered the place every day. Some had become a little insane: A woman of about forty, shriveled under a sheet, begged to be allowed to return to her home, though she had none. Some of the dying folded their hands to us in *namastes* but did not speak. There was an exhausted young mother with a dying baby in her arms. The exactitude of death prevailed over all those who lay waiting for it on the stone floors. Outside, the wreck of Calcutta, obscured by its slime of people, dragged its huge body onward to its own final demise. What the residents of Bombay fear their city will become, Calcutta already is—one of the worst places in the world.

Mother Teresa herself appears to have been slow to see that there were too many people in the city. If she saw it, she was slow to analyze the cause. She was opposed to the introduction of contraception to the people, despite the dying children in the roadways. Eventually, she decided to make her health workers introduce the rhythm method to poor mothers: They were issued with thermometers and by taking their own temperatures were supposed to plot monthly charts of safe and unsafe periods for intercourse. Two of these workers, Mrs. Lovejoy and Mrs. Domingo, took us around various slum areas, to demonstrate how their program operated.

The houses to which they took us mostly consisted of one or two small rooms, the water supply coming from a public tap at which the wives started to queue in the frightful hour before dawn. The average income of the couples who lived in these tenements was between sixty and seventy rupees a month. That is about ten dollars a month, or four pounds. The average number of children they had was between four and five. The mothers talked to us, their doe eyes wide, about the impossibility of feeding or clothing the children, let alone educating them. They could not afford to offer us anything to eat or drink: They tried to offer us air, gently fanning the flies off our sweaty faces with their little calloused hands.

These women kept their thermometers and their charts; they clearly hoped not to have any more children. How successful the rhythm method had proved was difficult to ascertain. The women do not use it simply because they are Catholics—some are Hindus and Muslims who heard about it while taking their children to Mother Teresa's clinic. The workers tell them about other contraceptive methods but don't supply any devices apart from thermometers. Mrs. Lovejoy said in a disappointed way that some of the acceptors abandoned the thermometers in favor of pills or the loop, though she did not explain why. The women themselves smiled a little blankly when asked.

But they looked, with their wide, harmed, harmless eyes at their children. In the small, dark, surprisingly neat rooms beyond the shallow sills of the doorways, the children played. Sculptured into the skin, their ribs swelled outward at every breath. The last children in nearly every family we visited had the swollen and weak ankles symptomatic of rickets, and some had the mild white stare of the mentally defective. Mrs. Lovejoy herself had five children; she was a member of the community in which she worked, and her husband brought home eighty rupees a month, about eleven dollars. The Lovejoys, husband, wife, and five children, lived in a place called Crematorium Street.

I went to see Mother Teresa in her clinic: a withered, wiry little woman, with vividly blue eyes under her wimple and a voice that manages curiously to mix Albanian gutterals with a very Indian lilt. This voice is very low and very intense, and when she spoke to us we heard it against the slow float of voices from a choir in the chapel above. In the courtyard outside an Alsatian basked on a leash in the sun, and the street beyond was filthy and crowded and fierce. "Why are people so worried about world population?" Mother Teresa asked. "There is plenty of land in India for people to live on. It is so rich a country. Why are people worried?"

A child with a broom as minute as herself swept up dust in the courtyard, the bristles whispering in the dust. "Children should be a joy and a pleasure," Mother Teresa whispered, "I am not trying to stop people from having children. I am only trying to ensure that they plan them, so that it is a joyful occasion when a child is born." Her wrinkled face had the peace of certitude. She was very still as she talked, economic with her energy when it was not necessary to use it to any purpose. I did not agree with very much that she said, but I didn't say so: There seemed no point in arguing with a saint, even if one wished that saints were more of this world.

Dr. Biral Mullick lives in Calcutta, where his father started the Humanity Association for the uplift of the downtrodden in 1924. Dr. Mullick was born three years later and has operated the association since his father died. In 1956 he attended the International Planned Parenthood Association conference in New Delhi, where he met Margaret Sanger and other family planning dignitaries. In 1960 he was asked to carry on an experimental program with the loop in Calcutta. It proved a failure. "It is only the answer," said Dr. Mullick, "if it is inserted by a properly trained person and is properly followed up to obviate complications." He said he had once said this to Dr. Jack Lippes, who invented it. After the failure of the loop experiment, the Pathfinder Fund in

Boston allocated Dr. Mullick a sum of money to try out the pill.
"It has been a real success," he said. However, for some reason
he did not clarify, the money from Pathfinder then dried up. "But
I am using a new technique," said the doctor, "menstruation regulation, for an early abortion. If a woman has missed her period
and does not want the child, I can induce the period very simply,
with a syringe and a cannula. I have done thousands and thousands
of abortions. This equipment is very simple, not like all the
paraphernalia the government requires for abortions."

He is a clumsy mover, like many Bengalis, and talks a lot, also
a characteristic of his people. We drove to one of his city clinics,
in the Pilkhana slum across the yellow Hooghly River that divides
Calcutta proper from Howrah. The slum was crammed with industry, with people, with little, dirty shops, with unspeakable odors,
and with rubbish, like a gray fitted carpet, across every alley. The
clinic was down one such alley and was full of neat, slight women
who were the patients. "They are the wives of industrial workers,"
Dr. Mullick said. "They have dressed in their best to talk to you.
Talk to them. You will find them not unintelligent."

Dr. Mullick interpreted for me, and surprisingly he changed
completely as he did so. His movements became sparse and
masterful, and his words terse. The women were obviously eager
to answer questions. Some were Hindus, some Muslims, but they
all clamored responses to each query. Since the Pathfinder money
had stopped, Dr. Mullick had run out of supplies of the pill. The
women complained that since this had happened several of them
had become pregnant. Some bought Nirodh condoms or local
pills in the market but were dubious of their value. Others made
their husbands practice the withdrawal method, but they said
that this created some sexual problems.

They were surprisingly frank for Indian women. None of them
had practiced contraception before the pill, but they had all
wanted to, and their husbands had wanted it as well. There was
no exception to this, and there must have been forty women
there. They had heard about the pill and the clinic through local
workers and through friends. They took it because they felt they
could not feed or clothe their children, and they all wanted the
children they already had to be educated. The Muslim women
said their husbands and the priests had no religious objections.

Dr. Mullick told them about menstruation regulation, but they shook their heads. They wanted the pill.

One woman said that even if her husband were rich, she would not want more children. "Because," Mullick said laboriously, "of mental peace and no trouble. And she also thinks of her own health." There was a chorus of agreement. They didn't want tubectomies. One woman said it would make her weak, but they all frequently reiterated that they wanted the pill. "I think about it like this," one woman said. "There is a water shortage here. With the water I have, I cannot bathe the children I have. Rationed food is getting less, and the price of everything is rising. In a country like ours I can't afford to have children. That is why I want the pill."

When I started my trip, in Delhi, I had known little about the problems of population. Like most literate people of my acquaintance, what I knew was simply that the world had too many people, that it was likely at some unspecified future date to have more than it could feed or even contain, and that it was therefore necessary to limit population, particularly in undeveloped countries, by means of contraception. When I ended the Indian part of my trip in Calcutta I had become aware, simply through having been immersed in the whole problem for some weeks, of its height and breadth and of the appalling complexities that surround it.

There was foreign aid in India, and foreign experts and advisers who had crossed the world to try and help the country control its population. There was the central government and the state governments, their heavy machinery turning in an effort to control the population. There were dynamic men in the field, like Pai and Chacko, fighting. There were men like Aggarwala and Pisharoti, thinking and planning. There were the voluntary bodies like the FPAI and the Humanity Association, and there were people apart from the main force, like Mother Teresa and her workers—all, in their different ways, concerned with the same immense problem: how to control the population.

The application of all this energy and intelligence and expertise would not, in the opinion of most people I talked to, be able to stop the population from doubling itself between the next twenty and thirty years. The complexity of the problem lay partially within the reasons for this apparent lack of success. The reasons lay embedded within a peasant logic, simple but relevant, whereby children meant security, hands to work, a kind of wealth, within a traditional way of life in which tremendous importance has always been attached to procreation, within religious beliefs, and the normal human instinct to reproduce as a way of fighting one's own inevitable death.

Indians, it seemed to me, could be told how to limit their families, but it was not easily possible to tell them why they should—especially when three-quarters of the population still lived, entrenched in tradition, in remote rural areas. The urban population, most people in the program said, were more receptive to the idea of family planning than the rural population; but that was a further problem, since in Bombay and Calcutta at least, the more people come to the cities, the more those cities fall apart, unable to carry the overload. The more economically sound your life is, the planners say, the more educated you are, the more receptive you will be.

The Government of India has made a tremendous effort since independence: Over twenty-five years they have made agriculture and industry thrive as never before. Had the Indian population stayed the same as it was in 1947, the country would today stand on the desirable edge of prosperity. There would be some measure of economic stability for most people and some measure of education. But the population has swelled like a lunatic balloon, and the target of proper education and economic stability for all falls away behind it as it rises. Even for the educated ones, work is hard to find: Unemployed engineers, unemployed doctors have become something of a commonplace.

And the balloon swells and rises all the while: There are large numbers of people in the country of an age to marry and produce children, and before they have ceased to be capable of doing so, the adolescents of today will also be breathless in one another's arms on millions of beds. What basically I had realized in India was that the population problem was not merely a matter of handing out condoms to happy peasants. It involved social life, and economic life, and medicine, and necessities, and love, and indeed almost every one of the chessboard entities that combine to make the life of a man. What India was fighting for was its own life, that is, for the life of every Indian.

Maybe the politicians needed to be educated before the people—somebody had said that to me. In Calcutta, used as a political toy for many years by demagogues who knew nothing beyond their own rhetoric, a city now derelict and broken apart by the weight of its people, I could see what the whole country might come to at some rapidly approaching date. I was glad to step into the plane that took us away from it, to the bulky islands of the Southeast Asian archipelagoes, set in their deep blue seas, where something less depressing was, possibly, happening.

CHAPTER FOUR

"We have no problem of population here that
we cannot solve—yet."

Hong Kong, where I had been based for two years, working
for a magazine, is one of the last British colonies in the world.
It has Gurkhas and a governor and is occasionally visited by
royal personages. The colony consists of the main island of Victoria, several other islands, and a portion of the Canton mainland
that comprises the commercial city of Kowloon and the New
Territories. The total area of all this is 398 square miles, and an
estimated 4.5 million people occupy it; though, since much of the
land is uninhabitable, the bulk of the population is packed into
some sixty square miles, mainly on Victoria and Kowloon.

In some of the more crowded parts of Victoria, the population
density is one of the highest in the world: It is 165,000 persons
per square mile in the Shaukiwan area, where people live not only
in houses but on houses—they erect squatter huts on the roofs.
At peak hours in Central, the main commercial district of Victoria, it can take up to an hour to find a taxi because of the press
of people. There is a mild sense of claustrophobia in the colony
caused by its lack of size and the population density. My work
took me out a lot, however, into the rest of Southeast Asia, so I
didn't feel this claustrophobia as much as Leela, who mainly
stayed at home while I traveled.

To come to Singapore from Hong Kong was always a pleasure.
It is a green island a short way off the Johore coast of Malaysia,
built in the last century by Sir Stamford Raffles. He now stares
in stone from a plinth in one of the squares, and the most famous

hotel in Singapore was named after him. The British left Singapore and their Malayan settlements in 1966, and Singapore became part of independent Malaysia. A year later, under the leadership of Lee Kuan Yew, a taciturn, intelligent, Westernized Chinese, Singapore broke away from Malaysia. It is now an independent republic, though a minute one: The island has an area of only 220 square miles.

Lee Kuan Yew cleaned his little republic up quite literally. Singapore was once a littered and dirty city: People threw rubbish about in liberal quantities. Lee instituted a fierce system of fines for litterbugs; today to throw a cigarette into the street in Singapore is a punishable offense, with the result that it is the cleanest city in Asia.

Lee also put down the triads, or Chinese criminal bodies, that operated in the new republic and made it safe as well as clean. He had a number of old buildings pulled down, including the death houses of Chinatown, and put up neat, comfortable, wholly unattractive but desirable blocks of government housing. The tourist industry flourished, and while ten years ago Raffles was the only large hotel on the island, there are now literally dozens—indeed, in the opinion of many people, an excess exists. The euphoric mood of the inhabitants, who are friendly and cheerful and very talkative and feel that they inhabit the best of all possible worlds, is contagious.

This city was my favorite stopover. At night you could eat cheaply and very well in the food stalls that abound in Singapore: There was *satay*, a Malayan version of *shashlik*, skewered bits of chicken, pork, or mutton that you dip into a hot peanut sauce, or Hokkienese or Fukienese food. Or you could drive to one of the beach restaurants outside town and devour chili crabs. Everything around you was prosperous and peaceful, a change from most of the rest of Southeast Asia. You had the feeling that nothing could possibly go wrong in this society.

But something has now gone wrong with it. It had already gone wrong when, a couple of months before this visit, I had last come to the city, though I hadn't realized it then.

The present population in Singapore is 2.1 million, and it lives very comfortably. After World War II, however, there had been a boom in babies, the aftermath of family limitation during the

Japanese occupation when many couples were separated. The
babies born then are adults now, they have married, and they
are producing children. The growth rate in Singapore shot up
alarmingly in 1972. It has been said that in thirty-nine years, that
is, by 2012, the population will have doubled to 4.3 million. After
that, if the present growth rate is maintained, it will double once
more, this time faster.

The difficulty about this is, of course, the size of the island.
The government has a Housing Development Board that is rapidly
erecting blocks of cheap high-rise flats. The skeletons of new
ones rise everywhere in Singapore, waiting to be fleshed out with
brick and plaster, and 40 per cent of the population now live
in these flats. It is estimated that by 1980, 75 per cent of the
population will do so. Dr. Peter Chen, a sociologist at Singapore
University, thought that because of these high-rise flats, Singapore
could still cope comfortably with a population of 4 to 5 million.
"After that," he said, "the problems will really start."

But Lee Kuan Yew and his ministers are, typically, aware of
the coming problems. The Health and Family Planning Board
has launched massive family planning campaigns, simplified by
the small area of the republic and the high literacy rate of the
population. Now 96 per cent of the married population is estimated to have heard of family planning, and 52 per cent of eligible couples practice it. Different ministries cross and correlate in
the propagation of the program, so that not only the Ministry of
Health but the ministries of Labor and Finance are involved. So
are the mass media.

Government policy has swiveled towards disincentives for the
people. That is to say, they are not offering people money to have
operations, as in India, but are threatening to take away existing
benefits if parents do not limit the number of their children. This
is being tried out in India now: It started in Maharashtra some
years back. In Singapore tax relief could once be claimed for up
to five children. Tax relief can now be claimed only for up to
three. Hospital fees for pregnant women are low for the first
child but rise steadily for every subsequent pregnancy. Paid maternity leave used to be available up to the third or fourth con-
finement. It now stops after the second.

But the most important disincentive is in housing. Housing in

Singapore, because of lack of space, is a very serious problem that the Housing Development Board flats were built to resolve. It is impossible for people of the lower-income brackets to afford private flats, and their ambition is therefore to obtain a subsidized HDB flat. Until 1970 there was a high priority for couples who had several children. The priority has dropped and from August 1973 will be reversed: The highest priority will be for couples with three children or less. These are the disincentives, and there are no incentives.

Contraceptives have to be paid for. At government clinics these are cheaper, because of subsidization, than if they are obtained privately. I visited one such clinic in a huge new HDB estate at Toa Payoh, a little way out of the white city blocks of Singapore proper. The population of Toa Payoh is around 200,000. The particular clinic I went to specialized in the twinned entities of family planning and mother and child health care. It was a large place, more disciplined and cleaner than any Indian hospital or clinic I had been to, and it was packed with women, mostly Chinese, with a sprinkling of Indians and Malays, most of them clutching small children to their breasts. It serves about 12,000 couples.

"So far as contraception is concerned," Dr. S. C. Hu, the spry lady who ran the place, said, "pills are the most popular." This was the opposite of India: Dr. Mullick in Calcutta was the only person I had met there who had claimed success with the pill. In most places in India the pill seemed to have failed, because of the difficulty of storing it or taking it in privacy or because illiterate women couldn't keep proper count of the days. "Some of the women who take the pill from us," Dr. Hu said, "are illiterate, but if they are keen on it, they keep to it. Most of them are Chinese." The remark rang a faint bell in my mind, and I suddenly thought of Hong Kong.

The family planning program in Hong Kong has been very successful. This, in the opinion of many, has been because 98 per cent of the Hong Kong population are Chinese, and the Chinese are shrewder, and more practical, than most other Asian races. They are aware of the dangers of producing more children than they can support, and they therefore submit readily to sterilization operations or opt for less than terminal methods that they practice in a precise and capable fashion. In Singapore 70 per cent of the population are Chinese. They are the descendants of immigrants who had to fight to make their way in a new country: They are used to being practical and efficient.

Perhaps it is because Singapore is basically a city, where the incentives to a better life for their children are constantly before the eyes of the Chinese, that so many of them accept family planning. We drove on from Toa Payoh through bright fields bedewed by the occasional leak from the clouds above, to a rural clinic at Yio Chu Kang. Dr. Ho May Ling, who ran this clinic, showed us around: a small waiting room, a dispensary, an examination room, an operation theater. She said, "Rural areas are different from the city: Here the mothers-in-law live with their children. The wives have no privacy. If they take the pill, it's known.

"These older women don't think of the future. They feel children in the family are an excellent idea, the more the better. The people are mainly Chinese from Hokkien: They breed pigs. They farm. Girls are married, sometimes, at thirteen or fourteen. But the younger Chinese do think of family planning; they read the papers or listen to the radio. The Malays are opposed to family planning, however, because they think the Koran is opposed to it and because they really love children around. The Chinese wives are more positive. Some sign on for ligations (the sterilization operation known in some other countries as a tubectomy) without the knowledge of their husbands."

Singapore is so small that Yio Chu Kang would, in another country, be described as a suburb of the capital. Yet even here the rural beliefs of the Asian recurred: the belief in numerous children as financial assets, rather than as physical liabilities. In this small village, Dr. Ho said, people want sons: If they have a number of daughters to start with, they will keep trying; and when they beget one son, they want another for safety's sake. It was exactly like rural India, even to the question asked by the Malays, according to Dr. Ho: "If my wife practices contraception, can you guarantee that she will be faithful to me?" Dr. Ho said, "It's a question of education."

The village women came in and out of the clinic: mostly Chinese in blouses and skirts or trousers and tunics, but also

Malays in the *sarong-kebaya* and Indian women in dresses or *saris*. Dr. Ho looked at them and said, "Economic factors play a part in the acceptance of family planning, yes; but education seems to me the main factor. The Chinese are better educated than the Malays and Indians, and that is because as a mass they are economically better off. They are the best acceptors." The women smiled blankly at us as we left the clinic under an eddying rainy sky. There were only women in the clinic—and children. In Singapore, as in India, women accepted family planning better than men.

But in India in 58 per cent of case studies the decisions are made for a family by the husband. In Singapore the husbands were decision-makers in only 32 per cent of the families studied. A united decision by husband and wife was most usually made in Chinese families in Singapore. Among Indian families on the island, the husband was the decision-maker in 47 per cent of cases, among Malay families, in 49 per cent of the cases. Nevertheless, in the rural areas of Singapore, as Dr. Ho had said, even the Chinese were difficult, at least the older ones; and there, only a few miles outside a prosperous city, the ancient village values of Asia were still preserved.

Dr. Wan Fook Kee, the chairman of the Singapore Family Planning and Population Board, smiles a lot, and seems relaxed and friendly, and has not yet acquired the nervous edge to his voice that most family planners in India have when they talk about population. "The growth rate here," he said, "climbed in the years between 1971 and 1973. Partly this was because most acceptors of family planning here seem to want to space their children rather than limit them. For example, according to a survey we recently had, the number of children a couple wants to have ideally is 3.6. But the actual number of children most couples in Singapore have is 4.3. An acceptor isn't somebody who wants two kids."

What the Singapore Government wants, in fact, is to achieve zero population growth. That is to say, a couple should have no more than two children, so that as the parents die the children will replace them in society, not augment the number of the parents. "We hope to reach a crude birth rate of 18 per 1,000 by 1975," said Dr. Wan. "But quite frankly I don't think we'll reach it. The point is that any delay now means that the problems will be increased. The program now allows the people to have the number of children they desire, but the number is still too large. We're trying, through population education, the mass media, social disincentives, to bring it down."

The family planning program started in Singapore in 1966. "The first phase," Dr. Wan said, "lasted until about 1970. The aim was provision of good clinical services to family planning acceptors. In 1971 a stage came where this wasn't good enough: We had to cut down on the number of children. The program became more expensive, and we started to probe into the sociological aspects. Now we have fifty-four clinics, enough to cover the whole island. There's no transportation problem; it's a small place. The favorite contraceptive is the pill; 53 per cent of acceptors use that. The next highest method is the condom. But 6,000 women a year have opted for sterilization."

The campaigns launched by the Singapore Government to promote family planning have won prizes at the Asian Advertising Congress. "When you think of the energy and effort," Dr. John Cool of the Ford Foundation had said to me in Delhi, "put into selling things like soap, it's difficult to see why the same kind of expertise can't be used to sell family planning." The Singapore Government was doing this. Even if it had caught on to the problem a little late, it had done so earlier than many other governments. Now they were fighting it in a brisk methodical way, as they had fought the litter problem on their tiny island. They had, I thought, a fair chance of success.

Yet even in Singapore the complexities of the population situation recurred. For example, industry now flourishes on the island. At Jurong, where there is also a bird park containing two of the very few penguins in Asia, sad, black-clad birds like butlers or diplomats, an industrial estate has started up. Foreign firms, beguiled by tax incentives and the convenient situation of Singapore athwart the routes between Europe, Australia, and America, have opened factories there. Manpower is needed, so workers travel across the short sea from Malaysia or come from as far off as Indonesia. Thus the population is being added to by immigration, but it can't be helped.

It was formed by immigration in the first place. The Malays

themselves have streaks of Indian and Chinese blood left by
traders and invaders in the remote past. Chinese merchants settled in on the Malayan coast and Singapore for business reasons
or because they were driven from home by Manchu persecution.
The Indians were shipped over by the British at the turn of the
century to provide cheap labor, and many remained as traders.
There seemed world enough, and time, for all these races to
prosper in Singapore. But today it seems that, even in Singapore,
there is not world enough—or time enough—to control the relent-
less upsweep of the human race.

Malaysia is a small, verdant country where people have lived
since prehistory. It is no wonder: The black soil is lush and moist;
one has the feeling that a seed dropped in would sprout hugely
within seconds. Flowers blaze in the strong trees. The rivers are
slow and deep. Whoever has lived here, even thousands of years
back, has found it a kindly land. Kuala Lumpur, the capital, is
less than an hour's flight from Singapore, but its atmosphere is
completely different. Life here moves more slowly than it does
in the island republic. Things are less down to earth: There is a
mosque that looks like a railway station next to a railway station
built like a mosque.

It is a Muslim country, about half the population being Malay.
The remainder is mostly Chinese and Indian, with a sprinkling
of Europeans who liked the country so much in its colonial days
that they have never been able to pull themselves away from it.
Malaysia is one of the more prosperous and stable Asian countries,
and a large proportion of its land area is unexploited. But it also
has a population problem and recently opened a Department of
Family Planning to look into the matter. This department is run
by Dr. Shamsuddin Abdul Rahman, whom I went to see. He
was small and friendly and laughed a lot and confessed that he
had forgotten all the relevant statistics.

The problem, as I discovered elsewhere, is basically one that
arises from the rapid urbanization of an essentially pastoral
society. The growth rate in Malaysia is 2.9 per cent, which is
higher than that of India, but the population in relation to the
available resources is not difficult to manage. However, people are
moving to the cities; the result has been that there is an 8

per cent unemployment rate. It is with an eye to a future rather than to a pressing immediate problem that family planning has been introduced into Malaysia. The politicians, moreover, are averse to committing themselves utterly to the program; they haven't yet done so.

When family planning first came to Malaysia—a program was started up by the Family Planning Association as early as 1953—some Muslim leaders attacked the idea of contraception as being anti-Islamic. This explains the present hesitancy of politicians to commit themselves. The voices of the critics are now publicly silent, but there is no reason to believe that they are privately so, especially in the small *kampongs*, or villages, where the bulk of the Malay population traditionally lives. The Malays have been a pastoral people; the Chinese and Indians, in particular the Chinese, have been more urbanized and often merchants.

When Malaysia became a republic, a process of Malaysianization started. The Indians had traditionally worked on the railways or as government clerks, when they were not traders or rubber tappers. They were gradually replaced by Malays. I recall a conversation I had with Ghazali Shafie, a Malay and one of the most dynamic of ministers, in 1971. Ghazali, thumping the table excitedly, pointed out that the average Chinese had a per capita income of twice as much as the average Malay. The per capita income of the Indians was higher than that of the Malays, though lower than that of the Chinese. This, Ghazali averred, was because the Malays had been kept down.

"We are told that they traditionally are an agricultural people. This is untrue. Historically, they are a seafaring people who indulged in trade. They were pushed into *kampong* life because the British offered preferential treatment to the Chinese and Indians. Now we are trying to offer them help to come back into trade." The result has been that a number of young Malays have left the *kampongs*, entered the cities and towns, and looked for work there, raising the unemployment level. The Department of Statistics says that in 1967 20.2 per cent of the Malays had had no education at all, and 87.5 of the educated had not advanced beyond primary school.

The job shortage is acute anyway. The hundreds of miles of tall, tapped rubber trees still suppurate their blood into small tin cups fastened to the trunks, but the price of rubber fell two years back. The minerals such as tin, once a great source of income, are rapidly becoming exhausted, according to one informant. Now Malaysia is trying out palm oil, but, the same economist informant told me, the glut must come soon, since palm oil is now so popular. Jobs are therefore more easily available to educated people, and Malays by and large have suffered from a shortage of education. It is mainly because of this that family planning exists.

"If the economy expands fast enough," said V. T. Palan of the Department of Statistics, "we'll have no population problem. We need economic expansion first; then we can tackle population." He is a shy, intelligent Indian, who quotes statistics from memory, then finds he was right and smiles in a nervous, pleased way. Outside his office the green palm trees lolled back in the temporary sun, awaiting the inevitable rain. "Malays produce more children than any other community," said Palan. "There was a 27.6 birth rate per thousand among them in 1970."

He scanned his files. "The Chinese birth rate by comparison was 23.7 in the same year, and the Indian birth rate 22.0. The Chinese are the highest acceptors of family planning, the Indians come next, and the Malays have the lowest number of acceptors. The Chinese are the most urbanized of the communities, and in Malaysia family planning is basically an urbanized activity." It is also a fact that the Malays, apart from religious scruples, have the idea that family planning, in connection with them, will lead to a decimation of their numbers, which will enable the Chinese to obtain the upper hand in Malaysia. Some of the Chinese have the same fear in reverse.

A curious fact, however, is that family planning has been practiced for some time among the Malays. In the *kampongs*, abortions have been induced through manual massage and through eating raw pineapple or raw papaya or wild herbs. So long as this is done privately, the religious leaders of the village turn a blind eye on it. If birth is stopped by means of a technical method that stems from modern medicine, there may be trouble. I was told this by a girl reporter from the largest Malaysian newspaper who had been brought up in a *kampong*. The older women of the village, she said, had learned abortion techniques handed down through generations. But they objected to new techniques.

A pregnant woman, once she had delivered her child, had to put up with the old methods. She was confined to her room for forty-four days, during which she was fed on rice, pepper, ginger, wine, and occasionally chicken. These were considered to be foods that generated heat and therefore helped both mother and infant. She was not allowed to eat fresh fruit or vegetables or to drink water, since these were alleged to be a cooling influence on the blood and hence unhealthy. Before her pregnancy, she would have been locked in a shuttered room, since it was felt that fresh air was full of bacteria. This, of course, had an element of truth in it—some tribal wisdom has.

The result of the diet was sometimes beriberi, and usually both mother and child suffered from malnutrition. Moreover, lack of exercise and fresh air usually told on the health of the mother, hence, on the health of the infant. "In most *kampongs*," the girl reporter said, "women look old by the time they're forty." I have seen this myself. In areas of Malaysia well outside towns, I have often visited villages of thatched houses on stilts, where chickens and livestock browsed in the shade under the houses, the men puffed cigarettes idly in the local cafe, and the women pottered about with a swarm of children around them. The women either looked young and ripe or old. There seemed to be none in between.

The Family Planning Association of Malaya started as an independent body. Their aim was to raise money and provide clinical services for the women in the *kampongs*. The Selangor Association, based in the state in which Kuala Lumpur stands, was one of four state associations that banded together in 1958. They received a government grant in 1961, and in 1962 the other seven Malaysian states started their own associations, under the FPA banner. The FPA recognized early on that a voluntary association could not function on a nationwide basis. Its role now is supplementary and complementary to that of the National Family Planning Board.

We drove into the suburbs of Kuala Lumpur, hemmed in by effusive shrubbery, to the headquarters of the Family Planning Association. These are contained in a large white complex of buildings where midwives and staff nurses are trained, with a fair-sized library that is available to university students. In a con-

ference room lined with chairs, I met three FPA officials, two of
them somewhat dominated by the third, a sturdy, elderly, and
incisive Englishwoman called Mary Butcher. The FPA in Malaya,
as it then was, had started out, she said, in 1953, an offshoot of
the Singapore FPA, which had started in 1949. The reason for
its commencement, she said, was simple.

It was because of the high rate of infant mortality in the
kampongs, the high number of deaths of mothers during or after
delivery, and the rate of malnutrition. "In 1965," said Mrs.
Butcher in her terse, clipped way, "the long-term implications of
population growth became apparent." The program concentrated
on the spacing rather than on the limitation of children and in
this was akin to Singapore. "Chinese have been the best acceptors," Mrs. Butcher said, "but there's a historical reason for this.
In most parts of Malaysia where there's a high population concentration, you get a Chinese majority. The rural population, as
you know, is largely Malay."

The work on family planning in the *kampongs* started only
after 1969. But Malaysia has an excellent health infrastructure,
and the family planning pill was wrapped up, as in most other
places, within the scented capsule of mother and child care. "Since
family planning at the beginning wasn't part of the national
program," said Mrs. Butcher, "we don't have special workers
within the health program as it now stands. We anticipate that
we will have some, but the idea is that our nurses and midwives
won't be identified with family planning in the eyes of the *kampong* dwellers, as the nurses and midwives in India are identified
with the red triangle. Do you see?"

She hurled her final question at me rather ferociously. I nodded
and said I did see. "Good," said Mrs. Butcher. "Now to continue.
To go solely by the number of acceptors is misleading. It's the
persistent users who are important. People are flocking to us now
for mother and child care. A younger type of couple, with one
or two children, is coming to us now asking for help to space
their children." It was the same all over Asia, I thought. Nobody
wanted to lose their children and have none left. It was like
money—even when you had a lot of it you wanted more, as
insurance for a bad future.

But limitation, as Mrs. Butcher was now saying, is unacceptable in Asia, with children as with money, unless you know that the children you have, like the money you have, will last. "Even unemployment," she said, "won't make people accept family limitation easily, at the moment." But Malaysia had time: India hadn't any because of the sheer numbers at which the already unwieldy population increased every year. Singapore hadn't much because of its size. Malaysia, with 11 million people in an area 130,000 square miles, much of which is still virgin land, had plenty: Despite government diffidence and some religious opposition, the program had been forced into birth and could grow tall.

The Economic Planning Unit plays an important role in Malaysia today. It is built on the tilt of a hill up which the invading vegetation swarms. In a small office, air conditioned and womb-like, through which one could look down at the marching armies of trees, I interviewed Aris Othman, who works for the EPU. "It is true," Othman said regretfully, "that the unemployment rate in West Malaysia is now 8 per cent. We are still waiting for an analysis of the 1970 census because perhaps the figure may not be reliable. The 1970 picture is not clear yet." He did not seem hopeful that the clarification of the picture would produce much difference in the unemployment rates.

"We have disincentives as in Singapore. Female workers are now only entitled, if they work for the government, to payment of maternity services up to and inclusive of three children. There is no free maternity leave. Only 3 per cent of national expenditure is now devoted to the family planning program, but it may increase. We must expand our economy to deal with unemployment; family planning isn't essential yet. The World Bank has commented that income in the modern agricultural sector in this country is higher than in the traditional urban sector. So we are proposing a movement to modernize agricultural techniques in modern development areas."

These areas are sited in the triangle of Johore and Pahang states, in Trengganu, and Bintulu. "It is very, very heavily forested," said Othman, shaking his head. "Unemployed people will be used to clear land. Then a combination of industry and agriculture will grow up there. We recognize the importance of *kampongs* as part of our Malay culture—there will be *kampong* dwellers who refuse to move into new areas. But the type of industries we want to create will be based on agricultural produce: canning factories, processing factories for rubber and timber, and industries that cater to exports. We are trying to foresee all possible problems so that they don't happen."

At the moment, the highest unemployment is in the industrial sector. "They have no prospect at all when they move to the city," said Othman, delicately leaving his "they" unqualified. "The per capita income in Malaysia now is $1,100. We have measured the GNP." There was an implication somewhere in this remark, but it was difficult to follow up. "We have no problem of population here that we cannot solve," Othman said, "yet." That morning in Kuala Lumpur the head of EPU, Dr. Thong Yaw Hong, had stated that if the growth rate were controlled and kept within its present limits, there would be full employment in Malaysia by the year 1990.

Outside Kuala Lumpur is the expensive industrial satellite of Petaling Jaya; swinging the other way, into the hills, you reach the Genting Highlands where there is a casino and row upon row of greedy shiny fruit machines awaiting those who do not play "chemmy" or roulette. The coffee shop at our hotel was frequented by sleek young people, Chinese, Malays, and Indians. I have something of an obsession about the way people speak English: In the mouths of these young people its iron and leather was pulped into pap. They sang to one another like imbecile birds. "Cannot come to Highlands tomorrow? Why no, ah? Plenty fun there, no?" And the girl, faceless behind her lipstick, "Cannot come, lah. My fadah, muddah, you know, ah." And the reply, "Fadah, muddah, yes, I know, lah, helluva t'ing, what?" These were not rich young people: The girls would probably be secretaries, the boys clerks of some kind. The point was that they could afford these small luxuries: the hellish coffee shop for a milk shake, the trip to the Highlands to force small coins down the throats of the occasionally spewing machines. "Highlands are beautiful, no, ah?" "Yes, lah."

Nothing in the streets of Kuala Lumpur, or in the *kampongs* in the forests, yet really threatens people. The unemployment there has been caused by urbanizing *kampong* dwellers—a policy that is now being reconsidered. It is something that can be solved. And yet beyond it there is the inescapable fact that one day there will be too many people; it won't be all that easy to have a milk shake in an "international" hotel or lose your play money to the machines at Genting.

The tragedy of the population problem is that though every single individual born is desirable, people in the mass can be lethal without their wanting to be. By the time governments realize this, it may be too late.

CHAPTER FIVE

"They come to the clinic very unhappy and leave happy."

The Philippine islands number about 7,000, some of them no more than broken skulls of rock that protrude coyly above the enfolding arms of the sea. The largest island in the south, Mindanao, kneels in an unplumbed deep and lifts its fierce head, feathered with palm trees, towards the sun and the typhoons. To this island, as well as to those in the north, the Spaniards came in the fifteenth century. The Muslim rulers who dominated the local tribes were no match for their technology, such as it was. Nor were the tribesmen, mostly aborigines or people of Malay stock. The Spaniards occupied the islands without too much difficulty and settled them.

Small white churches were put up amidst the trees, for the benefit of the rather surprised natives. The gun, the whip, and other contemporary instruments of Western culture were brought into play, and the population found itself kneeling in these churches. It watched as ports were built and Filipino produce was taken away in the tall, winged foreign ships. It suffered the Inquisition. It lived under the dispensation of Spain for 400 years. The Spaniards offered the natives benefits, such as the mingling of Iberian blood and diseases with the blood of the local women, and also the opportunity of education in distant cathedral-burdened Europe.

When a colonial power started to offer education in its own country to the people it colonized, it nearly always created an educated and rebellious intelligentsia in the colonies. Towards the end of the nineteenth century, José Rizal appeared as a

61

prophet of liberation in the Philippines. He was a remarkable man but had few followers, and the Spanish arrested and shot him in 1896. Every nationalist movement needs its martyrs, and the Spaniards had conveniently supplied the Filipinos with their own indigenous Christ. In 1898, in response to a Filipino appeal for aid in the fight for independence, American ships under Admiral Dewey arrived in Manila Bay.

On the gunmetal sheet of the bay, they broke the Spanish fleet and ended an empire. The newly made republic of the Philippines only lasted a few days, however; the Americans then, with avuncular firmness, took over. Though the Filipinos were allowed their own President, all actual power was in the hands of the Americans. To all intents and purposes, the Philippines were a colony once more—now an American colony. Shortly after the outbreak of World War II, following the dramatic if abrupt departure of MacArthur from Bataan, it became a Japanese colony. The course of the war swerved back towards the Allies, and MacArthur returned for a Roman triumph in 1945.

The next year, with a magnanimous sweep of the pen, the Americans again made the Philippines an independent republic. But the successive waves of rulers had left a mark on the people. Gentle as a rule, the Malay races can occasionally be ferocious in the extreme—the admixture of quarrelsome Latin blood did not help. The islands were now mainly Catholic, and their habits mainly Spanish, but all this was overlaid by the cosmetic of American culture. The people of the new republic were often, in the opinion of others, lazy, but they were also violent. Guns were owned by many people, and the crime rate in Manila rose. But the churches were still full.

So, it was discovered in the 1960s, were the cradles: The growth rate in the islands was exceptionally high, even by comparison with other Asian countries. The economy, by comparison, was exceptionally low. By the 1970s there were civil disturbances between the Muslim remnant in Mindanao and the local Christians. There were also Communist disturbances in Luzon, northward, the island where Manila stands. In October 1972 a state of martial law was declared and was still in force when we arrived in Manila in April. Things seemed quieter, though there was sporadic fighting in the south. Guns had been outlawed for

civilians. The crime rate had dropped. When it came to population control, the government saw the problem early, and despite
the numbers of conservative Catholic priests who opposed the
family planning program, it was braced with official support in
1970.

Manila, perched by its famous bay, is a scruffy city of occasional skyscrapers, colonies of squatter huts, affluent villas, and
slums. The traffic is in a constant tangle, which is not helped by
the gaudy presence of the "jeepney." This is a popular form of
public transport, a converted Land Rover that is usually packed
with people. The owners of these vehicles deck them out as the
peasants of South India deck out their oxen. The jeepneys have
names; they are painted in vivid basic colors that are then daubed
over with complex patterns and adorned with tassels and bells.
They provide a welcome touch of color in a mainly shabby city,
and also a traffic hazard.

Manila is, once you forget its appearance, an attractive place.
The people are friendly and very hospitable. There used to be a
vivid night life, now curtailed by the midnight curfew. Even now,
the crowds at dusk on Roxas Boulevard, the main avenue by the
bay, are noisy and happy. They look at the lights of the ships at
anchor and eat nuts or *balut*, which is a duck egg with an embryo
inside and is inexplicably considered a delicacy. At dawn race-
horses are bathed in the bay, an extraordinary sight, their elegant
heads and pricked ears raised above the shallow waves. But beyond all this, one is conscious always of the squatter huts and the
slums.

There are 40 million people in the Philippines. A few of them,
in Mindanao to the south, are Muslims; an even smaller number
are animists, like the Tasaday tribe, a collection of twenty-four
aborigines who were discovered in 1971 living in caves in the rain
forest of Cotabato. The overwhelming mass of the population is
Catholic. Every *barrio*, or village, has its white church and its
brown priest, and several of the churches, both in Manila and
the provinces, are very old. Catholicism has been in the Philippines long enough to become part of the blood of the people,
as in Mexico. But, also as in Mexico, it is intermixed with old
beliefs and traditions that the Spanish priests fought in vain.

The Philippines is the only Catholic country in Asia. This was something that the family planners, when they first started out, thought would be the main obstacle. But family planning seemed a necessity in that the bulk of the population lived in rural areas in hard conditions, and the peasants who moved to the cities lived even worse, in squatter shacks made of any available material. They were highly fertile, but the children they produced suffered from disease and malnutrition, and infant mortality was high. As early as the 1920s, two Protestant missionaries attempted unsuccessfully to introduce family planning based on mother-child health.

In the 1950s and 1960s, Filipino social workers and doctors became alarmed by the rising growth rate (as the improved health services interrupted the normal processes of death) and also by the consequent drop in standards of life. Several private bodies started to propagate family planning as a health measure. In 1969 it became apparent to the government that, if the growth rate stayed steady, the population would double within little more than twenty years. The government therefore appointed a commission to examine the problem. In 1970, when the commission made its report, a Population Commission was set up to implement the recommendation made in the report.

The role of POPCOM, as the commission is known, is to formulate policies first of all. It receives funds from a number of foreign agencies, including the U.S. Agency for International Development (AID), the Oxford Committee for Famine Relief, the U.N. Fund for Population Activities, and the U.N. Development Program. It then distributes these foreign funds amidst thirty indigenous agencies and works to coordinate and supervise what these agencies do. So far, according to Dr. Lorenzo, who heads the commission, there are 2,000 clinics all over the Philippines, with trained doctors in all of them. Dr. Lorenzo said that through the thirty agencies there were over a million acceptors of family planning, out of 5 million eligible couples. Most of them —over half—were on the pill.

These figures are often disputed. There is, for example, a Catholic organization in the field, known as the Responsible Parenthood Council, or RPC. The RPC members were pioneers of family planning, and they have proved to be excellent motivators.

They go into a province and organize a seminar attended by school superintendents, bishops, administrators, and health officers, so as to ensure their support. Then they recruit full-time staff members in the province, train them in Manila, and send them back to hold further seminars attended by local mayors, parish priests, and health officers. After this, seminars are held for the *barrio* captains, the village headmen.

Having thus set up an infrastructure of support, the RPC staff select volunteers to propagate family planning in each *barrio*. These people have some stature in the community and are personally known to the other villagers. According to Horatio Morales, one of the chiefs of the RPC, this method of motivation has been a success, and the RPC claims 100,000 acceptors, or 10 per cent of the entire number of acceptors throughout the country. But, as a Catholic body, the only method propagated by the RPC is rhythm, hence the support of the local bishops and priests. "We tell the acceptors about other methods," said Morales, "but of course we don't provide the services."

The critics of the RPC, however, say that its *barrio* workers actively impede the family planning program as a whole. Women who have accepted the loop are told by the local priest that hellfire awaits them if they do not remove the loop and take to rhythm. Women on the pill stop it and start rhythm. The rhythm method, the critics say, is unreliable because it is basically a male method. You can give a woman a thermometer and a chart and teach her how to ascertain her safe and unsafe periods, but if her husband does not care a damn about safe and unsafe periods, the method will fail.

The critics say the RPC figures are basically inexact. That is to say, their acceptors are not necessarily following the method with success. Morales denied this. Since a local volunteer works in each *barrio*, he or she ascertains and reports the degree of success in each case, and it is on the basis of these eyewitness reports that the RPC estimate of acceptors is based, he said. He added that all workers were told not to interfere with acceptors of other methods. The RPC were not responsible for what a *barrio* priest might say. Also, he told me, the rhythm method was cheap. A Japanese thermometer cost only thirty cents, and a woman, once supplied, did not often need to be supplied a second time.

Some critics, particularly from foreign aid missions, dispute not only the RPC figures—though these are mentioned frequently as being unreliable—but the POPCOM figures. No incentive is offered in the Philippines, as it is in India, to either acceptors or motivators. Nevertheless, the motivators are supposed to produce a quota of acceptors per month to earn their salary. It is alleged that the motivators put people on their lists who are dead or do not exist at all. In defense of the motivators, it is said that many women visit rural health clinics for the pill or IUD without the knowledge of their husbands and give false names and addresses.

In this way, in the Philippines as in India, the exact number of acceptors is difficult to ascertain. Moreover, a large number of acceptors already have anything between four and eight children who will shortly start to produce their own offspring. There are also a certain limited number of young people with few children who accept the program because they would like to space their progeny. The desired number of children for a Filipino couple is still around six. What this means is that the family planning program has skimmed the cream of the acceptors, those already mentally prepared to accept, and now faces the hardest part of its task: to penetrate the hard core of couples who don't want to know about family planning.

Dr. Flora Bayan, a sharp, wryly witty woman who runs a number of health clinics in the Philippines, said she thought that a weakness of the program had been that it was so much aimed at the wives. She felt it should be aimed at the men: The country had, after all, a paternalistic society. She felt also that the average Filipino did not sufficiently associate family planning with health; he or she thought of it as a segregated activity designed to limit children. This, Dr. Bayan said, should be changed.

I asked Dr. Bayan if I could smoke. She said yes, looking at my cigarette, I thought, wistfully. Only after I had smoked a couple of cigarettes, did she suddenly pull out her own pack. "Excuse me," she said, "I smoke myself. But I didn't want to do it in front of a strange man." This seemed to me somehow typical of most of Filipino society, but it was strange to see this embarrassment towards the male in a highly intelligent and efficient woman.

Filipino society is very oriented towards the comfort of the male. The concept of *machismo*, not exactly a concept of male superiority but of a permitted male domination, which comes not only from Spain but from the old Filipino culture, is extremely prevalent in the islands. This *machismo* is basically also that of the cock that treads all the hens it can reach. You see it in the attitude of the Filipino male towards women—all women. It is obvious that in the minds of most Filipino men their personality, their pride, is tied up with an idea of their own virility.

It seems to me that these areas of the mind have not yet adequately been explored by most researchers. I think demography is a long and foolish word, but if you want to try and understand people, which is what demography is about, more research ought surely to be done in these curious, inherently forested zones of the human psyche. They have developed over centuries, slowly.

But now the trees in these forests are tall, and much of the difficulty with family planning now, it seems to me, is that its propagators can't see the trees for the wood, the basic wood of an immediately insoluble problem. Children are a product of the mind as well as of the chance collisions of bodies in the night. The exploration of a racial or national mind takes time, but it should be done. Contrary to most outside opinions, the Church in the Philippines does not appear to be an obstacle to the success of family planning. *Machismo* is, but the main block is the Asian peasant tradition, a tradition based on the reality of the area.

In the Philippines, as in the rest of Asia, children represent security, hands to work, hands that will feed the parents when they are old. There is also the fact that all Asians are extremely fond of children. A peasant has a small choice of recreation: Drink and tobacco cost money. The pleasures he does not have to pay for are sex with his wife and time with small creatures he himself created—the only thing he can create—scrambling around his dusty feet when he comes back from the fields. This is also something deep in the inherited mind. People say that if Asian peasants had social security they wouldn't have so many children. It is not, I feel, that simple.

Stefania Lim, the Philippines Secretary of Social Welfare, is a member of POPCOM. She is neat and competent and was trained as a clinical psychologist. "Mental health," she said, "has a direct relation with poverty. When I talk of mental health, I am not talking of sanity or madness. I'm talking about the state of the mind, as a doctor, when he speaks of physical health, would talk of the state of the body. The poverty in the Philippines, she thought, was wrecking the mental health of the poor—the mass, as doctors say. It is wrecking their physical health. A steep rise in population of the kind prophesied by the experts would now be disastrous without concurrent economic growth.

"The Filipino family structure has changed," Mrs. Lim said. "The family lived together once, dependent on each other, because of economic pressures. Now the economic pressures have increased and also become different. Mass communications and a high literacy rate make the people have higher expectations for themselves and for their children. They can't afford to have dependent relatives now. They have more ambitions, more demands, you might say." To explore the traditional mind of a people is to be desired, before you start to resculpture their lives and their minds. But there is no time in Asian countries, and the demands will have to be met.

Dave Finnegan, an intense young man from AID, with spectacles and hair that looked as though it should be red, though it wasn't—I mean this purely in terms of his personality, not his politics—said one hot day in Manila, "I'm a population hawk. There're population doves. The POPCOM are doves. They don't want to offer the people incentives, because they think it would be coercion. I don't agree with the term, but it doesn't matter. There's a huge problem in Asia, and it has to be tackled now." I agreed with Finnegan. The Philippines has no time to develop its economy fast enough to catch up with the rise in population and the resultant needs of the people.

All that can be done, therefore, is to try and hold the population increase down, and to start doing it immediately, and as hard as possible, by the offering of incentives, by the switching of program pressure from women to men, by any means readily at hand. POPCOM says that the growth rate was 3.1 per cent in 1970; it says its target is to bring it down to 2.5 per cent by 1976. Most foreign experts say this is impossible to achieve. If the growth rate is not much changed, the population will have doubled by 2000 at the latest, and the living standard of a people whose per capita income in the rural areas is now seventy-five cents a day will have dropped to an irretrievable level.

The RPC wanted me to see what they were up to in a *barrio*. Our friend Tristram Eastwood, the UNFPA coordinator in the Philippines, suggested that Leela and I visit an RPC *barrio* in Tarlac province, north of Manila, then shed the RPC and continue northward to Baguio, a hill resort where a population education course was to be offered to school superintendents. This course was financed with UNFPA funds, so Tristram said he would be in Baguio and would meet us there. The night before we were due to leave, Leela slipped on a highly waxed staircase at a party and sprained her ankle. In the morning, the ankle was worse; so I left by myself.

It wasn't unpleasant weather, hot, but the air conditioner purred in the car, and my driver told me excitedly that it was the first time he was visiting Baguio, and I felt pleased for him. We picked up two RPC workers, Beybs Pizarro and Rebecca Dorres, and rumbled slowly through Quezon City, which is one of the linked towns that compose Manila, on to the open road to the north. Miss Pizarro talked indefatigably, describing the activities of the RPC. Miss Dorres said little. The driver and I smoked, listened, and looked around. The landscape, despite a recent drought, was vividly emerald, and there were hills standing idly at the back of the fields.

There were also buffaloes in the fields, the same sort as in the rest of Asia but called in the Philippines *carabaos*; they were frequently ridden by peasants in shorts and stetsons and are in fact a mode of transport. In the first small town we passed, I noticed a number of very shabby shacks with large signs above them saying, for example, "Jack's Cocktail Bar." There was also a Chinese restaurant called the "Ever Wanton," presumably after the dumpling. Children ran around in the narrow dusty roads, shouting to each other in Tagalog, the national language. They seemed happy but very thin.

As we got farther away from Manila, the fields of paddy shimmered under heat haze. The *carabao* cowboys were more frequent, romantic silhouettes against the glaring sky. We drove through a *barrio* with twenty shops within a compass of fifty yards, and hanging outside each shop an identical leering young lady advertising Coca Cola from a poster. "Whose influence do you think that is?" I asked Miss Pizarro, with a laugh. She frowned very seriously and said, "That is a very popular liquid refreshment called Coca Cola. It is excellent for quenching the thirst. Are you thirsty?" I said I wasn't and ceased to attempt ironic queries. It was probably as well. The driver smoked.

His smoke and mine filled the air-conditioned car, and presently my eyes started to water. I had already told Miss Pizarro and Miss Dorres about Leela's ankle, in order to explain why she hadn't come. They both patted my shoulder. It would be fine, they told me, I shouldn't cry, though they knew what I felt. One of them told me all about how she used to weep for her sister, who had been given a black eye by her boyfriend. We arrived, none too soon, at Tarlac city, the capital of the province. Here a young man, a Mr. Leynes, was awaiting us with a Land Rover. Tarlac was small and dusty, with the usual shacks brandishing their "Cocktail Bar" signs. We turned into the town.

There was a small RPC office here, with field workers, all of whom stood to attention at our arrival. Carmelita Campo, the young woman in charge—she was very pregnant—told me about Tarlac. There were 17 municipalities in Tarlac (the Filipino provinces are divided according to the old Spanish system) and 476 *barrios*. There were also 67,275 eligible couples, 24 per cent of whom had accepted the rhythm method. The twelve field workers, all of whom were stiffly and attentively present, went into the *barrios* from time to time to supervise the work of the *barrio* workers. There were 1,554 of these in Tarlac province. The acceptors were said to number 16,299.

But there was a follow-up, Mrs. Campo said, through the *barrio* leaders. These are the RPC *barrio* leaders, volunteers, and they aren't the same as the *barrio* captains or village headmen appointed by the government. The permission of the captain, however, has to be obtained before the volunteers can operate. We then went to see one of these *barrio* leaders, in a place called Mapalaciao, some distance away. The road was bumpy and dusty, like most roads in the countries I had been to, and it passed sugar cane fields that rustled irrelevantly since there was no wind at all. It also passed by a sugar factory, and Leynes said, "It stinks, *oh-oh*" (*oh-oh* meaning "yes" in Tagalog).

Mapalaciao, some distance beyond the sugar factory, was a *barrio* of little compounds, fields beyond, shabby houses, dust, heat, etc.: Asia. We came to a house with a wooden stairway leading up to the living quarters and climbed it. At the top, one of the local *barrio* workers, whose name was Mrs. Grafil, awaited us. She was stout and gray, and she beamed and pointed to the RPC certificate on the wall, which appointed her a volunteer worker, a contradiction in terms, it seemed to me. The small wooden main room where we sat was, in Filipino terms at least, prosperous: There was a glass closet, full of knick-knacks, also chairs.

Mrs. Grafil has a daughter in Canada and another in Holland. She herself, when younger, had three miscarriages, the last in 1955, when a doctor in Tarlac told her she should plan her family but didn't explain how. She looks after one section of the village, three other RPC volunteers administering the remnants in her section; and there are, according to her, fifty-five eligible couples, all of whom have accepted the rhythm method. Only four, she said, had dropped out, that is, become pregnant. Apart from her two daughters overseas, Mrs. Grafil said, she had seven other children. In the old days, miscarriages apart, people had had manual abortions if they thought that they could not afford any further children.

Mrs. Grafil's husband, while I was talking to her, stood on the cool landing of the stairs that led up to the main room, smoking cigars. He was dressed in his underwear. As we left, he yawned, laughed, and offered me a cigar. He was unemployed. We descended the stairs and went to a house opposite, where the entire village appeared to be assembled. Inside the front room, a television set flickered with vaguely kicking soccer players. Unlike the Grafils' wooden house, this one was solid, concrete, and not very attractive. Ofelia Walath, the wife, came out with a baby on hip and said it was due to her husband's prosperity (he worked in the sugar factory) that they had the television and house.

She was thirty-four; it was her fifth child. The husband came sulkily away from the indistinct screen and stood by her. She said she had accepted the rhythm method for her health; he said he couldn't afford any more children, darted a poisonous look at his wife, and returned with his giggling friends to the unsteady soccer players. The wife said maybe she would have another child. It was up to her husband; she would have liked to space them. She adopted the rhythm method after the third child but had two more in rapid succession. "Of course," said Mrs. Grafil, "this isn't a failure. The children were desired." I asked Mrs. Walath if they had been. She smiled.

The *barrio* was full of children but also of men asleep on their porches on which their industrious wives also sat, chipping away with immense *bolos* at the coarse muddy hides of sweet potatoes. We arrived at a house on whose front porch a woman sat with a baby in her arms, trying to entertain two slightly older and very noisy children. Her husband also sat on the porch, smoking. At our approach, he arose and fled into the house. The wife smiled at us and said she thought three children were enough, but her husband wanted more. She had therefore abandoned her thermometer and was now pregnant for the fourth time. "What" she asked "can you do?"

She was in the process of making various disparaging remarks about the idleness and randiness of her spouse when he reappeared, a small man (also dressed in his underwear) but one whose appearance was rendered far more impressive by the fact that he had in his hand a *bolo* nearly as large as himself. He seemed to be prepared to use it, whether on his wife, the RPC workers, or me was not entirely clear, but it seemed unwise to allow the situation to clarify itself. We backed off the porch and returned in fairly good order to the cars. "He is not," said Mrs. Grafil, "a cooperative man," a statement that I thought extremely redundant. We drove back into Tarlac town.

Here the driver and I abandoned the RPC workers and continued towards Baguio and the mountains. The provincial towns and villages by the road were crowded with people and full of the usual shacks posing as cocktail bars and also of *sari-sari* shops, a Filipino institution that does not sell Indian clothing, but disposes of anything from safety pins to canned food. The driver smoked peacefully, and I looked out of the window at the lush paddy fields of Pangasinan province, at intricately carved wooden houses that stood on stilts by the road, and at the approaching mountains. Then we entered the mountains, which were heavily forested, and the car choked, retched, and stopped.

After a while, much besmeared with engine oil, the driver and I resumed our trip. The car limped round hairpin bends, past ravines spanned by a single bamboo pole devoid of railings, a bridge for the local aborigines, which reminded me uncomfortably of similar bridges I had had to cross in New Guinea. Eventually, the car stopped once more. "What's wrong with the engine now?" I inquired crossly. "There is nothing wrong with the engine, sir," replied the driver, "but there is something wrong with my stomach. I wish to defecate." He disappeared into the hillside brush for a considerable time. When we eventually reached Baguio, I was three hours late for my appointment.

Josie Chua, Tristram's marvelously efficient secretary, met me in the hotel lobby. "You had a breakdown, *oh-oh*," she said. "But Mr. Eastwood is waiting to have dinner with you, no?" When Tristram, magnificent in a *barong-tagalog*, the embroidered shirt worn by many Filipinos, had emerged from his room, we went out to dinner. I phoned Leela in Manila, and she said all was well, so I felt less worried. Next day, Tristram informed me, he had arranged for me to interview various officials of the Family Planning Organization of the Philippines in Baguio: Indeed he had asked them to breakfast—at six A.M.

At six A.M., I bestirred myself with some reluctance and went out to meet the FPOP officials. There were three of them, all ladies, all talkative. Baguio, they told me, had an area, including outlying villages, of fifty-nine square miles; there were 90,000 people around. One of them, Tony Apawa, is a faith healer who, said the ladies, did surgical operations with his bare hands. People from all over the world, they added, flocked to Baguio to be cured by Apawa, a trip facilitated by the fact that he runs a travel agency with international branches. "He could be an excellent ally," one said, "for the program. He would make it more respectable."

Ths was in some ways a debatable point, but the ladies pointed out that while having your stomach sawed open by the bare hands of Apawa was considered, locally, desirable, family planning was not—so much so that women from Baguio would travel down to the lowlands for a supply of pills or an IUD insertion and would cross, on their way, lowland women coming up to Baguio for the same purpose. "So that the neighbors should not know," said one of the officials. "In some cases even the husbands do not know." The International Planned Parenthood Fund and the Pathfinder Fund supplies the Baguio FPOP with pills, which are the most popular method of contraception in the area.

Six different organizations, as well as private doctors, are in fact propagating family planning in Baguio. The missionaries started the program in the 1960s, and, according to the ladies, the Baguio drive for family planning was one of the earliest in the Philippines. Rural people in the area tended to marry very early. The aborigines in the hairy hills around, who were divided into five tribes, had a system of trial marriage to prove that the girl was fertile. The young men and women also lived together in communal houses. This did not conduce to family limitation. The movement, however, had initially been confined to Baguio city.

Now there were motivators in the hills. "We are stepping up the program," said Anastasia Marzan, the promotional secretary, who has been involved with family planning for a long while. "For example, our newest project is to follow up the first acceptors. That is something that is long overdue." They took us to a city clinic, a small neat place, empty because it was Sunday. It was a clinic like any other, but they were proud of it. It exuded memories; it was theirs. They had distributed pills to over 1,000 women here, over a few years, and inserted 600 IUDs. "Ours is a successful program," said Mrs. Marzan. "Baguio is a small place, and everyone knows us."

It is a small place, with a busy crowded center, but with handsome villas, one of which is Tony Apawa's, sitting back near the hills. The church bells were chiming, calling the faithful to prayer. "The church hasn't hindered our work," said Mrs. Marzan. "Sometimes it has helped." She is a stout, motherly woman who has several children herself. "I used to be a schoolteacher," she said. "Now I teach adults. It's a privilege to be told personal secrets by women. They come to the clinic very unhappy and leave happy. It's not like teaching children, where it takes years to see what result your work has had. Here you see the results of your work immediately."

The FPOP officials I met in Baguio, the RPC workers at Tarlac were all fairly typical of the people involved in family planning in Asia. Many of them were women who had themselves experienced childbirth and its consequences and who believed deeply in their work. They were mostly educated people of the middle class, and some worked for free—Mrs. Grafil in Mapalaciao received $1.50 per month from the RPC to cover her expenses. But in the Philippines, as indeed through most of Asia, there is a certain cachet in being identified with an organization. This is as much of an incentive as hard cash.

There is, however, one unique and peculiar organization in the Philippines that does not seem to need workers. All over the countryside, and in the cities as well, one passes churches of uniform architecture, square and spired. These are the churches of the Iglesia de Cristo, Church of Christ, a controversial body in the Philippines. The Iglesia is neither Catholic nor Protestant: It says that it corresponds to the original church of Christ in Palestine. Its observance are austere, indeed Calvinistic. It claims that anyone who is not a member will descend straight to hell, while anyone who is will zoom up in the opposite direction. There are no exceptions.

Tristram and I visited one of the churches in a suburb of Manila. A mobile van was parked on the turf outside. It was surrounded by a crowd of people, mostly women and children. A girl sat at a table beside the van, putting down names on a list. We talked to a small man who was one of the deacons. He told us that most of the church members were poor people, but they helped one another and were helped by the church, if they were true members. True members do not drink, they attend the church service every Sunday without fail, they do not marry outside the church, and they shun such dens of iniquity as dance halls or bars.

The members of the church are therefore united in a sort of puritanical stance that sets them a little apart from other Filipinos. They are closely interlinked with one another and with the church, which helps them in times of need. In return for entry into the brotherhood, the church demands that its members are united in everything. The head of the church makes the decision, in a political election, who the Iglesia de Cristo should support, and all the eligible voters amongst the church members then vote for the candidate he has named. The Iglesia has churches all over the Philippines, and though it will not divulge its numbers, estimates have been made.

On the basis of these estimates, it is certain that the Iglesia has well over 4 million communicants, possibly more. But one of every ten Filipinos is certainly a member. For this reason, they are politically very important. Their bloc vote can be the decisive factor in a national election. They are wooed by all parties. A few weeks ago, Carrie Lorenzano, a dynamic lady in the family planning field, had, after long discussions, got the head of the church to permit her to send her two mobile van clinics around the churches in Manila, providing health services like vaccination and also family planning. This was, in its way, a stroke of genius.

"The head of the church has not said definitely that we must practice family planning," said the deacon. "He has said that we may do so if we wish to." The very fact that the head of the church thinks family planning permissible, however, had clearly acted as an incentive. During the hour that Tristram and I were there, an overworked lady doctor, working inside the steamily hot van, inserted three loops. The pill was handed out to some women. Children were vaccinated. Prescriptions were issued. In the five weeks since Carrie Lorenzano had got her signal from the head of the church, there had been 1,400 acceptors from the Iglesia de Cristo.

Since, as the deacon said, the members of the Iglesia came mainly from the poorer people, this seemed an excellent idea: It gave people with no money to pay for their children a little time to stabilize themselves before they had more. If all the members of the church all over the Philippines could be reached, the existing problem of the national growth rate could be somewhat alleviated. "But I need more vans," said Mrs. Lorenzano, "and more funds." Tristram nodded. He was off to UNFPA headquarters in New York within the next few days. "I'll ask them when I reach New York," he said. "Write me an official letter tomorrow. I'll try. That's what I'm here for."

CHAPTER SIX

"To die of hunger was an offense."

Leela's ankle swelled up, and she found it more and more difficult to walk. It was decided that she should stay behind in Manila with two friends, Chino and Pacita Roces, rest for a few days, fly on to Bombay, rest some more there in her parents' flat, and then follow me to Kenya. Meanwhile I committed myself once more to the unsteady air and set off for Nairobi on the first of a series of flights that kept me in the sky or in airports for the next twenty-four hours. I was exhausted and sleepless by the time we came to the blue edge of the Arabian Sea and saw below us, sad and tawny as an ancient lionskin, the immensity of Africa —Ethiopia, the pilot said.

It was my first visit to black Africa, and I stirred back into life and looked down at a continent that has fascinated me always. The plane droned on over the endless sprawl of Ethiopia and across the border of Somaliland. The green hills of Africa were not in evidence: The earth below seemed parched and lifeless. "It is the drought," said my Zambian neighbor. "Everywhere in Africa now there is drought. On the west coast it is worst. There is drought in Asia too." He relapsed into an indistinct mutter, the gist of which was that the drought had been induced to visit Africa and Asia by Western scientists who wanted to destroy the new nations.

Africans tend to express their opinions with some violence, and sometimes the opinions are rather odd. "Look at the matter of population," said the Zambian. "The more people a nation has, the more powerful it is. But these white fellows tell the African

77

countries and the Asian countries to practice birth control. Why? So that they can wipe out all the people in those countries and be able to take them over." It was the first time this particular idea was put to me in Africa, but by no means the last. I thought the Zambian an eccentric; he was not. He was expressing an opinion held by numbers of more or less literate people all over the continent.

The country below us became more hilly, checkered with fields and rivers and patches of forest. We were now over Kenya, and presently we slanted steeply down out of a cloudless sky and landed at Nairobi. The airport was full of brusque black officials. They seemed aggressive and eager to be offended: A customs officer spent several minutes loudly telling a European woman that she must address him with respect due to him, he wasn't her servant. Eventually, I cleared my suitcase and drove into town. It was a mild, blue day, with a little wind, perfect weather, and Nairobi had an attractive look about it and seemed to like to be visited.

Grassland and hills surround the city. It sprawls somewhat, but the actual center, a place of neat white offices, banks, and hotels, is very small. Most people were dressed in European clothes, but loping down a crowded street, wrapped in a red robe, copper ornaments round his neck and a staff in his hand, I saw a Masai tribesman, and suddenly I had a full sense of having arrived in Africa. The hotel was anonymously international, but shortly after I had checked in, the sky clouded over, as abruptly as it does in England, and a loose, wild rain fell. After the rain there was a marvelous smell of wet leaves and earth. Nairobi didn't smell like a city.

Kenya is a country of savannahs and mounts, deserts, forests, and huge lakes, a temperate climate and a sufficiency of wildlife. All this is spread over an area of 220,000 square miles, inhabited by a little over 10 million people. They come from a number of tribes, the most important of which is the Kikuyu tribe that lives under the shadow of Mount Kenya. The Luo around Lake Victoria are also important, but there are others, some rather primitive, like the nomadic Masai of the savannahs and the Turkana who inhabit the desolate areas on the Somaliland border and have something of a reputation as cattle thieves. Not all these various tribes like one another.

There are also a relatively small number of Asians—Indians, Pakistanis, and Ceylonese—resident in Kenya. None of the tribes like the Asians. Until recently the commerce of the country was in their hands, and they had a reputation, not entirely undeserved, of cheating African customers. They also, when Kenya was trying to become independent, sided with the British, and this has not been forgotten. It is perhaps surprising that the British who have stayed in Kenya, perhaps because parts of it are not unlike England with a better climate, are not unpopular. Some are still government officers, and a number of them have adopted Kenyan citizenship.

With a comparatively small number of people in a large area of land, population control did not seem particularly important to many observers. Family planning was practiced from the standpoint of mother and child care, but it was practiced on a very small scale. Then, after the 1965 census, some curious facts came to light. The crude birth rate in the country was one of the highest in the world, about 50 per 1,000. The crude death rate had dropped to about 20 per 1,000. The growth rate, therefore, was exceptionally high: about 3 per cent per annum. This means that the present population will have roughly trebled itself to 30 million by 2000 A.D.

The whole affair was further complicated because the land area available to a soaring population was by no means as ample as it seemed on paper. The population density in 1962 was calculated at thirty-nine per square mile, but a survey showed that because of irrigation difficulties, soil erosion, and various other reasons, only 25 per cent of the land area was suitable for agriculture, by which most Kenyans live. About 75 per cent of the population were concentrated in a few areas, where the population density reached an average of 300 per square mile. These areas included the two main cities, Nairobi, the capital, and Mombasa.

Even if the population dependent on agriculture were to be evenly spread out over the available land, the average size of agricultural holdings would still be small. Already, it was noted, there was a trend on the part of farmers who held two or three acres of land to leave their families to work the land while they went into Nairobi or Mombasa to look for work. The population in the cities was increasing three times as fast as the population of the country. In 1972 the growth rate of the population of Nairobi was 10 per cent. What really proved a terrifying statistic was that the city unemployment rate was 20 per cent.

But there is also, in the countryside, what is technically referred to as disguised unemployment. That is to say, a man with a very small piece of land would probably be unable to work it for large parts of every year, while awaiting his crop. The crop would, obviously, be scanty because of the size of the farm. So the man would try the city. The actual unemployment in the cities was thus in part caused by disguised unemployment in the country. A further fact, revealed by a Population Council survey in 1965, when the population was 9 million, was that at the existing growth rate the population would reach 144 million in less than 100 years.

In addition, as the survey pointed out, the death rate would probably drop still further over this period, due to improved health services. The population would therefore rise still further, unless the birth rate—the fertility rate—were to be brought under control, rapidly and drastically. In 1973 the desired number of children, for most Kenyan couples, was six or seven. This desire, according to one observer, was based upon an awareness of the formerly very high infant mortality. The more children you had, the more you were likely to finish up with.

The infant mortality has dropped, but most people in the countryside are still not aware of it. It is the old story brought over from Asia: the more children, the more hands to work, the more social security in age, the more status in the community. There is a further complication, reminiscent to me of the situation as regards the Indian states. The tribes have proportional representation in the Kenyan Parliament. The larger the tribe, the more elected members it has to speak for it. In a situation where most tribes suspect and distrust each other, this is obviously no incentive for a tribal chief to tell his people to limit their families.

In 1967 the Government of Kenya rather warily said that it supported family planning, so long as it was accepted voluntarily —which meant that no incentives should be offered—and so long as it was done for reasons of health. The Kenyan Parliament is a highly vocal body, and the government and family planners in the country were verbally assailed by a number of professional politicians, including ministers. They continue to be so assailed, and perhaps the noisiest critic of all is the Assistant Minister for Home Affairs, the Honorable J. M. Shikuku. The week I arrived, he said in a speech that family planning was intended to wipe out Africans.

When I met Shikuku in his office, he was dressed primly in a dark suit and was shouting violently in Swahili at a telephone. Eventually, he slammed down the receiver and eyed me with some suspicion. Then he proceeded to tell me what he felt about family planning and, once under way, went on for the next two hours. He said, for a start, that Kenya had inherited a capitalist system from the British, which was not in keeping with what he described as African socialism. By this, he said, he meant that in the old days a tribe owned land in common, and the chief would see that no member of the tribe starved. "To die of hunger," said Shikuku, "was an offense."

While the African tribal system seemed to him admirable, he said the British tribal system was terrible. "Once in London," he said, "I was strolling in Hyde Park with my friend. I saw a man lying down. He was covered with pigeons. He had pigeons on his head. I thought this man was dead. I took away the pigeons from his head and asked him 'Are you dead?' The man said no, but he was Scottish, and because of that no English would employ him. He said he was a Master of Arts, and he had not eaten for thirty-six hours. I gave him ten shillings, because, as an African, I am traditionally generous. He went off.

"There is enough for all in Kenya," Shikuku continued. "The problem is one of equal distribution. The wealth in Kenya was held by Europeans and Asians for seventy years, but after *uhuru* it was grabbed by a lot of Kenyans. So you find people who hold twelve different company directorships and other people who cannot find employment. Equal distribution of wealth will solve this problem. Arid areas can be irrigated. We have lots of water in Lake Victoria and Lake Rudolph."

He then turned to the actual question of family planning. "Pills," he said firmly, "make a woman very fat. Loops cause women to bleed to death and have awful pains. Also, with both the pill and the loop, women either lose all interest in sex or they become very sexy. Women in Nairobi are very reckless. Homes break up and divorces increase. This is OK," said Shikuku scornfully, "in the United Kingdom and the United States but not in our country. We should not copy the United States. All this is due to birth control, which is why I oppose it." He paused a moment.

At this point I intervened to put in a question about the economic future of Kenya if the growth rate stayed steady. "I am not an economist," Shikuku said with a modest smile. "I am only a silly little politician." He paused once more, "But I am telling you the facts. First, like General Idi Amin of Uganda, we should throw the Asians out and take over the commerce of our country. People say that the economy will suffer." He shrugged. "Most people in Kenya are so poor they won't feel the pinch anyway." After a while, he added, wealth would be widespread in the country.

Freda Mudoga runs the Family Planning Association of Kenya. She is a large, friendly lady, and, so far as African tribal tradition went, she said that a form of birth control had been practiced throughout history. The Luo around Lake Victoria had for centuries used a kind of herb for birth prevention; this was at present being studied by a doctor on a research assignment. "Also," she said, "traditionally, a couple had no intercourse while the wife was still feeding a child, and sometimes it took two or three years for a child to be weaned. That prevented further children during the time.

"It's also not true to say that many children were a status symbol, at least, not always. If a husband had many children and no money to keep them with, he would be reprimanded by the village elders and so lose prestige. There was polygamy too, a common practice. If a husband had several wives, he would not want to have them all producing babies at the same time. Then, in some tribes, the wife had to return to her parents before the delivery, and she would stay there for two years. Finally, there were a number of ceremonies performed before the child was two years old; these ceremonies forbade intercourse between the parents.

All this contributed to a natural pattern of spacing children. It did work, on the whole."

When family planning started in Kenya, Miss Mudoga was involved. "This was prior to 1955," she said. "Doctors kept finding that women patients were ill from too many pregnancies. The Family Planning Association of Kenya was formed then. There were three separate committees in Nairobi, Mombasa, and Nakuru. In 1957 the FPAK affiliated itself with the International Planned Parenthood Foundation. Then we expanded, and not only into other urban areas, but into many rural areas." Miss Mudoga thought the growth rate in Kenya in 1973 was 3.5 per cent, not 3 per cent. "We estimate that we have 120,000 acceptors," she said. "But there's a lack of follow-up in these matters."

It is not only difficult to follow up acceptors, except in the towns and cities, it is difficult to talk to women in the first place, to persuade them to accept family planning, certainly in the countryside. Many tribes have taboos involved with talking about their children, and women won't tell a stranger how many they have, for fear of witchcraft or simple bad luck. Moreover, so far as I could gather from Miss Mudoga and other Kenyans involved in family planning, a large number of the acceptors were couples who had already produced the six or seven children desired by most Kenyans. Also, some of them were wives rather than husbands, and they did it secretly.

"The husbands do not like their wives to take the pill or have loop insertions," Miss Mudoga said, "because they are afraid of unchastity." Maybe, I thought, Shikuku had been right, or at least typical of many Kenyan men when birth control is mentioned. "The husbands in rural areas," Miss Mudoga added, "are often away in the cities looking for work. That's difficult too: The husband fears the wife will be unchaste while he's away, and the wives think if they are on the pill, which is the most popular device here, that they needn't take it till the husband comes home. He may come home unexpectedly on a visit from the city. And then what happens?"

What indeed? According to the Population Council report, "even a major program that would be judged as very successful, would still lead to a substantial increase in the population of Kenya." The report adds that even if there was a 50 per cent reduction in fertility, the population of the country would have doubled by the year 2000, that is, it would be 19 million (allowing for the year 1965, in which the report was published) rather than 30 million. Even a doubling of the population would probably be too much for the country to contain under existing circumstances. Under existing circumstances, moreover, the possibility of halving fertility is minimal.

Two Americans, Jim McCarron and Jason Calhoun, are working for the Health Education Unit, a government organization in Nairobi, on the implementation of media to assist family planning programs. They put out a poster showing a happy couple with two children. Under the picture was a list, also pictorial, of the advantages they would obtain by family limitation. On the other side of the poster was a couple with numerous children and no pictorially portrayed advantages. The tribesmen, when they were confronted by this poster, had a uniform reaction: The couple with two children were rich but sad, for unlike the philoprogenitive couple, they were unfulfilled.

"Nothing's been planned for the rural areas," said McCarron, a quiet, rather flushed man in his forties, "except seminars, where people involved in the program talk to tribal chiefs, schoolteachers, and so on. There're only three areas in the whole of the country chosen for rural development. One of them is Vihiga, near Lake Victoria. There's a terrific population density there." Miss Mudoga had told me there was to be a seminar at Masena, not far from Vihiga, over the coming weekend. I felt it wouldn't be a bad idea for me to drive down and look at Vihiga, and what was being done there, even though I was not tremendously anxious to attend the seminar.

When you leave Nairobi by road, heading down into the Rift Valley, you realize how curious a country Kenya is. The road we were freewheeled down by a young U.N. driver called Johnston, from Nairobi, ran, some miles from the city, through pastoral, emerald country not unlike the landscape around Oxford. By the road there were small stalls that were festooned with sheepskins and with sheepskin caps. Then the countryside turns African: You slide down from Cotswold country and see under you an enormous expanse of yellow earth, patched with bushes and pocked with blisters, that is the Rift Valley—a fault in the earth that extends northward through Africa.

Through the first part of the trip, before we came down to the valley, rain fell. It was a pervasive, soft rain, like English rain, that made the landscape around one more familiar, except for the tin shacks in the forest and the black people. Leela, who had been carted off a large plane in a small wheelchair the day before, was with me, and Johnston beamed and talked about his own wife, currently in Mombasa with his parents. When we struck the valley, the rain stopped, and there was a hot sun out. The earth smelled rich and wet, and the car roared down a road on either side of which, feathered with tamarisk, the savannah lay. Johnston ceased to speak.

We didn't see many people: once, a couple of Masai herdsmen in their red blanket robes, huddled, chin to knees, by the roadside, far from their own country. What they were doing north of Nairobi, Johnston, come to life once more, couldn't explain. Now and then there were buses packed with people, and off the road were tiny isolated churches and farms. Then we came past the lakes, Naivasha and Nakuru, huge dingy pools of water lying amidst the arms of the hills. We stopped for lunch at Nakuru, where the surface of the lake seemed covered with a pink scum: flamingoes, whole aviaries of them, lying tinted and packed on the water like swans with a disease.

We descended through a national park to the lakeshore to look at them where they lay on the unmoving water. The shore stank of decayed fish and was molted over by drying pink feathers. When the wind shifted inshore, one could tell the flamingoes stank too, and as they moved listlessly, in their incredible numbers, on the water, they exuded a curious sound like that of a burst beehive. Johnston stirred restlessly on the shore, kicking up the gravelly sand with a well-shod foot. As we drove back through the park we passed bushbuck and waterbuck where the thick trees were, and, in the open spaces of savannah, impalas on tiptoe, ready to quiver into flight, birdlike and light.

Johnston, as we bumped off down the highway once more, said the buck and antelope were excellent to eat. "Flamingoes," he said, "maybe some other tribe eat them, not mine." He swerved up a road that took us into what are called the White Highlands, where the British colonials, apparently, built houses and farms, where the Mau Mau were particularly active during the independence movement, and where the landscape was more like the Cotswolds than ever, especially because a thick shroud of cloud floated above us and presently released itself in rain. This was not English rain; it fell in hard and heavy spears, berating the windshield, till we dropped from the hill.

The rain having stopped, we ran quietly through an emerald countryside dotted with exotic trees. People were now visible in fair numbers: women, wrapped around in colorful cloth and bandannaed, hoed the fields or carried loads of firewood on their heads down the trails to their clustered beehive huts, and men, mostly in European clothes, but a few in Biblical robes, sauntered homeward, too.

The sun dropped quickly; the trees cut surrealist shadows into the red earth. A long glimmer appeared in the distance. "Lake Victoria," Johnston told us—the source of the Nile, a huge crinkly transparent sheet of water, with rushes stiff as soldiers on parade or collapsed drunkenly to one side in the offshore shallows. These, I had been told, were full of bilharzia, deadly parasitic worms. At Kisumu, a small, pleasant town on the shores of the lake, we stopped and checked into a hotel. The mosquitoes sang shrilly in the darkness outside our bedroom. I tried to contact Freda Mudoga in Masena, seventeen miles from Kisumu, but the telephone didn't work properly. I gave up.

Instead, I sat down and thought about the day. After Asia, the landscape through which we had passed seemed very sparsely populated; also, after Asia, there seemed to be comparatively little cultivation. Coming down from the White Highlands, we had driven through miles of tea plantations, the squat round bushes dripping in the rain. But tea, like coffee, was introduced into Kenya by the British, and these were commercial plantations. Tea, after all, is not something that people usually eat, except in Japan, and Kenyan farmers usually cultivate edible crops. We had seen, in the small fields by the road, plantations of maize and plots full of sweet potatoes.

Maize is a staple food in Kenya and is usually eaten in the form of *posho*, a sort of porridge. In Africa as in Asia, people fill up the corners of their hunger with starch, which does not make for a balanced diet. By no means all the tribes are hunters and fishermen, and so far as hunting goes these days, there is also a matter of game licenses to be considered. So it is difficult for people in the hinterland to balance their diet, especially since vegetables are normally produced as a cash crop rather than for domestic consumption. The farms we had passed were tiny, so there was no room to cultivate much except maize, and this year the rivers were dry.

To expand the area of arable land, I had already been told, was very difficult. Now I had seen this for myself. After the heavy rains along the way, the highland slopes had seemed to dissolve: The top layer of red soil, stripped away, swam in a surge of water down the highway, and the raw underside of the earth had been exposed. Very few soil conservation methods have been employed in Kenya. One method that works in Asia is to terrace the fields: Witness, for example, the tremendous tiers of paddy on the slopes of Banaue in the Philippines, which I had visited in the past. Kenyans, however, are averse to terracing their fields. The reason is odd:

During the time of the emergency in Kenya, when the Mau Mau were slaughtering white farmers and those considered to be collaborators, the British tried to bring in a soil conservation program. They introduced it by way of terracing, and the people they put to work on it were political detainees. The Kenyans apparently feel, therefore, that to terrace fields is a colonial idea: they associate terracing, according to a Swiss expert I had met in Nairobi, with forced labor. They are now independent, but the aversion to terracing remains. Perhaps one reason why people are always a problem is that their reactions tend to be so excessively instinctual.

The Rift Valley had been dry and broken by boulders. Irrigation, the Swiss expert had told me, was possible in that loose yellow volcanic soil, but the spread of water was liable to cause a spread of disease. It might be possible, he said, echoing Shikuku's dream, to pump water from some of the lakes into the valley, though it would be extremely expensive, but the likelihood was that the water would carry bilharzia with it and set the whole health program back. In Kenya, as in Asia, the whole problem of people turns in a vicious circle. It seemed to me that it would be exceptionally difficult to unmake the circle, at least in our time.

That night in Kisumu, at dinner, we bumped into Jerry Owuor, who is the Deputy Secretary of the government Family Planning Unit. He had been at the seminar in Masena but didn't know where Miss Mudoga might be. He is a thick-set man in his early forties whom I had met earlier in Nairobi, where he had not been particularly sanguine as to the future of family planning in Kenya. He had said then that the growth rate was 3.3 per cent, thus differing from Miss Mudoga, who had said it was 3.5, and from the Population Council, which estimated it as 3 per cent. The inability to obtain proper figures about population had now begun to seem to me endemic in the Third World.

Owuor had told me, at the time of our interview, that another worrying point was that 48 per cent of the population was under fifteen years of age. Though the average life expectancy in Kenya is between forty and forty-five, there are a number of old people, and their presence, as well as that of the children, means that there is considerable dependency on young married couples, adding to their economic instability. Though the government had approved of family planning in 1967, up to a point, the program had still not started up properly: The implementation had been delayed till 1974 so that the program would become part of Kenya's 5-year plan, which starts then.

Even so, the outlay on it was not tremendous: $230,000 had been allotted as the budget per year over five years. The intention was to reduce the growth rate from 3.3 to 3.05. "If we reduce it that far," Owuor had said, "it will have, at least, *some* effect." But he had been a bit somber. "Unless there is a definite plan, it is no use," he said. "And there are too many foreign agencies dabbling in the program in order to try and help us, as they say. They get in one another's way, and in ours. We are also very short of doctors. We will have to run the program through paramedics, midwives, auxiliary nurses, and so forth. It's a question of health, really."

Tonight in Kisumu, things were different from the way they had been in his neat office in Nairobi. It was dark outside and cool, with the Ugandan border not far off, and we were able to talk to each other not as interviewed and interviewer. Owuor said, "If you look at the Family Planning Unit, there are two Europeans and myself running the operation. We don't yet have enough trained Kenyan personnel. The clinics will have to be part of district hospitals or of health centers. We cannot direct the program in terms of limitation. We have to direct it in terms of spacing. He shrugged. "I'll give you a letter to the FPAK man here; see him tomorrow."

Next day he left for Nairobi. I walked down the road to the FPAK office, past trees and the distant lake, the hard smell of leaves and water in the air around me, the Luo people of the lake loping by me with their boneless African stride, and found, in the large empty office, a nice man who said that since it was Saturday no family planning clinics were open. "We give seminars in remote villages," he said "but no such seminar is scheduled for the next two days." Since I could not possibly await this event in Kisumu, I felt a bit disappointed. "But I think," the FPAK man said, "you will see the local conditions. Perhaps."

I had every intention of trying to see the local conditions, but felt we needed a guide: Johnston, since he was from Mombasa in the south, didn't really speak the Luo language; besides, neither he nor I had the faintest idea where we should drive to. Vihiga was only about fifteen miles off, and there were supposed to be some American advisers there. But having come all the way up from Nairobi, I wanted to look at a reasonably large area. The FPAK man, however, informed me that at weekends it was his custom to return to his farm in a village thirty miles from Kisumu. He did not manifest any intention of asking us to look at it. "I relax," he said, "there."

This was entirely understandable. On the other hand, he did not proffer any ideas whatever about where I should drive to or whom I should see. We sat on the terrace of the hotel, to which I had brought him, staring at each other in a deeply depressed way. Johnston appeared and asked what I wanted to do, and I said we probably wanted to return to Nairobi. Johnston raised his eyebrows, smiled, and returned to the car, in which, not very long after, he fell fast asleep. Meanwhile, a procession of other cars arrived: Out of the front one, on which a dusty national flag fluttered, climbed a man in a Kwame Nkrumah suit. He turned out to be the Minister of Finance.

He was followed by a train of attendants, one of whom was an Englishman, a mild, softly spoken man called Malcolm Milne, who had been the planning commissioner of the province, and was now the planning adviser. The minister, Milne told me, had come to inspect the progress of new road and water schemes in the area. He added that if I cared to follow the minister's procession in my car, he would be glad to ride with us and explain the difficulties around Lake Victoria. The FPAK man looked dubious, but I said we'd be delighted to follow the minister. The FPAK man then looked relieved. "Next time you come to Africa," he said, "you must visit my farm."

The minister took off, his limousine, flag flapping, plunging down an unmade dirt road into the hinterland. The limousine was followed by three other cars, which were followed by ours. The red dust rolled up in clouds so convulsive that it was impossible to see the cars ahead. Also their tires kicked up stones and rocks that flew like shrapnel through the indistinct air. "I think," said Milne in the front seat, carefully, to Johnston, who appeared to feel that he was in competition with the other cars, "it would be wiser to leave some space between us and them. We can follow them by the dust, y'know. Lots of it here."

There was, certainly. As it wrapped us in its wounded arms, Milne said, "You know, people here live at subsistence level, hm? Yes . . . subsistence level, y'see. They're building a waterworks for irrigation; hm, and, hm, there are various projects going on." He pointed to the side of the road: beehive huts, children waving still, even though the ministerial chariot had roared by, and men and women standing by the road or in the fields and staring. "Suffer from malnutrition, y'see," said Milne. After Asia, it was extraordinary to think these people did: They were tall, and they looked as though they should be in excellent health. They weren't, Milne told me.

"Malnutrition, y'see," he repeated, blinking his blue friendly eyes. "Bilharzia, too. All the way around Lake Victoria. Very bad, bilharzia, hm? Can be fatal." He was like Edgar Wallace's Sanders of the River, with those blue eyes and the limp he had because of arthritis, and the safari suit he wore, and the shooting stick he carried. "Where are you from?" he asked Johnston, who told him. "Hm, a long way from home," Milne said. He had been in Kenya for some years, and before that in the Cameroons: He was an old Africa hand. "People here," he said, "are much nicer than they are in West Africa, y'know. If you're going to the west coast you'll find out, hm?"

We pulled up, after thirty miles or so, in a small village that was built in peeling plaster and had a few shops and bars. A crowd stood in the sun, eyeing our minister with respect. Awaiting him also was the Minister of Natural Resources, who carried an ostrich-feather fly whisk in the crook of his arm. The ministers welcomed each other, then we all climbed back into the cars and were off once more. We drove for another thirty miles, to a mission school where drums thumped and a Luo in his full ceremonial costume, including feathers, capered slowly in imitation of a crane. The school had a water supply that was to be deflected to the surrounding villages.

Milne sat on his shooting stick in the shade, under a wall draped with lurid bougainvillea. A priest sat with us, fanning himself with his hat, a Dutchman. He had planted the bougainvillea himself. The drums thudded in the distance, trailing the ministers around the school. "Why do the villagers need a water supply?" I asked. "Lake Victoria isn't very far away." The priest said, "We are a little inland from the lake. Too far is it for the people to walk for water, and in these villages there are no pipes to connect with the lake. Also the lake, she is polluted with bilharzia. Too polluted is she to drink safely. Of course, most of the people have bilharzia already. That is why if they are to be cured, they need pure water."

I decided to pull out, since Milne said the ministers would be on their tour till nightfall. Johnston, who appeared relieved, sped down the road, then abruptly slowed down. I asked him why. He pointed to the people on the roadside, women in their body-cloths and bandannas, tall tired men: "These are poor people," he said simply. "Why should they eat my dust?" The clouds of red dust settled outside the car, and I was touched by this quality of compassion in Johnston. We drove on slowly past hills contorted with strange outcrops of rock, Lake Victoria below us, to

Kisumu. Johnston went off for his lunch, and we went into the hotel for ours.

The headwaiter told us that a wedding reception was to be held, and after lunch, as we sat on the verandah awaiting Johnston, a battered bus drew up, full of singing people and bearing on its roof a host of wedding presents. These included a small refrigerator, a stove, and a live goat. The guests, the men in tight, badly cut suits and shoes, the women mostly in fantastic hats and bright dresses, though some were dignified in their native dress, sat on the verandah and ordered vast amounts of beer. The electric appliances were borne into the dining room, where the reception was to be held. I didn't see where the goat was taken, maybe into the backyard.

Afterward, we drove up to Vihiga, past a sign, on a slope above Kisumu, that stated that we were now on the equator. It was cool, and the roadside was crowded with people, women with bales on their heads, men with staffs, chewing sugar cane and spitting out the pith. We had nearly reached Vihiga when a tremendous storm broke, the rain lashing and spitting in the red mud. The American advisers for the rural development scheme were not to be found, and the rain was too heavy to move around in. So we turned back. Next day we returned to Nairobi. It was Sunday, and in the fields, to attentive congregations, black priests clad in white were saying Mass.

In Nairobi there were occasional squalls of rain punctuated by sunshine. I had now seen a few of the most thickly populated areas in Kenya, as well as some that were thinly populated, and I looked at the city with new eyes. Around Lake Victoria I had seen people who lived at subsistence level and who suffered from endemic diseases. Poverty in Kenya, where the average per capita income is $140 a year, is not as blatantly obvious as it is in Asia: Illness is less obvious too, and this may be because the people as a rule are taller and better built than most Asians. But it exists, and for the first time I started to notice beggars in Nairobi.

The situation, so far as population was concerned, seemed on the surface to be under control, but what the eye sees isn't always the true picture. The Population Council had recommended that the Kenyan Government aim for a 50 per cent reduction of fertility, but this the government could not do. Not only had they to tread warily in a situation where several politicians and minismers were bitterly opposed to the idea of famly planning, they had also to consider that many of the literate populace thought family planning was a white plot aimed at wiping out the blacks, and some tribes thought it was a plot by other tribes to decimate them.

The psychological difficulties apart, there were purely physical difficulties involved: the shortage not only of doctors but of any trained personnel, the remoteness of certain parts of Kenya, and the lack of any clinical facilities in these parts. The government hoped for a drop in the growth rate through family planning, but apart from certain people in the Ministry of Finance who are much involved with the program, their target was a relatively minor drop; they aimed at it with leisurely arrows.

It is very difficult to see that Kenya is threatened by a problem of overpopulation unless you are acquainted with the mathematics of population. These are complex in the extreme. Population increase tends to move like a wave: It rises to a crest and then curls down into a trough, then rises once more. The increase over the years, however, is a constant. The population of Kenya, therefore, is bound to have risen steeply by the year 2000, and unless this is accompanied by a concurrent economic development, the cities will become chronically overcrowded and the unemployment rate will rise. Jack Kisa, the principal economist of the government, is closely connected with planning for the future. I went to see him.

Kisa is a stocky, intelligent, busy man. He seemed a little remote at the start of the interview. As we continued, he became interested in the conversation, picking up every point, his quick eyes in perpetual quest of my face to see if I had followed what he said. "The levels of living in urban areas are far better," he told me, "than they are in rural areas. We need to narrow the income difference between urban and rural areas to prevent an excessive migration to the cities. Some of the rural areas, we plan, will become urban. We'll create areas of concentration provided with a proper infrastructure and a sound economic base."

He added, "Our economy is quite advanced in comparison with other African nations. Our industry is fairly sizable, and it's growing at the rate of 8 per cent per annum. Agriculture is on the increase too. Our view of the future is one of increased industry, where we will process industrial products for our own consumption. Our policy is not to depend too heavily on the export market. We export tea and coffee, but we have no control over those markets." He paused a moment and looked out of his window at the vivid flame trees. "Unemployment is our main problem now, though you must remember that the concept of employment is an imported concept.

"However, in the so-called modern sector, the wage sector, there is a labor force of 4 million men and women between the ages of fifteen and fifty-nine. Only 700,000 of them can be employed. Nevertheless, there is a yearly employment increase of 3 per cent in the modern sector. Our policy now is to try and create incentives to induce industry to come into what are now rural sectors, and not to concentrate on Nairobi and Mombasa." He turned to the family planning program. "The program, as you know, started in a minor way in 1967. Between then and 1970 only $150,000 were allocated to it by the government—a very small percentage of its budget.

"Between 1970 and 1974 the allocation doubled. Now the program is to be aided by the World Bank. For the program in the new 5-year plan, the World Bank will bear half the cost. There are other donors, but the Kenyan Government will bear most of the other half of the cost. We will spend it on vehicles, on clinical facilities in the rural areas, the training of workers, the purchase of contraceptives, and the motivation and education of the people. Originally, the program aimed at the spacing of children, but now we've started to talk of family limitation. There are a lot of obstacles to this, as you probably know." He rubbed his brow pensively.

He is a young man and resilient. At times he looks very tired, then suddenly springs back into the conversation with a rapid rush of words. "Family planning is by no means the only way in which we hope to control the population," he said. "Our socio-economic programs will play a very important part. We have noted that the more education and income people have, the more they resort to family planning on their own, without motivation. As our educational program expands, more and more young people will be in a position to know what methods are available for family limitation, and they'll see it as a way to a better life for their children.

"And our educational program has been a success. We've been spending 20 per cent of our national budget on education. At present 60 to 70 per cent of our children attend primary school. Our long-term objective is free primary schools. The secondary schools are very heavily subsidized. Only 1 per cent of the population attend the universities, so university education is free. By 1985 we should have universal free primary education as well." He studied his watch. "I'm afraid I have a conference in a few minutes. But I'd like to say that even if the worst predictions about our population growth come true, we are trying to provide an infrastructure able to support it."

Several agencies now work on the family planning program in Kenya. Lars-Gunnar Remstrand, who is the administrative adviser to the Kenyan Government Family Planning Unit, and himself belongs to the Swedish International Development Authority, was rather sarcastic about them. "They come here and spend a day talking to someone," he said. "Then they promise aid and sponsor a plan and fly home. The aid never comes on time; sometimes it never comes at all. It also happens that one finds the government, the agency headquarters, the local agency chief, and the field workers all fighting each other. The success of any program is dependent on the flexibility allowed by the sponsors. Most allow none."

SIDA supplies the Kenyan Government with all the contraceptives used in the family planning program except the loop, which is provided by the Population Council. It is also busy in information and training activities, and finances the printing of pamphlets on family planning. "There are about 48,000 acceptors a year now," Remstrand said. "But nobody knows how many have dropped out. We have an evaluation department, but no staff to evaluate. We are trying to launch a cooperative venture with Nairobi University. Follow-up is essential, but follow-up depends on the workers. Without sufficient workers, it's impossible to evaluate success."

Of the other agencies at work in Kenya, the International

Planned Parenthood Federation provides training for medical and paramedical personnel. It also provides seven mobile units for family planning, which, according to its officials, account for a third of the acceptors every year—that amounts, at present, to 16,000 a year. It supplies the various Kenyan voluntary associations with family planning posters, brochures, and so forth. The Ford Foundation finances the FPAK, up to a point, sends students to America to study population, and funded a study of tribal reactions to family planning, edited by Angela Molnos. But it may be pulling out of population work in Kenya soon.

"You see," said Susan Fisher of the foundation, "there are now twenty-one donor agencies in Kenya, all of whom are supporting family planning. But we'll continue to look for input opportunities, probably into training programs." The foundation had a representative on the Population Council team in 1965 and now has a representative at the Ministry of Health. The IPPF set up its office in Nairobi in 1967. Other agencies moved in about the same time; some came later. Remstrand was sour about them. "They are trying to solve problems," he said, "that should be solved on other levels. First, they should try and raise the living standards of the poor."

Our time in Kenya was over. I was sorry to leave it. However brusque and abrupt the officials might sometimes be, the blackmen loping down the streets had superb white smiles, and they seemed to love life in a way that Asians didn't. The trees were smeared with flowers, and there were brilliant butterflies even in the city. The rain when it fell brought its crisp smell of wet earth. We had made friends in Nairobi, too, and it was sad to leave them. On this trip I found it peculiarly so. As a writer, one wanders the world, and leaves one's books and articles as footprints. Had I come simply as a writer, all the farewells would have been easy.

Had I come simply as a writer, I would have interviewed politicians, looked around me, and said to my friends when we parted, "See you sometime, somewhere," and been pleasantly surprised when I next bumped into them in some unexpected corner of the world. Because I had come as a writer on population, I was unable to do this simple thing. I had started to see all the countries that I had so far visited as scarred, difficult battlefields on which wars nobody else was aware of were being fought. I saw these countries in terms of whether or not they would survive this mysterious and unknown series of wars, and I saw my friends as the possible victims.

If this sounds overstated, I can only say that, covering my first shooting war, before I knew much about what actual war was like, I had feelings that were radically the same. There are, of course, an enormous number of experts behind every war, plotting its course, swinging its armed puppets this way and that. Behind this particular war stood a host of demographers and of world agencies, fronted by its opposition. Demographers are fine, world agencies are fine, but in Algeria and Israel, Vietnam and Belfast and the Indian border, it was always the helpless ones on the torn earth who were the people that mattered. I thought about this before Leela and I took off for Gabon.

CHAPTER SEVEN

"They want to reach a 100 per cent level of
school attendance. Ha, ha."

To get to Libreville from Nairobi, we had to fly through Entebbe
in Uganda and Bujumbara in Burundi to Kinshasa, the capital
of Zaïre, for an overnight stopover. Kinshasa was once known as
Leopoldville, and Zaïre as the Belgian Congo. The plane, as I
shortly learned was normally the case in Africa, was late, four
hours late. At last, however, we took off, and several hours later
were flying over forests of a surprising, clotted thickness. As Leela
said, it was like looking down onto a mass of broccoli heads. This
interesting view was soon wiped away by a thick cloud, and we
came down on Kinshasa in the midst of a violent electric storm
and torrential rain.

The storm had stopped by the time we left the airport. It was
very hot and very damp outside, with rough primitive trees rising
amidst scattered clumps of white houses. Most of the women we
saw wore their traditional robes and bandannas, but the people
as a rule looked much less cheerful than the people in Kenya.
They had, in the main, a sullen and burdened look to match the
weather. What I couldn't get used to was that they all spoke
French, though I suppose it was no more or less peculiar than all
the people in Kenya speaking English. We booked into an exceptionally uncheap hotel, and, suffering from lack of sleep, attempted
to amend this.

Midway through the night, I awoke with the impression that a
revolution had broken out. I went to the window and looked out:
Every few seconds a crippled tree of lightning sprouted and died

in a ripped black sky. There were such fusillades of thunder as I have never heard anywhere else in the world and a blinding, driving rain crackling into the slack yellow waters of the Congo as it slouched immensely by. Sleep was impossible, and I started to wonder about the feasibility of flight under these conditions. Next day, however, things cleared up. It was a gray, slow day and was made considerably slower by the fact that our plane this time was six hours late.

Eventually, after numerous false alarms, we took off, and presently arrived over the broccoli forests and slow sea of Gabon. The airport formalities at Libreville took a long time, but there was a U.N. driver outside to meet us. He was a large man, and much of the black skin of his face had turned pink and swollen. I later discovered that this was due to a traffic accident, but at the time thought that he was the victim of some frightful equatorial disease. Even if we had known the truth, I doubt if it would have comforted us much, as he proceeded, in the manner of a hurricane, to take us through boiling clouds of yellow dust into the small and scattered town.

Libreville stands on the bank of the Gabon Estuary, which at this time of year, the end of the rainy season, had a dull corroded look about it. Overhead the sky was full of a dark fleece of cloud. The driver informed us that even when the dry season came, these clouds would still be there. "The sun only shines," he said mournfully, "for a month or two every year in Gabon." This might, I thought, explain the surly looks of most of the people we passed on the road and of the people at the hotel. Several of them seemed to have skin infections of one sort or another. There were surprisingly few children around. The low white houses of the town had a deserted look.

Gabon is a country that was artificially created, an area of impenetrable forest that the French colonists arbitrarily demarcated and named after what the Portuguese navigators, the first Europeans to arrive in these parts, called the estuary down which they sailed. *Gabon* in Portuguese means the sleeve of a matelot's uniform, and the shape of the estuary apparently reminded the navigators of this. The Portuguese were followed in due course by the Spanish, the Dutch, the Danes, the French, the English, and the

Americans. The main reason for their frequent calls was the fact that they were able to remove from Gabon a plentiful number of slaves.

The Portuguese, when they first arrived in 1482, were looking for ivory and spice. At that time the tribe that inhabited the banks of the estuary was the Mpongwe, who were fisherfolk. There is no record as to how many of them there were, but historians do not think that there could have been more than a few thousand. Beyond the estuary was the thick, dark, unknown forest, between whose immense trees a handful of pygmies flitted with their blowpipes and poisoned darts. The forest, at least the kind of forest that exists in Gabon, is by no means the natural habitat of any human creature.

The likelihood is that the pygmies arrived there through no choice of their own. That is to say, they probably, in some unimaginably early time, inhabited the savannah country to the north of the forest, until driven out by the arrival, through migration, of larger and more ferocious people. These tribes, in turn, were driven from the savannahs into the forest, either because of the incursions of even more warlike tribes or because of the depredations of the Arab slave traders, armed with swords and rifles of a sort. The Mpongwe, on the banks of the estuary, found that another tribe, the Akele, had emerged from the forest. They lived a little way beyond the Mpongwe, farther back in the forest. A third tribe, the Boulou, then turned up, beyond the Akele.

The three tribes, the strongest of which was the settled Mpongwe, started to make occasional forays against one another. The captives taken became the slaves of the victorious tribe. In Libreville today there is still an Akele quarter; the divisions persist. In any event, the Mpongwe started to realize that they had trading assets far more valuable than forest honeycombs, wood, and so on—they had people. They started to sell their own criminals, and the captives they had taken from the Akele and the Boulou, in exchange for raw spirits, flintlocks, mirrors, and Manchester cloth. The Portuguese were by no means displeased.

As other Western nations arrived on the shores of West Africa to prospect this profitable market, the slave trade increased. The slaves, who were often under the impression that the white men were loading them on to their ships as a source of nutrition for

the duration of the voyage, were bundled, hopeless, terrified, be-
trayed, and abandoned by their own race, despised and treated like
animals by their white purchasers, away to an island called São
Tomé, off the Gabon coast, where, in the slave barracks, they
awaited the arrival of the ships that would take them away. How
many people were taken from Gabon itself has never been worked
out.

It is unlikely, considering the nature of the terrain and the
consequent sparsity of the population, that an immense amount
were. However, according to Gaston Rapontchambo, the keeper
of the Gabon National Archives, over a million men, women, and
children were carried away from the west coast of Africa over the
period of 300 years when the slave boom was on.

It is a curious fact that the diet of the tribes of the interior
changed because of the slave trade. Apart from hunting, the
tribes before the trade really started subsisted on taro and wild
bananas. But on São Tomé, the slaves awaiting shipment had to
be fed, as they had to be fed on the voyage. Manioc, potatoes,
and breadfruit were therefore imported, mostly from East Africa
and sometimes from America. They spread over the sea from São
Tomé to the hinterland.

By the sixteenth century, many of the visiting Europeans were
writing accounts of Gabon: one was Jean Barbot, who said of
the islanders of Korisko, at the mouth of the estuary, "They are
governed by a chief, who is lord of the island, and they all live
very poorly, but have plenty enough of cucumbers, which grow
there in perfection, and many sorts of fowl. . . . As to the government in Gabon," he continues, "every free person lives for himself, without any regard for king or chiefs, neither have those
dignified persons any shew of state or grandeur; for the king
follows the trade of a blacksmith, to get his living, being like his
subjects very poor, and is not ashamed to hire his wives, at a
very cheap rate, to the Europeans." Barbot also remarks on the
fondness of the Gabonese for strong waters.

"Many of them are excessively fond of brandy and other strong
liquors of Europe and America, and spend all they can upon
them. . . . their excessive greediness for strong liquors renders
them . . . little nice and curious in the choice of them." For this
reason, the Europeans profited, for liquor was an article of trade

and, "tho' mixt with half water, and sometimes a little Spanish soap put into it, to give it a froth to appear of proof, by the scum it makes, they like it, and praise it as much as the best and purest brandy, and do all they can to have a stock of it. . . ." If Barbot and his friends thus attempted to swindle the natives, one feels it not unlaudable that the Gabonese did it back. Nevertheless, some Gabonese paid an ivory tusk for liquor.

Other payments were made: "They besmear their bodies with elephant's or buffalo fat, and a sort of red colour . . . which makes them stink so abominably, especially the women, that there is no coming near them, without turning a man's stomach . . ." despite which the sailors seem to have come very near them: "They sell their favours at a very cheap rate to any of the meanest European sailors, for a sorry knife or some such trifle, of no value. . . ." Barbot also talks about what the Gabonese ate. "They depend chiefly on hunting and fishery and do not seem to mind tillage." They also consumed potatoes, yams, roots, bananas, and beans, "but in no great plenty."

They drank "palmwine, or a particular liquor which they call *Melasso* made of honey and water" (presumably the source of the English word "molasses"), which Barbot says "tastes much like our metheglin, and none drink without spilling a little of the liquor on the ground for his idol." Barbot did not make any close study of these idols but notes that previous sailors had found on Branca Island a small hut "wherein was an earthen pitcher covered by a net" and in the same hut "the figure of a child cut in a piece of wood very oddly, with some small fishbones thrust into and round about one eye . . . supposed to be the idol of those people. . . ."

It was eventually the British who put an end to the slave trade, and they were in a position to do so after the defeat of Napoleon. The Congress of Vienna, when the treaty between the British and French was signed, provided the British with an opportunity: They introduced a clause into the treaty that called for the abolition of slavery. In spite of this, a number of ships, some of which were American, continued to sail up and down the west coast in search of slaves. British warships patrolled the African waters in an attempt to seize these ships and rescue the human cargo. Later the French did this too. They were able to minimize British influence and to claim Gabon as a French possession.

In 1839 the French Admiral Bouet Villaume signed a treaty with the Mpongwe ruler, Rapontchambo, known to the French and to subsequent history as Le Roi Denis, whereby the French were allotted a small tract of land on the point facing what is now Libreville. In 1842 a chief named Dowai, whom the French called Louis, allotted them a portion of land on the other side of the estuary, where they built a fort and where the cathedral of Libreville now stands. The natives on this side of the estuary spoke a kind of English, because British and American influence had been stronger here. They wore, to some extent, European clothes and the French Marshal Daumal described them as being "clean."

The extraordinary, hermetic, frozen world in which the Gabonese lived seems to have been more or less unexplored by the slavers and sailors: firstly, because to them the blacks were articles of trade, like cattle or horses; secondly, because the contacts they made were only with the coastal tribes, never with those still sealed in the dark crypt and cradle of the forest. They may not even have been aware that people lived in that immense, mysterious, and dangerous mass of vegetation that they could see beyond the villages on the coast. But by the time slavery ended, other tribes had been driven from the savannahs, including the tall, cannibal Fang. That tribe, for example, was unheard of till 1842, when an American missionary came upon a party of them some fifty miles inland from the estuary.

Then came the consolidation of French rule in Gabon. In 1848 a Brazilian slaver, the *Elizia*, carrying 300 members of the Loang tribe, was captured by a French warship. The Loang were settled around the French fort on the estuary and given land, trousers, stovepipe hats, and a Christian baptism. To celebrate the fact of their freedom, the French named the new town that was now spreading out around the fort Libreville. It was full of French military personnel and missionaries.

The American missionaries already present were asked to leave; French missionaries replaced them. Conversion of the natives was difficult: Gabon was an area that was full of secret societies based on animist beliefs. Magic and witchcraft were very real to the people. The tribes had their individual taboos, and most people carried *gris gris*, charms and amulets, a practice that was reported by as early an observer as Barbot. The missionaries therefore enlisted the aid of the navy. On Sundays and any religious holidays that might come up, processions marched to and from the cathedral, carrying banners and accompanied by ceremonial cannonfire from ships in the estuary.

This greatly impressed the natives, and they were converted in large numbers. Most Gabonese are now, at least nominally, Christians; but *gris gris* are retained by most of them and in the interior secret societies still flourish, and magic and witchcraft are believed in. However, by the commencement of the twentieth century, Libreville was in essence a French city, with a population of between two and three thousand. In the 1960s, when the French started to pull out of black Africa and declared their intention of leaving Gabon, the Gabonese appear to have been rather dismayed. They said they had nobody who was equipped to replace the French administrators. But the French went. That is to say, Gabon ceased in name to be a French colony.

The Gabonese Government is heavily staffed with French advisers still, nearly everyone speaks French, and most restaurants in Libreville serve French provincial food. That doesn't mean that most Gabonese eat it. The prices in Libreville are fantastic; Zaïre and Gabon must be two of the most expensive countries in the world. The recent discovery of oil and of minerals in the interior has made Gabon rich. It has not done the same for the Gabonese, though the World Bank report says that the annual GNP per capita income is $630 a year, and that would make them among the richest people in Africa. But the World Bank may have been mistaken.

Gabonese history has been, to put it mildly, unusual. Gabon itself is an abnormal country in that it has today one of the most abnormal population situations in the world. When most people think of population problems, they think in terms of rapid population growth. The point is that a population problem is a problem of people. If the population of a country suffers from endemic diseases, that is, true enough, a medical problem, but it is also a population problem. If there is a very high unemployment rate in a country, that is a population problem too. If the country has too few people, rather than too many, that is a population problem—and serious.

Gabon has an area of 272,000 square kilometers, of which about 210,000 square kilometers consist of dense, nearly impassable tropical forest. The country has never been what anyone could call densely populated, but in the nineteenth century the French were of the opinion, though admittedly no proper census was held, that about a million and a half people lived in it. Assuming that this is true, what has happened in Gabon is something that has hardly happened anywhere in the world: The population, instead of rising, has fallen. What slightly confuses the whole issue is the impossibility, in Gabon even more than in other Third World countries, of obtaining correct population statistics.

In 1969 the government held a census, as a result of which it was announced that the total population of the country amounted to 550,000 people. This gave an average population density of 1.9 per square mile. The census was financed by the French, but it is noteworthy that a World Bank report supported the figures. Shortly after the census, however, the Gabonese Government announced that the real population figure was 950,-000, giving a population density of 3.6 per square kilometer. Uncharitable critics have said that one reason for this sudden expansion of population is that the higher it is in a country, the more that country qualifies for certain forms of U.N. and foreign aid.

In any event, the French demographer who had worked on the census was expelled from Gabon. The government, at the time it reassessed the population, made no attempt to explain the reasons for its reassessment; but officials I talked to—Gabonese, not French—had two explanations, neither of which seemed to me entirely feasible. The French, as colonists, had a habit of milking each of their African territories of one specific item. In Senegal, for example, it was groundnuts. In Gabon, which was more or less one colossal forest, it was wood, more especially, the wood of the gigantic *okoume* tree. To obtain this wood, the French used forced labor drawn from the villages.

They paid the conscripted workers, but not very much, and conditions in the lumber camps were exceptionally hard. For this reason, some Gabonese officials told me, large numbers of people ran away to neighboring territories like Guinea or the Cameroons. Later, when they had heard of the economic boom that followed the discovery of oil and minerals, these people had allegedly returned to their native land. I found it hard to believe that, as this statement implied, 400,000 people had come back to Gabon within the short space of time between the census and the government reassessment. Moreover, nobody I spoke to in the government could produce any records whatever of their entry.

The second reason, though rather more valid, was not entirely convincing either. When foreign visitors first came to Gabon, the tribes they met lived on the estuary. In later years, as the hinterland was opened up, the French found a number of tribes living on river banks. The main mode of transport was by boat, since nobody in his right senses would attempt to travel far through the forest. The French built roads, and many tribes either moved voluntarily, or were moved by the French, to where these roads were. Some Gabonese officials say that the census-takers, for obvious reasons, could only count people who lived on the rivers or on the roads, easily accessible people.

They say that in the interior of the forest, which the census-takers could not reach, enormous numbers of people may live, unbeknown to anyone. It is certainly true that there are pygmies in the forest; it may even be that there are other tribes who live there. But it is difficult to imagine that 400,000 people can at this moment be in the Gabon forests, unknown to everyone except themselves. Also, the forest is obviously not a place where anyone who had a choice would want to live. Though it is possible that some people who live in the forest went uncounted by the census, I doubt if there can be many.

But whatever the actual size of the population, certain facts are perfectly clear and have been vouched for by experts, disinterested and otherwise. There is only one doctor for every 6,000 people in Gabon. In 1960 the life expectancy for a man was twenty-five years. In 1973 it had increased to thirty-seven years. Infant mortality, which is very high, contributes to these figures. The death rate is therefore considerable. But a curious fact is that the birth rate is very low. The fertility rate in Gabon is

1 per cent, the lowest of any country in the world. So in terms of growth, the Gabonese population is virtually static.

Pierre Sallée is an expert on music who works for UNESCO but is at present in charge of a museum in Libreville. This museum should have been full of items of Gabonese art, but, when we visited it, wasn't. Everything, Sallée said, had been sent to an exhibition in Germany, except for a few pieces. These included musical instruments, which looked rather beautiful and were obviously used and real. There was a xylophone with a musical scale surprisingly like that of the West. Sallée tapped it into life and did the same with a drum. The dark museum momentarily hummed with a dark sound, the sound of an old religion, an old art, a sound out of dank forests where few strangers came.

There were a few masks left as well: white masks that Sallée said symbolized death, slits for eyes, with a curious manic look; also long, glaring masks that looked so truly evil they were terrifying, hanging there on the dark walls and looking down with their absence of eyes. "The civilization here was the most purely African in the entire continent," Sallée said. "Picasso took much of his inspiration from Gabonese art." But it struck me—I had thought Picasso had studied masks and art from the inner Congo rather than from Gabon—that while his work, derived from them, had had a quality of celebration, of life, the Gabonese masks, if they celebrated anything, celebrated death.

"The population here," Sallée said, "is characterized by its sadness. The people have a philosophy that is fatalistic and deeply connected with death, not a dynamic philosophy. There is a lot of pessimism in the Gabonese character. Also, according to a World Health Organization doctor from Spain, who has made a biogenetic study here, their sexual habits are very strange. There is a lot of impotence, and the men quite often do not know how to perform the sexual act. One reason may be the way they feel about their women. In the villages the women are the creative ones; they hold the life force. They bear children, they cook, they plant and harvest the crops. They are the workers of the community.

"The man will visit the forest to hunt, to collect wood, but much of his time will be spent in a secret society that practices initiations and sorcery; and in the old days he also fought in battle. Basically he was the unproductive one; the woman was productive. Because of this, the WHO doctor feels that the man is in some awe of the woman. This may lead to impotence for psychological reasons. There are also," added Sallée, "some purely physical reasons. Ever since foreigners first came here, they have noticed how addicted the Gabonese are to liquor. They also take a lot of drugs, mainly a root known as *iboga*. The drugs and liquor may very well lead to impotence and infertility."

Iboga, I was later told, was a stimulant that keeps one awake and excited. According to Sallée, it is only found in Gabon, though I was not able to check on this. It is often associated with religious rituals. "The people who came into Gabon," said Sallée, "were dispossessed people. They were driven from the savannah country to the north and to the south by powerful invaders and forced to come into the forest, which was inhospitable and savage. They were surrounded by darkness, trees, pygmies, and wild animals: gorillas, leopards. Naturally, they spent their time in fear at first, hence the rituals and the secret societies. Every detail of the societies was secret, because of fear of enemies.

"There are approximately forty ethnic groups in Gabon," said Sallée. "And they all have linguistic and cultural differences. They have a god in common, Zambe, who is associated with a first ancestor—Zambe who breathes, Zambe who creates. Otherwise they are different, even physically so: The northerners are taller and more dynamic, the southerners are more refined in appearance, more civilized . . . more effeminate. The tribes fear and suspect one another, even today. The most dynamic and powerful tribe now is the Fang tribe, who are relatively recent arrivals here."

We left him in the museum. The masks on the wall stared at us, and I was relieved to escape those eyeless stares.

Libreville was sunless yet hot under its stifling shroud of cloud, but it had a few small, charming aspects. One day we saw a chimpanzee preening itself in the driver's seat of a dilapidated bus. Our own driver, Georges, explained that the bus driver kept it as a pet and that it drove everywhere with him. Once, he added, there had been a gorilla in town that used to smoke cigarettes, but its owner had had to have it shot: *"C'était un scandale,"* Georges said. Also, in the schools we passed, black and white children seemed to mix freely and be happy together. But there were aspects of the town that were far less agreeable, and in some ways I found it a deeply depressing place to be in.

For example, the back of Georges' neck, which was something I was constantly looking at when he drove us: The black skin was peeling away in pink patches of ringworm. He was an exceptionally nice young man, and we were friends. But I couldn't, however hard I tried, control my little spasm of disgust when I looked at those pink patches. It must be added that a number of people I saw in Libreville appeared to suffer from afflictions of the skin and from a perpetually unsmiling look that sometimes manifested itself in bursts of sharp temper. They were also very slow both in their physical and mental reactions. This was also true of the many French advisers whom I met in the city.

It is not, physically, an unpleasant city except for the absence of the sun. It lay by the estuary, and on the shores men waded in with nets that came out dripping with living silver. Women prowled the rocks at low tide, collecting stranded shellfish. In the streets, which were plentifully provided with trees, you saw tall Hausa in their robes and caps, and Dahomey women, usually amply padded and swathed in brightly colored wraparounds, bandannas on their heads. But there was something in the atmosphere that was not dying but already dead. Maybe the slave trade had a lot to do with this, for it seemed to me that the atmosphere came not so much from the city as from the people.

One day Georges took us to a village a couple of miles from town that is apparently famous for its artistic productions. Every house was full of sullen men chipping at lumps of soapstone, from which, in the final stages, gods, devils, and animals emerged. This was admittedly for the tourist trade, but there was a joyless and lifeless air about the carvers; and they did not seem to be doing anything that they particularly wanted to do.

Independence Square was a tarred patch of earth like a school playground. The presidential palace while we were there was surrounded by scaffolding—whether they were trying to renovate it or simply prevent it from falling down, I could never really ascertain.

I decided to try and travel out of Libreville and was advised to drive to a place called N'Toum, where there is a U.N. horticultural program. N'Toum, I was told, was surrounded by interesting villages in which I could observe the real life of the people. So we set off, piloted by Georges, under thick cloud. Beyond Libreville we passed into what is locally called *la brousse:* which had nothing whatever, so far as I could see, to do with bush country. On either side of the road, which was cratered and potholed beyond belief, vast, thickly leaved trees heaved themselves upward. Between them a tangle of undergrowth rose, and there were no flowers, only those huge trees and the undergrowth.

As we bumped down the pockmarked road, we passed occasional villages, tucked into a small space from which the trees, incredibly, had been cleared. They were built mostly of the wood from packing cases that still bore stenciled inscriptions describing the wares they had contained. The roofs were of tin. Nobody seemed to be around in any of these villages, which seemed to be signposts towards a life that didn't exist. The trees thickened, and suddenly, with a crash of thunder like those I had heard during our night in Kinshasa, and zigzags of lightning all over the sky, the rain that had threatened to fall since morning fell. It roared in the trees and on the glass and metal of the car.

The trees did not bend or shake: There was no wind, simply this endless, solid fall of water from the furious sky, ripped open every few seconds by lightning, and every so often the thunder, so close and loud it was as though some presence had leaned down from the sky and shouted into one's ear. The road was flooded within minutes, with yellow water pouring down from the forest and into the potholes that bubbled with liquid, as Georges swerved this way and that to avoid them. Then, as suddenly as it had come, the downpour stopped. The yellow water from the forest slowed in its flow, but there was no sun, only the clouds overhead pressed like a lid over the tops of the tremendous trees.

Some of these were *okoume* trees, higher and thicker in the waist than anything I have seen except California redwoods and some English comedians. The villages we passed now, and these

were less and less frequent, looked more as though they should
be where they were; that is, they weren't built of modern materials but of materials as old as this huge, frightening forest, bark
and wood, and they had shapes vaguely like the beehive huts of
Kenya. Outside some huts were stalls on which lay small wooden
or tin platters that contained vegetables or fruit. "If they grow
these things," Georges explained, "they don't eat them. They
sell them. Some lorry drivers come down this road."

Nobody was visible in these villages, even now that the rain
had stopped, save that we passed a couple of drenched women,
holding banana leaves over their heads against the drizzle that
continued still. Eventually, however, we reached N'Toum, a small
town with three or four stores, where we had to abandon the
tarmac road, which was bad enough as it was, for an unmade road
of red and runny mud. Georges, as he turned off on to this road,
drew to a halt. Passing us was a small boy holding, all four feet
bunched into one hand, the carcass of a pygmy antelope, a grey,
plump little beast with faint smears of blood on the fur around
its throat. The child told Georges it had recently been killed.

Georges asked how much he wanted for it. The price was five
dollars, which seemed to me not excessive, but I was relieved
when Georges declined. Leela, who because of her foot was in
the roomier front of the car, beside Georges, had no space to
spare for dead animals, and I felt a strong aversion to the idea
of having to spend the next few hours seated by a muddy, bloody,
murdered, and possibly flea-ridden antelope. We drove on, and
I inquired of Georges, who appeared a bit disappointed at having
missed his chance of procuring the dead beast at a suitable price,
what he usually ate. Georges was a U.N. driver, and I assumed
that his salary was, by Gabonese standards, fairly high.

Georges told me what he ate: basically manioc, yams, and occasional meat or fish—apparently very occasional. He lived, with
his wife and two children, in a shack in Libreville that had no
water and no latrine. His life in town, even though he was comparatively highly paid, did not seem to differ very positively from
the life of the tribes in the forest. We bumped on up the trail
of red mud and presently emerged into open fields dotted with
red brick houses. In a species of shed off the road, we saw a
truck, several Gabonese, two Frenchmen, and large quantities of

vegetables lying on the floor. I deduced that this was the horticultural experiment, so we stopped.

The Frenchmen waved at the red brick huts and told us that
twenty Gabonese farmers and their families occupied them. They
were being trained to grow vegetables with modern techniques,
"but" said the Frenchmen, "they are very lazy." Some cattle had
also been introduced into the area, but these were European cattle, who rapidly acquired diseases that the Frenchmen were unable to diagnose. "Of course," they said, "here is also the tsetse
fly. Most people here have sleeping sickness, and animals, they
also have illness from the bites." A number of insects wavered
around us in the damp hot air, and I eyed them rather uneasily:
Sleeping sickness didn't seem a disease Leela or I should have.

The Frenchmen told us that there was a village farther on,
inhabited by Fang people, that was the kind of village forest
tribesmen normally lived in. We set off down the rough red road,
Georges repeatedly swerving to avoid the flooded potholes, and
reached an area where huge felled logs and tree trunks lay under
the faint drizzle. The timber trade still continued, apparently,
in Gabon. The trees are cut in the interior of the forest, and then
have to be brought up, apparently on some primitive form of
rollers, to the road, where a truck will eventually pick them up
and carry them into Libreville. It is apparently the same system
as the French employed in the days of forced labor.

Georges had been told that the village we needed to see was
beyond a bridge. We reached, up a slippery mud road that kept
climbing, a village whose huts were of bark and a primitive form
of thatch. Beyond it was a terrifyingly rickety wooden bridge,
and beyond that the road went up, with mud and water pouring
down, at a slope of about sixty degrees. At this point we decided
to abandon the idea. The difficulty was that the road, apart from
being awash with mud and water, was very narrow and flanked
on both sides by a steep drop into thick undergrowth and forest.
We tried to reverse down the road, but it was too slippery.
Finally, Georges decided to turn the car around, or try to.

For the next five minutes the tires slithered and slid in the
mud, the back wheels on the thick vegetation on the edge of the
road, vegetation so thick that one couldn't really tell where
the edge was. At last, Georges, whom I admired more and more

during each of those five eternal minutes, managed to turn the car around. We recrossed the bridge to the first village we had passed on our way from N'Toum, and at this point the sky broke open once more. Lightning crackled, thunder roared, and the incredible walls of rain stood all around us. In the village there seemed to be nobody except two women crouched on their haunches in a bark hut. They were both pounding manioc in a mortar.

Beyond them the hut was full of smoke from a fire. This was, at least for them, a sign of something that could be identified with human life, because they were utterly abandoned otherwise: nobody else in the village, a monstrous and primeval rain falling, and the terrible forest all around, shielding its secrets. Perhaps you become used to this sort of situation, if you live in the thickest forest in the world within a tribal system, but I honestly fail to see how anybody could. The women in their hut had a look on their face that was by no means either happy or placid. And their ancestors, in the same situation, without cars passing —what may they have thought might not walk up out of the trees.

Georges, on the way back from N'Toum, said he was hungry. He therefore stopped at one of the tiny stalls outside a village and obtained an immense quantity of what he called garden eggs and what Leela thought were baby aubergines. An urge for shopping then seemed to possess him. He stopped in another village, deserted, the rain slipping down, and obtained some yams from another wayside stall. A little further on he stopped once more to buy some manioc. While he was bartering with the stout lady whose stall it was, loud shrieks came from the huts across the road. A chicken hawk spiraled lazily up into the dull sky from amidst the trees that clenched themselves around these huts.

The chicken hawk, it happened, had come down and killed a chicken belonging to a woman in these huts. Georges, before this became clear, told me that it was probably a leopard that had committed this outrage. In any event, the shrieks and wails of the owner of the assassinated chicken suggested some really drastic event, and presently she appeared, walking towards her hut with a dead, battered, bloody hen in her hand. "They will eat it tonight," Georges said with some disgust. Meanwhile, he had piled up his purchases beside me. I may say that manioc smells like nothing else in the world, which is fortunate for those who don't have to smell it. I'd have preferred the antelope from N'Toum.

We came back to Libreville; we ate our enormous, expensive, French provincial repast at the hotel. I started to think about Georges and his manioc and yams and garden eggs and about the grief of the woman whose chicken had been killed. When I was a boy and I lived in India, I had an elderly friend, a writer since dead, who used to take me for walks around Bombay. He showed me the way the beggars lived and said, "Men should not live like that. It is a shame that men should live like that." Georges and the village woman were by no means beggars, but I thought it was a shame that they should live like that—Georges eating manioc in his hovel, the woman desperate over a dead hen.

Because of all the unfacts concerned with population in Gabon, I think perhaps I should say what I, quite personally, perceived to be possible facts. When people flurry and flounder over the reasons for the infertility in Gabon, they proffer explanations that are not only numerous but absurd. Before I left New York on my long trip, I was "reliably briefed" by officers of the United Nations that the main reason was that all Gabonese had hereditary syphilis bequeathed to them by the slave traders. It is true that there is quite a lot of venereal disease in Gabon, but this does not seem to me by any means the sole cause. It seems to me for a start that nobody should live in areas unfit for human habitation.

The tribes who inhabit Gabon didn't want to live there. They were driven there from the savannahs by more powerful tribes. They were placed in a hostile environment and, for reasons that are very human, they, or at least the men, defended themselves by the excessive consumption of alcohol and drugs. This—perhaps together with some kind of psychological block towards the sexual act with their women, who did the work and, in a way, did what the men should have been doing—created a physical and psychological inability to procreate. The Gabonese who have had, or whose families have had, a history of producing many children are the rich and the powerful.

Moreover, the children of the village people in Gabon go more or less straight from the breast onto a diet of manioc. This is not nutritionally a particularly brilliant idea, and since the staple food is manioc, Gabonese men suffer from a Vitamin E deficiency. Vitamin E, I am told, is what ensures virility. If you eat nothing but manioc as a child, you are likely to die, which is the reason, in part, for the high rate of infant mortality. If you eat little but manioc as a man, you may become sterile. And apart from this, the forests are full of nasty little creatures that have a habit of bestowing frightful diseases upon you if you live there.

A French official said to me in Libreville that the Gabonese tribes were people who were on the verge of extermination when the French took over. They had been artificially preserved, he said, by the introduction of Western civilization. I do not believe that any race can be artificially preserved unless it has the will to survive. I therefore wondered what is being, and could be, done for the future of the Gabonese; and during the time that remained to us in Libreville, I visited François Nguema Ndong, who is the Minister of Social Affairs. He is a Fang and was educated mainly in France, though he came, himself, from a remote village in the forest where he had a wealthy father.

Ndong surprised me by telling me the exact opposite of what most of the French officials had told me. He said that not only was the population growth not static, but it was rising too rapidly. "According to a book written in 1913 by Albert Schweitzer" (whose hospital at Lambaréné is southeast of Libreville), he said, "the population of Gabon was around 2 million. It dropped for a number of reasons. As you know, many people fled to avoid forced labor in the forest. Also, Gabonese who accompanied French expeditions into the Congo forests brought back sleeping sickness, which killed numbers of people. Many men died in the forced labor convoys. Women became sterile because of venereal diseases and tuberculosis. So the population fell."

At one time, he added, twenty out of every hundred women in certain areas of the country were sterile. This was no longer so, because the health services had improved. The rural areas had been developed, and now the population was on the rise. Medicine from hospitals and public dispensaries was free. There was social security for workers: He thought the average income all over

Gabon was about $200, but could be $500, if one included salaried people like white advisers in the count. Because of this newly come prosperity, he felt, the population was increasing, and he had personal reasons for believing this. "My eldest brother," he said, "has five wives and seventeen children."

I expressed surprise and awe, and Ndong smiled proudly. "But my second brother," he informed me," has four wives and twenty children." The children would come to the city to study, he said: Their wives would be able to have children in city hospitals, "which means that the infants will have a 60 per cent chance of survival." This figure did not seem to me high, but Ndong seemed to feel that, comparatively, it was. "I myself came here from a village," he said. "When I first saw Libreville I thought it was huge. Now there are other urban areas in Gabon, especially where the mines are. People are no longer unaccustomed to towns and the services that you find in towns. It is good."

The government has started to build a railway that is to extend over 600 kilometers of the country. Rumor had it, however, that they had been unable to find sufficient labor to build it in Gabon and therefore had to recruit people from neighboring states like the Cameroons and Upper Volta. If the population was rising so fast, I asked Ndong, why was no labor available in Gabon itself? He hedged a little. It was a tremendous enterprise, he said, and many men were needed for the labor force. "There is no shortage of people," he said. "Look at Libreville itself. The population now is 130,000, and there are more coming every day. It is a growing city."

But the growth of Libreville, it seemed to me, could be measured more by the spread of shantytown slums than by the sprouting of skyscrapers. I put this to Ndong, and he admitted it. He also made another statement interestingly different from any I had heard before. The prosperity of Gabon now, he said, was admittedly directly due to the discovery of oil and of minerals, but it would not be so in the future. The Gabonese had always lived by agriculture. He felt the development of agriculture would build up prosperity in the future. "It is very fertile soil," he said. "The trouble is that at the present time all that a farmer cultivates is used as food for his family."

However, President Albert Bongo, over the past five years, had created a system of roads all through the country, said Ndong. If these roads were properly exploited, produce could be fetched into urban areas from the surrounding countryside and sold. "Now," he said gloomily, "it is quicker to fly things in from abroad than to bring vegetables from a village forty kilometers from Libreville." A curious fact about Gabon is that nearly all its food—at least, all the food the moneyed eat—is imported, which is one reason why it is such an expensive country. Moreover, a large percentage of its imports comes from, of all places in the world, South Africa. The Gabonese don't like to admit this.

They are also reluctant to admit that, as a French statistician told me, 43 per cent of their imports are liquors of one kind or another. I thought it tactless to raise either of these points with Ndong, so I didn't. But I did ask him why, if the health services were now so widespread and so improved, the only dispensary I had seen on the road to N'Toum had been a tumbledown roadside shack devoid of patients, doctors, equipment, and even furniture. "It is possible," said Ndong without so much as a blink, "that it was a holiday on the day that you passed this dispensary." He was an intelligent, bland man and very conscious of the fact that he was educated and a minister.

A French adviser came to have a drink with us in our hotel. We sat out in the open, at a table under a sort of thatch umbrella, by the murky waters of the estuary. Rain occasionally spattered over the thatch above us. Listless people walked around on the rocks below us looking for shellfish stranded by the tide. "The sun only shines here," the Frenchman said, "for a month or two every year. Literally as well as metaphorically. Can you blame the Gabonese for looking so miserable all the time?" His work was to do with education, and he was rather sour about that as well. "It's a carbon copy of the French system. They want to reach a 100 per cent level of school attendance. Ha ha."

He had studied the education system. "Three-quarters of the students of any course leave before the end. You see, for one thing, there is not much to do with a degree. You could become a priest, or many people, for example, study because they want to become ministers or members of the National Assembly. Or people want to become lawyers, but they don't know what a lawyer is. Anything that will bring them security. . . . It's said by a French sociologist that the Gabonese are without ambition, but I think it isn't that, simply that they are without opportunity. There are few channels open to an educated Gabonese. The reason there are so many French advisers is that no Gabonese is properly equipped."

Only about 2,000 Gabonese had had higher education, he said, and many of these were rich people who wanted to travel. "For example, in Paris now there is a student who is doing a medical course. He is fifty-four years old and has been there for ten years. I don't want to make—how you say—generalities, but the Gabonese don't like to work more than is necessary to keep themselves alive. Maybe it's this terrible climate; maybe the French colonizers wrecked their tribal life without replacing it with anything of value. All their traditions are smashed; most of the village arts are lost; they have a mongrel kind of religion, a mixture of Catholicism and voodoo." He threw up his hands and laughed.

Inland from the estuary, from our thatch umbrella, from Libreville itself, in the dank, pathless, dripping forest, there was no population problem as the man in a New York or London street understands it. There were not too many people but too few. Compared to other African countries, or to some Asian and Latin American countries, Gabon is very rich; but the wealth, as in all countries, developed or not, is inequally distributed. The level of poverty in Gabon, as in other Third World countries, is too low for people from developed nations even to start to understand. And in Gabon the poor have stayed poor, uneducated, and sad; and therefore what is happening in Gabon is as much a problem of population as is what is happening in India and—because people are the problem—of equal importance. Talking to my French friend, I remembered the huts in the forest, the crouched women, the *gris gris* of feathers tied to a pole outside a hut, the white death masks inside the hut, the atmosphere of pain and fear. Obviously one cannot make a mask laugh, but one should at least try to make it possible for people to do so.

CHAPTER EIGHT

"Nous manquons de bras."

We chose a wing seat position on the way out of Libreville to Dakar, the capital of Senegal. In front of us sat a young black man who had a taut look, like some kinds of intellectual, accompanied by a solicitous elder man in a *fez*. There were four stops between Libreville and Dakar, and the plane, as is usual in Africa, was hours late. At our first stop, in Togo, the young man in front of us rose to his feet. He was clad in the *bubu*, the flowing robe of the Senegalese. Because of Leela's foot, neither she nor I had left the plane, and I was rather glad I had not done so when, after a short while during which he stared fixedly at the carpet, the young man raised his head.

A hostess was passing by. She was white; the other hostess was black. To this slightly nervous white hostess, the young man announced, "I am mad." The white hostess stared at him in the silence owed to such a remark. "I was supposed to have a sedative before I left Libreville," said the young man, "but my political enemies stopped it. Unless I have my sedative now, I will take all my clothes off. Then I will become very violent." The white hostess fled, and the black hostess replaced her. With her was a doctor with a syringe. The young man's companion, who one now realized was his keeper, produced a boxful of ampuls. "Is it to be intramuscular or intravenous?" the doctor asked.

The keeper didn't know. Meanwhile, the young man, in a sober and deliberate way, removed all his clothes. He was then given an intramuscular shot of whatever the ampuls contained. He kept saying sadly, "I must go to the lavatory." Eventually, the black hostess took him there. As he passed us, I noticed that, apart from his nudity, the oddest feature of his appearance was that his arms were festooned with amulets. "An enemy," he said to the hostess, "has bewitched me." The hostess shook her head in real sympathy. "But with all the *gris gris* you carry on your arms," she said, "it shouldn't have happened." The extraordinary thing was that she was utterly serious.

We then moved several rows back and sat there for the remainder of the flight, some eight hours. The black hostess, who appeared to be not only compassionate but far more courageous than anybody else on the plane—the lunatic and his companion now formed a small island in the midst of rows of empty seats—approached frequently and kept handing the young man cold towels, both cloth and paper, which he placed upon his head. She also handed him napkins, in the interests of modesty, but he placed these on his head as well. At every stop, astonished women paused and stared at the young man, and, as they passed by, laughed in a Rabelaisian way. How false an idea the Victorians had about women!

Leela was convinced that we should never reach Dakar, that long before we had, the young man would have broken all the windows and murdered everybody else—but we did. I must confess that even I, veteran of many hazardous flights, was surprised that we did. The young man reclad himself and left the plane in a modest and quiet manner. A large number of his relatives awaited him at the airport. While they welcomed him in the effusive Muslim manner (Senegal being largely Muslim, due to Arab influence from the north), he stared back at the empty plane. "I wish," he said, "I was back there. There I was happy," a remark few of his fellow passengers would have made.

In Dakar the sun shone, there were violent outbursts of flowers in every tree, and lepers strolled around with ivory smiles or sat on the pavements with tin boxes for alms beside them, waiting for their fingers or toes to fall off. There were 4 million people in the country, and a lot of them were in Dakar, because in the north there was drought and a hot wind out of Mauritania; thousands of people and cattle were dying in the wind, and of starvation because the crops had failed, and of thirst because the sparse rivers had dried up. This had been going on for five years. It was the season for rain, but none fell. The sun and the lepers smiled —the opposite of Gabon.

We arrived on a Friday, and since everything in Dakar closes up for the weekend, I decided to drive out into the drought area and look around. In a place called Kongoule, in the midst of the drought area, the Senegalese Government was attempting to resettle people—to populate the desert. I hired a car and told the driver to take me to the Kongoule area, where I was to look for a French adviser whose surname was Gérard. We could stay overnight, I was told, in a town called Kaolack that was on the way. The driver, Niang, a gangly young man from the Wolof tribe, the largest in Senegal, did not seem very happy about the assignment, but money had changed hands, and so he drove.

Dakar sprawls by a blue sea. In the center of town there are cinemas, French bistros and restaurants, white houses, tall, dignified women in *bubus*, tall, dignified men in *bubus* or suits, tall, dignified lepers. A little way outside the town the whole landscape changes. There are huts with tin roofs, miles of empty red earth, and huge billows of red dust. The trees by the road become more skeletal, mile after mile. Sometimes you see herds of cattle, skeletal also, humped and of the zebu type prevalent in India. They are driven by skinny boys, and they kick up huge halos of red dust that swirl around their horned heads; usually they are moving towards the city, not into the dry countryside.

The earth was horribly parched, with cracks in it: We took bridges over rivers that had ended long back, leaving, as memory, eroded, water-worn rocks and pebbles in their yellow beds. Every so often we passed a village of beehive huts, and I asked Niang to pull up at several of these villages so that I could talk to the people. They all spoke French, and they were mostly Muslim; but outside the huts there were totem poles with *gris gris* of various sorts attached, and there were more *gris gris* inside the huts. Of that long hot afternoon I remember most entering the hut of a village headman: a 2-room hut, with a kind of small altar to one side, adorned with *gris gris* to placate God.

The headman showed me his stomach, which had stretch marks on it, like those on the stomach of a woman who has borne children. "Now," he observed pleasantly, "I am not as stout as

I used to be." The red dust from the desert blew around his hut.
Outside there were a few head of scrawny cattle, dogs, fowl. The
headman had two loaves of French bread for himself and his
family to eat. The villagers didn't make this bread; it was sold
from bakery vans that passed occasionally. But apparently it had
been the staple diet of the people since the drought had started.
Before that they had cultivated millet and peanuts, had eaten
some of what they produced, and sold the remainder to merchants.

This particular headman didn't want to move to the city,
though some of the other ones I met did. This was his country,
he said, and the country of his people. He looked up into the
irremediably blue sky, his reddened eyes meeting the red eye of
the sun, and said that the rain couldn't stay away forever. Some
day the sky would relent and weep. The cacti in the desert around
stood still as statuary made by some very bad modern sculptor,
and the gales of hot wind colored them with dust. There was a
school in the village, and the gusty dust filled the empty class-
rooms. We drove off to Kaolack. The hotel we stayed in was like
a bad dream: a French provincial hotel in the desert.

The owners charged incredible prices and were suspicious about
my paying in traveler's checks. At night the air conditioner
creaked and wailed. All night the burning wind surged through
the town, slapping sand over the windows of the neat French
houses and throwing it through the open doors of the huts. In
the morning the pitiless sun was up once more, and now the
wind, not yet asleep, was bringing the dust up in spinning towers,
filling the air with it, so that as we drove towards our dubious
destination, Kongoule, it was like driving through an English mist
in November. There were cacti and tamarisk by the roadside,
otherwise only sand, sand, sand.

A few people labored with burdened limbs against the sand-
laden wind: Once I saw a couple of men loading a camel, their
arms up to protect their eyes, not very effectively. The wind
whipped at their tattered *bubus*, bent the leafless brown trees over
backward as though for rape, hurled the few badly briefed birds
who had strayed into the area out of their aerial courses, and
filled the car with a hollow booming sound, as though one was
driving at high speed through an endless tunnel. This wind, it
seemed to me, constituted a large part of the population problem

in Senegal. It drove people before it from the countryside into the city—into Dakar and the slums of Pikine.

Under the whiplash of the wind, we reached Kongoule and were directed by a friendly inhabitant to a small house with a corrugated iron sheet for a gate, and a well in the dusty courtyard. A large blue lizard with a yellow head scurried about in the dust. The front room of the house was cool and filled with music from a transistor radio. In it, amidst two refrigerators, a sofa, a set of armchairs, and a dining table, sat a young Frenchman, writing letters. This was Michel Gérard, and he had lived in the area for a year and a half. He was in charge of the Kongoule program; he was supposed to look after the people who were moved out from Fatick, halfway between here and Dakar.

Senegal consists of the Bassin des Arachides, the delta area where groundnuts are grown around Dakar, and the sandblasted country beyond. Fatick, which we had passed on our way, is a small, slow town some 120 kilometers out of Dakar. The people, Gérard said when he had recovered from his initial surprise at our appearance, were being moved out of Fatick, in small numbers, to Kongoule by the promise of free land. The Bassin des Arachides, he said, was overpopulated, and the earth was exhausted even for subsistence crops. Here, despite the sand and wind, there was a very interesting agricultural potential. The population density was only four or five per square kilometer.

The local people, therefore, had not put up any opposition to the idea of newcomers. "Indeed," Gérard said, "they welcomed them. The Serere tribe is being particularly encouraged to come here, because there are too many Serere in the Bassin, but there are also Wolof. We are trying for intensive groundnut cultivation here, as well as the cultivation of millet, which most Senegalese eat as a staple food. Also we are trying to introduce cotton. The climate and the soil are favorable to it here. There is much need for diversification of produce in Senegal, and the government wants cotton as the main new crop for diversification."

He opened his smaller refrigerator and took out beer. Golden and white, it sat well in tall glasses and traveled smoothly down the throat. It was intolerably hot outside, and the sand and wind still roared past the little house. Gérard, however, after eighteen months here, didn't seem unhappy. I admired him. "I go some-

times to Dakar," he said, "to make reports and buy provisions."
He opened the small refrigerator once more. In it were bottles
of liquor and of water and tins of imported foodstuffs. He asked
us to lunch, which was produced by an efficient servant. It started
with a mixed salad, which was followed by lamb chops, and concluded by cheese. With all this, we ate excellent home-baked
bread and drank a red wine that was by no means bad.

"In 1972," Gérard said over lunch, "we moved fifty families
into the area. By the end of this year we will have moved another
100 families, and next year we plan to move about 150 more.
That was our target, to move 300 families in three years, and if
it succeeds, we may be able to move thousands. So far it has
succeeded; the people adapt themselves well. We have agents
at Fatick who motivate the people to come. We have bore wells
here in Kongoule, so the water shortage is not as bad as in other
parts of the desert area." He poured some more wine. There
seemed an oddity in this kindly young man and his French hospitality, with the sandstorm thundering past his latticed windows.

Niang, exercising his accelerator to its limits, was able to take
us back to Dakar by nightfall. The shape of the dunes had been
changed by the wind, and where the sand had drifted away we
saw, like desert travelers in some Hollywood film, bones, whether
animal or human it was impossible to tell. Dakar seemed beautiful after the desert: The fountain opposite the hotel sprang up
like a mirage, quenching the thirsty eye. We slept deeply to the
morning; and then it was Monday, and the interviews started.
I had a bit of luck, since my first interview was with Dr. Jacques
Gagnon, head of the Department of Statistics, who is in process
of organizing a census for Senegal.

I was lucky in two respects: Gagnon was trained as a demographer and probably knows more about the Senegalese population
than anyone else in the country—that was one; the other was
that in him I found a friend. He is a French Canadian, irritable,
bossy, opinionated, absentminded, and entirely likable, entirely
a man. He has a pretty and equally likable wife, Constance, and
two small children, Anne and Eric, who have excellent manners,
though I took some exception to the fact that they called me
Monsieur Lapin, due to Leela's informing them that her nick-

name for me is Rabbit. Jacques Gagnon was thereafter of the greatest help to me in obtaining information in Senegal.

He himself, though brilliant at his work, told me that no real study of population had ever been done in the country. The President, Dr. Léopold Senghor, is a poet who spent much of his early life in France. He was one of the first proponents of the idea of *négritude*, of Negroness: all the people in the United States who are now saying "Black is Beautiful" were set off by him. Nevertheless, in his own life he is very European; he is married to a Frenchwoman. It is possible that he might have introduced the idea of family planning to raise the level of life in the cities to which the people are flocking and in the rural areas and desert where infant mortality is high, but there were obstacles.

These were from the attitudes of other politicians, who had the idea that the whites were trying to bump the black race off by means of birth control, and from what in Senegal are called the *marabous*, the Muslim religious leaders, who have considerable power. (Senghor is a Catholic.) This is an example of how, particularly in black Africa, the phrase "dangers of population" has either not been clearly conveyed by the world organizations that speak of it or has been entirely misunderstood by the people who have heard of it. The population problem in the world today is not a danger *of* population but a danger *to* population. This cannot be overemphasized, since it isn't yet understood.

At one time the slum dwellers in Dakar built their pathetic shacks along the highway that leads from the airport to the city. This was thought to create a bad image in the minds of visiting dignitaries, so they were moved to a place called Pikine, immediately outside Dakar. Here they built shanties, and endured. The migration from the rural areas started, and speeded up as the drought and flaming winds came. The people who fled to the cities, winnowed by these winds, also settled in Pikine. It is now a sort of satellite town of Dakar. Niang took us there, and I talked to a doctor in a local clinic. He was a grave, dignified man, and unlike some doctors appeared to be telling the truth.

He said the people in Pikine were much less healthy than the people in Dakar, even though the physical condition of people in Dakar left a lot to be desired. He said that the people in Pikine suffered from enteric diseases, pulmonary diseases, and fevers and that the infant mortality was high. The housing and sanitation was poor, he said, and when later I drove through the town, he seemed to have made an understatement. The sad, rickety shacks with tin roofs, huddled together under a rainless sky, swarmed with ragged children, few of whom had proper schools or health care.

There is tremendous comfort in another human body, when it is coupled with yours, and if you are very poor you need comfort. If you do not want children, or anyway more children, and you do not know how to stop their arriving, your problem becomes worse. You would only not know this in a country with no policy on family planning: Certainly, if you lived in a developed country, you would know how to achieve your aims in life, if you had any, and know how many children you could or could not afford, both for their security and for your own. Many officials in Senegal did not want to realize this.

Demographer Ferry of L'Office de la Recherche Scientifique et Technique d'Outre-Mer, a French organization known as ORSTOM which assists the government, was, like Jacques Gagnon, a little cynical about the feasibility of population studies at present. The estimated growth rate, he said, was about 2.3 but could be anything up to 2.6. "Population *is* a problem in this country," he said. "For example, there are important differences between the bush and the towns. The mortality rate in the bush is about 30 per 100. In the towns it's about 15. The birth rate in the towns is a little lower than in the bush, and the first-year infant mortality is lower too: In the bush it's about 150 per 1,000, and it's between 85 and 90 in the towns."

Migration from the bush was another problem, and this had not been studied in depth either, Ferry said. "The increase of population in the cities is around 3.5 per cent per annum. In Cap Vert, the area of Dakar and Pikine, there is a total population of about 800,000 with 250,000 in Pikine and perhaps 500,000 in Dakar. This leads to a considerable amount of unemployment, perhaps 20 per cent in Dakar. A Senegalese custom is that a relative who has money supports a relative who doesn't, so the unemployed don't actually starve. But it means that those who earn have less for themselves—a man may support twenty or thirty relatives and clansmen off a relatively low salary.

"The resistance of the *marabous* to any idea of family planning is not due to their Muslim heritage. There is nothing in the Koran that opposes contraception. The basis is animism and African tradition, which is all mixed into Islam here. The polygamy problems, for example, are quite different from those in the Arab world. Senegal has no attitude towards the qualitative nature of its population. Nobody here has studied cultural patterns or the effect upon the people of Occidental culture. Nutrition and health have not been well studied. So the population is in a bad state, physically and mentally: malaria, malnutrition, parasites . . . all."

Ferry said, "I am not a pessimist, but I can see a number of problems of population in Senegal. Essentially, it is a political problem. Family planning won't solve very much, and it will come very slowly. What finally makes problems is infant mortality and the control of the urban population. The urban migration is uncontrolled," and Ferry, a young man with the tight sealed face of a professional, added, "and uncontrollable." I walked around Dakar with Leela afterward, and though there were not the floods of people oozing down the streets that there are in, say, India, there were too many people who were poor and leprous, all flashing brilliant improbable smiles.

Samir Amin is Egyptian and persuasive. He runs an institute of population studies, a U.N. body, in Dakar. He is slight and has a quick rivery voice. He said that in the history of mankind the rise of population had been inducive to development. In certain areas of the world, he said, like India, this was not so. It was the opposite. But in tropical Africa it was so. "People actively don't want family planning in Africa," he said. "And growth in terms of population has to equal economic growth. The Senegalese Government has not the courage to face the opposed interests within the country. If the growth, economically, was quick, then perhaps family planning could come in to reinforce it."

As long as the problem of poverty was unsolved, Amin said, the question of family planning didn't arise. "There's a difference," he said, and I agreed with him, "between a national attitude and the attitude of a family. There's also a difference between the attitude of a nation and the attitude of an international body like the United Nations. When the Portuguese came to the Congo for the slave trade, they estimated there were a million people there. Three hundred years later, they estimated that there was a population of about 300,000. Black nations think of oppression on many levels, both past and present. If the whites ask black nations to reduce their population now, what are the blacks to think?"

It was another Sunday, and Jacques and Constance Gagnon said why didn't we all have a picnic on the island of Gorée, with their children. The island is a 15-minute ride by ferry off the harbor of Dakar. The Gagnons picked us up at the hotel, and we drove at Jacques' normal irritable speed to the harbor. A large number of people were awaiting the ferry. A lot of them were white: U.N. people, French advisers, and their children. Anne and Eric wanted to eat fruit, and a large bosomy Senegalese lady in a *bubu* offered to take them to buy some; Africans are incredibly tender and kind with children of all colors. They returned, carrying little leaf caskets full of fruit.

It was a very sour, rather smelly fruit, but the children liked it. "They eat anything they lay their hands on," Jacques said. "Nothing hurts them." A white ferry arrived, and we boarded it. It was a sunny day, the ferry was crowded, and the colors of the people were roughly two-thirds black to one-third white. The blacks laughed as the spray flew back from the cleaving bows, splashing them with foam; the whites drew back a little from it. The blacks had very white smiles. The teeth of many of the whites were black. But the foam was white in the wake, and everyone was happy. Eventually, we drew in to the island of Gorée, and there were pink and white colonial houses and fine beaches there.

On the beaches, girls in bikinis, and sturdy young men, of all colors, basked under the strong sun. Jacques said, "Do you know what this island is famous for?" I said no. "It was here," Jacques told me, "that the Senegalese slaves were brought to be shipped to the Americas. This is, I think, the only place where the slave quarters have been kept intact as a memorial." Constance and Leela drank beer under a beach umbrella, and Anne and Eric disappeared like tiny dolphins into the sea. We walked up through a not too unpleasant tourist village, with stalls selling woodwork and cloth and postcards, to book a table at a restaurant above the beach. The day being Sunday, it could have been full.

After that, we picked our wives up, and Jacques entrusted his children to a Senegalese boy—they wanted to fish—and the boy collected them and the bait and took them off to the pier. We strolled down the dusty streets, past colonial houses and a church, and came to a compound of pink buildings, and Jacques said, "This was where they kept the slaves." He knew the curator, an elderly man named M. Ndiaye, who very kindly took us around. He showed us the cells where the men were kept chained up, sardines in a can of pink stone; the cells where they were fattened, from troughs, before the slave ships arrived; the punishment cells, some by the blue friendly sea—those, he said, were the worst.

His voice shook with emotion. The tide flooded these particular cells, he said, and on occasion the prisoners had to sit up to their necks in water. He showed us the cells where the women were kept, the cells where the young virgins were kept, the cells where the children were kept. In area, each of these cells was of the size in which a fairly progressive English farmer would keep a single pig. There had been, at one time, thirty or forty human beings, the men chained, the women chained, the children, being harmless, left unshackled, in each. "It was not the only place on Gorée," said Ndiaye. "There were a number of such places. We have kept this as a memorial." His eyes shone wetly.

On the top floor was where the slavers lived. They had kitchens and large drawing rooms with fireplaces. By the time we came down from their apartments, a number of young Senegalese had linked themselves to our party. They were not all in *bubus*: Some of the young women wore miniskirts, some of the young men shirts and trousers. Ndiaye pointed at a slot in the wall facing the brilliant sea. "From here the ones who rebelled were thrown to the sharks," he said. "From here the slaves filed through to the holds of the ships. The tragedy for Senegal, for Africa," he added, fixing his young countrymen with a bitter eye, "was that it was not the white men who captured these people. It was our own chiefs who sold them into slavery, for alcohol, for mirrors, valueless trade items.

"Remember this," he said, but the young Senegalese looked at him with an absent sort of interest, as at some museum mask without relevance to their own place and day. They drew patterns in the dust with sandaled toes, murmured to one another dreamily, smiled. The girls giggled. Ndiaye looked back at them with an expression that was partly astonished and partly ironic and led us back to the exit. The Gorée barracoons have become a place where African statesmen come as pilgrims, to deliver speeches on the exploitation of their countries by the West, or, in the case of President Bongo of Gabon, to weep. But I wondered how much their people know about Gorée or how many really cared.

The Senegalese as a race are tall and willowy, their appearance in this respect being enhanced by the flowing *bubus* that both men and women wear. They move in a loose, nearly boneless way. They laugh a lot but seem quick to anger, and the week before we arrived there had been a strike at the University, during which some students had abused and kicked Constance Gagnon, out shopping in town.

The French recruited a lot of troops in Senegal, and some came back from French Indochina with Vietnamese wives, so that the *ao-dai*, the long fluttery butterfly tunic of Vietnam, is occasionally seen in the flowered avenues of Dakar. There are also Senegalese who have migrated to France. The national attitude towards France, however, is ambivalent. Constance, for example, was of the opinion that the students had attacked her because she was white and probably French. At the same time, Dakar is full of Frenchmen who assist the government as advisers or who have businesses in Senegal. The attitude of most average Frenchmen in Dakar towards an average Senegalese is a bit paternalistic: They are benevolent towards taxidrivers, waiters, barmen, the women you encounter in cafes, who, their infants slung on their broad backs, try and sell you peanuts, fruit, or flowers, in the same way that they would be benevolent to intelligent children or preferred pets.

This particular income bracket of Senegalese play up to the Frenchmen: They grin and allow themselves to be teased with that peculiar type of servility that is closely allied to mockery. Jacques Gagnon said one day, as we lunched under a very French, very lurid parasol outside a sidewalk restaurant, "There was a lot of difference between the colonization practiced by the French and, for example, British colonization. The British introduced their cultural patterns to the chiefs and leaders, not to the masses. The French made everyone learn the French language, eat French food if they could afford it—even today, as you saw yourself in the bush, the peasants eat French bread.

"In British colonies it was only the elect who spoke English; in French colonies nearly everyone spoke French, except for wild tribesmen in remote areas. The British adapted their educational system for their colonies, but the French didn't. So you have young people here studying in the French manner, which is totally unsuited to the needs of this country. The whole system should be changed." Curiously enough, the day after this I spoke to Dr. R. R. Bergh, who works at the University of Dakar, on loan from the University of Leyden. Dr. Bergh runs a research program financed by the Government of the Netherlands, and the research is on population in one of its many complicated aspects.

This research is related to urban planning, and it is supposed to be an interdisciplinary program between the universities of Dakar and Leyden. There is supposed to be a proper research center in Dakar by 1974, and the idea is that students in both universities will be involved, as an educational measure, in the research. Dr. Bergh, however, said that while he had found Dutch students to so involve themselves, he hadn't found any Senegalese. "It's because of the French system," Dr. Bergh said. "The French university system, which they use here, says applied research doesn't exist. The programs have been blocked by French professors and by Senegalese professors trained in France."

These professors, according to Dr. Bergh, say that they are training students to be teachers, not research workers. "The Senegalese students, more and more, are becoming involved in the problems of their own country, but in this respect they are more or less unable to participate in our program because of the unavailability of research training here. There are very, very few Senegalese researchers. The government does realize that research centers, Senegalized ones, should be created. We are sending students from here to the Netherlands," Dr. Bergh said, "for the kind of training they cannot obtain here. But naturally this is not on a very large scale, and it's a slow process."

The program is unique in Senegal in that it has a counterpart structure. Two commissions have been appointed to control its activities, one, composed mainly of university professors, in Holland, the other in Senegal, composed of various directors of government departments who are interested in applied research. "They orient the research we do," Dr. Bergh said, "towards problems that need to be solved by the policy-makers of the government." So far the research has been on a very small scale and has been almost entirely devoted to Pikine, but some of Dr. Bergh's findings were extremely interesting, because they were not afloat, like other population studies in Senegal, on a tide of surmise.

Dr. Bergh estimated that there was a yearly population increase of 6 per cent in Dakar and Pikine, especially since the drought had started. This was higher than the figures Ferry had suggested, and the research tended to show that the unemployment rate was more than 20 per cent—perhaps between 20 and 30 per cent. "The income of each earning man in the city," Dr. Bergh said, "feeds twenty people." Pikine, he thought, though a slum area, was better than the slum areas of Dakar itself. Pikine, when people were pushed into it first, was provided with an infrastructure of sorts: roads, water, electricity, dispensaries, and schools—not in plenty, but it was provided with them.

Dakar, however, had unplanned slums, where things were worse. Delinquency, which is the normal consequence of sudden urbanization, had increased in Dakar. In Pikine, Dr. Bergh thought, the way of life was more African, and the inhabitants were therefore happier. They were also able to build their own houses on government plots of land, and there were more stone houses built by the poor in Pikine than in the slums of Dakar. These houses are put up by a local labor force, and Dr. Bergh's people are trying to study this force "to collect data on how best to organize it and so help people put up houses more cheaply, which is one of the most important problems."

At present, it costs about $1,000 to build yourself a stone house. Of the urban population, a World Bank study says, 20 per cent earn more than $140 per year and can afford to build houses or obtain low-cost housing. Forty per cent earn between $40 and $140 a year and cannot afford either to build houses—proper houses—or pay for low-cost housing. The remaining 40 per cent have either very little income or no income whatever. Dr. Bergh's program is aimed at studying the second of the three sectors, the people with some, though not much, income. "At the present growth rate," he said, "both through natural increase and through migration, the Cap Vert population by 1980 will amount to over 1 million people. That will be difficult."

The control of migration is particularly difficult. "Either," Dr. Bergh said, "you stop it by dictatorial methods or you permit it. You have to spread development in the smaller towns, not only as ORSTOM plans, by shifting people back into the country but by developing the small urban areas that exist already and by developing agriculture. In the south of Senegal, it may be possible to develop rice and bananas, and it may be possible to produce sugar cane crops in the north and develop vegetable crops in the Cap Vert area. But basically there isn't much to develop in Senegal. A very large investment would be needed. A concentration of government funds on Cap Vert could be one solution."

He was an interested man, with blue eyes that were not inexpressive. He was building up theories and ideas as he talked. "Maybe it wouldn't be a bad solution. Apart from the groundnut crops, Cap Vert is a regional center with a good climate. If there is a very considerable population growth in the urban areas here, why not? The unemployment may increase, but then, in the rural areas, you have disguised unemployment. What foreign experts have warned the Senegalese about, if they want to develop the cities, is high-rise building: we learned our lesson in Europe. But the Senegalese want high-rises; they think of it as development. Conglomerations of people do not really constitute development.

"Those stone houses, the kind they have in Pikine . . . those could be the solution. The quality of the preventive medicine here is low, because it's badly organized. The clinics put up by the government are costly to build and staff—millions of francs worth—but if they put up clinics and schools located in this kind of native stone house, they'd have many more at much less cost. But the government must have data on population before it plans, and that is not yet readily available. We have to verify the population density in various areas. We have to verify what the family structure is. The old family structure, does it still exist—the reliance of relative upon relative? I think it does."

Outside, Dakar University, recovered from its recent strikes and riots, sat in the sun by the stertorous blue Atlantic. It had large, impressive buildings and flowered lawns, and the students who wandered around looked docile in the extreme. Most young women in Senegal have been to school at some point in their lives, though few of those over forty have. Most young men in Senegal have been to school, but comparatively few people of either sex ever arrive at the university, and then the percentage of men, as in nearly every country in the world, is higher. Dr. Bergh said, "It comes back, in a way, to education. No high-level research has yet been done in Senegal, as you know.

"There is very little economic research done—at least, there has been very little so far. The reason is that there are very few micro-economists in the world, very few to fix their research upon a small area and to explore it thoroughly. There are plenty of macro-economists, who work in a huge field; but I think what is needed in Senegal, which is a small country in terms of population, is a micro-economic structure, where each small town will be planned. The income of the people in each area has to be known and what their expenses are. What is the distance from the water supply of the farthest house in each area? And the placing and the nature of the shops? That's what I mean."

He sighed, and said, "As I told you before, it comes back to education. There are no proper research facilities because of the Senegalese acceptance of the French system of education. Research is difficult because there isn't any coordination. But all this needs research, and maybe a change in the whole educational system." The office was stacked with files and memos and cups of coffee unspoken for over a long period of time. When I said goodbye and came out to the smooth lawns by the sea, Niang was waiting for me. He opened the car door and asked me in his guttural, disconsolate French where I wanted to drive next. As we left the green grounds of the university, he said, sadly, "I didn't go to school much."

A long way away from the center of Dakar, in parched, blazing, Frenchified streets, Niang pulled up outside a maternity clinic, in

which I met Phebean Whest-Allegre, who to my considerable relief, since I read French better than I speak it, came from Sierra
Leone, and therefore spoke English. Mme. Whest-Allegre is a
stalwart lady with a rather suspicious eye, and when I put in my
appearance was in process of examining a young woman with an
infant. Mme. Whest-Allegre's clinic is basically a maternity clinic,
but she claims that it is also the only clinic in Senegal that offers
family planning, and she may well be right. "I cannot," she said,
however, "tell you much about it."

She wouldn't, for example, tell me how many acceptors there
were but said there were "several thousands." The family planning part of her clinic is open five days a week, in the afternoons,
and between ten and seventeen women visited it every day.
"President Senghor encouraged me in this venture," Mme. Whest-
Allegre said. "It was on condition that nobody should be urged
to use contraception: We should offer them advice, and then if
they wanted it they would accept. Most women accept because
of health reasons, their own, not their children's. IUDs are most
popular here, mainly because of the high illiteracy rate. They
don't know how to take pills, so they use IUDs."

The room in which we sat smelled of antiseptic and, for some
reason, vinegar. Mme. Whest-Allegre's voice was whispery and
hypnotic, and it was very hot. "Mostly they accept," she said
"with the consent of their husbands. Some don't ask the consent
of their husbands. We not only put in IUDs, we take them out.
You know that Muslim women cannot pray if they are in their
menstrual periods, because they are supposed to be unclean. The
IUD causes heavy bleeding, in some cases, in the first three or
four months, and some of these women come back to have it
removed because they are unable to pray. But not very many do
this. Mothers now are concerned about health.

"Conditions in Senegal are changing, because now with the
drought there is no need for the peasants in the countryside to
have more children to do the work. People want to live in the
cities. Children in Africa were always considered a blessing, but
now, perhaps, less so than before. The mothers say that, quite
apart from their own health, they don't want their children to be
in the same condition as themselves when they grow up. They
want them to have opportunities, though very few know what

exactly they would like the children to be. We keep instructing them, in our afternoon clinics, by means of pamphlets, if they can read, and films and verbal means if they can't."

Mme. Whest-Allegre worked "very discreetly" on family planning in Dakar as early as 1966, but it was officially integrated into her clinic program in 1970. "I like to see babies born," she said. "The mothers who have babies in my clinic can bring them back for a health check every week, until they are a year old, free of charge. It is good, this drift to the cities, because in the bush they have no proper diet—they don't eat vegetables, for example, and in the cities they do. I would say that in this country we used to lose 50 per cent of our babies, and now we lose perhaps 25 per cent. But in this clinic," she concluded triumphantly, "we hardly lose any at all."

Landing Savane worked with Jacques Gagnon in the Department of Statistics. "I feel we have no problem of overpopulation," he said. "It is simply that we are badly ruled. We have problems of population, yes: For example, more than 50 per cent of our population is under twenty years old. This is caused by high fertility and a short life span. But Western statistics are inadequate when they try and define our position. They are completely wrong when applied to African conditions. Let us take one example—that of dependency.

"In Western terms, a dependent is somebody over sixty and under fifteen, who is a burden on the earning members of the family. In African terms this is simply not true. In the bush in Africa, a child starts to do some sort of useful work by the time it is between the age of six and ten. The dependents in the bush are only the children below the age of six, or very old people." Savane had started the interview in French, claiming he knew no English. But in full flow, he switched to perfect English; he had apparently spent some time in the United States. He said the average per capita income in his country, so far as could be ascertained, was about $220 at the present dollar rate.

Twenty per cent, he agreed, was the unemployment rate in Dakar in 1973, but he added that people were still in the process of migration. "Many of the villagers," he said, "are aware that there is unemployment in Dakar and Pikine, but they also know that in the country there is no chance whatever of employment. In Dakar there is some chance. They know that family support has its limits: if they want to marry, for example. Say that you are one of the sons in a family of four children, which is the average size in Senegal "—I may add that estimates of this varied —"you cannot rely on the income of your family, if you are unemployed in Dakar, to marry you off. So often you migrate to France."

Savane sighed. "The Bassin des Arachides," he said, "was always heavily populated. The Wolof were here, and the Serere, and they cultivated millet and subsistence crops. When they were under French rule, things changed. The French wanted groundnuts out of Senegal, as they wanted timber from Gabon. So they planted groundnuts and built up a transport infrastructure in the Bassin. The hinterland was completely neglected. It was too far away, they thought. This is the cause of a lot of the problems in this country today." He also thought that urbanization made for a loss of value in things long prized in Senegalese society, such as virginity, and for the spread of gonorrhea.

"There is a unanimous opposition to family planning here. It comes from the Muslim *marabous*, from the Christian leaders, from the tribal leaders, and from the intelligentsia. Intellectuals in Francophone Africa, whether they are of the Left or the Right, are highly sensitive on the issue of slave trade. Can you blame them? '*Nous manquons de bras*,' they say, 'we have not enough men, because the slavers took the best youth of the whole country.' It's true. The slavers wanted the best: They didn't take old, infirm people; they took strong men, pretty and fertile women, and healthy children. The development of Africa would have been through people like these, and not, ever, through intellectuals."

I was supposed to return from Dakar to New York. Leela and I had been on the road for three months, the most exhausting and demanding three months of my life. In twelve weeks I had covered seven countries. It had been a fascinating trip, in the sense that I had suddenly become more aware of population and its problems than I had ever been before, but I was glad that we had to go to a place where we could put our suitcases down and our feet up. Jacques and Constance drove us to the airport, past the lipping, lapping sea, the white French houses, and the hovels. The plane was, of course, late, and we had to wait four hours at the airport. It was hot and awful, but the Gagnons stayed on.

In that last, though I hope not final, conversation with Jacques, I recapitulated, to him and to myself, some of the things I thought about population in Africa. There is no problem of over-population in the countries that I visited, that is to say, in the countries as a whole, as there is in Asia. There is a problem of urban overpopulation and a health problem. The health problem, ironically, is caused by the improvement in health services. Even if the birth rate stays stable, the mortality rate falls in every country in not only Africa but the world. Therefore the growth rate rises. In Africa, a social change is taking place: The rural population is moving to the cities.

Therefore, in the cities particularly, as well as in the country-side, the increasing population is pulling down the health services. Without a parallel economic growth, the African countries I visited would, I thought, find it difficult to increase the living standard of its people. Though in Kenya and Senegal many people were opposed to family planning, thinking of it as birth control rather than as planning, which is what it should be, it seemed to me necessary not to think of people as an abstract called population but as a collection of individuals who have to be cared for by the governments they entrust themselves to.

There is a fairly relevant peasant saying in India, in Hindi, *Sarkar mere ma-bap he*. This means "the government is my father and my mother," which is what an African or Asian government should be to its multitude of deprived people and peasants. In Africa, unfortunately, the horrors of the slave trade have branded a mark too deep to be excised for many years to come. It was the white nations that shipped the youth of Africa away, over 300 years, to the Americas. The Arabs started it all, but the Africans now remember the whites more vividly, because they did it on a considerably larger scale. It is now the white nations, perhaps motivated by a guilt memory, who are offering family planning to the African countries.

So, to the intellectuals who rule, this offering of a means of controlling population appears suspect. It seems to them another, more devious way of reducing the number of black people in the world, of keeping them eternally under the economic heel of the whites. They therefore do not exactly refuse it but keep it at arm's length: They are angry with it and afraid of it, though they realize it may be necessary. But the people of their countries, mostly the women, not only need it but often ask for it. If a government is the father and mother of its people—a loose definition, but valid in the Third World—it must supply its children with the necessities of life.

The plane was called at one in the morning. The Gagnons said goodbye, and we climbed once more into the belly of a steel bird aimed at America and roared away. It seems to me peculiar that the more one flies, the more frightened one becomes. To take off and land were simple operations once. Now they are immensely complex or appear so: One feels the vibration of every nut and bolt in the plane and feels they are going to fall apart at any moment. We thundered, sleepless, over the Atlantic to America. At a bleary hour that turned out to be the middle of the day in New York, we landed at Kennedy Airport. Coming down, I noticed a thick haze over the city. "Mist," I told Leela. "No," she said, "smog." It was the first time we had seen any for many weeks. I'd forgotten it existed.

CHAPTER NINE

"It's in their minds. Something has wounded them there."

New York, its skyscrapers like modernistic chapels, its dust-bins and prisons overflowing, its parks unvisited, is a city that Leela and I have always chosen to avoid, as far as possible. Now, however, it was headquarters. Now it was the place we lived in, though the place we lived in was a hotel suite and not our home. It is probably the chief city of the Western, developed world. Working in the hotel were Colombians, Poles, Irishmen, Haitians, Italians, and so forth, all of whom were Americans but not all of whom spoke English particularly well. In its own way New York is suffering from a population problem as large as that of Cal-cutta, though different. This one discovered, though one dis-covered it very slowly.

A short while after our arrival in New York, I noticed how unfriendly people were. There was a kind of open hostility about many people one came across by necessity, taxidrivers, waiters, and so forth. Friends muttered about the danger of being mugged in the streets. If delinquency is caused by urbanization, New York, one of the largest urban complexes in the world, appeared to be also an area crowded with delinquency and crime. This was a population problem, too, as serious as any in the world.

In the boroughs of New York City, the population varies very widely. Over the whole of it, the density is 24,000 per square mile. In Manhattan, the density is 75,000 per square mile. There is more garbage collected every day in New York than in London

and Tokyo put together: 30,000 tons. To collect all this, the city
has 1,450 trucks with 3 men on each, and the total work force,
including supervisors, amounts to 12,500 people. All these figures
were given me by Herb Elish, who was the Commissioner for Sanitation in New York City. "Each person in the city," he said,
"dumps about 5.5 pounds of refuse per day. Fantastic, isn't it?"

Elish thought this was because of the overpackaging of food
that exists in the United States. But also, he said, in the South
Bronx area, for instance, there are examples of people who have
a 10-foot-high garbage dump in their backyards. "I think this lack
of cleanliness," he said, "is caused by people's view of their lot.
The people there are mainly Puerto Ricans. There are more fires
there than anywhere else in the city. It is almost as though people
are trying to destroy their own community because they feel dis-
criminated against. There's always somebody at the bottom of
society in New York. And there are a number of reasons for the
miserable condition of the city.

"New Yorkers have never had a sense of community or of
neighborhood," Elish continued. "No matter if they're rich or
poor, you find people who don't care how they live. Actually, the
city now is possibly cleaner than it was ten years back, but the
problem had spread because the city itself is deteriorating. The
population is on a razor's edge all the time. Because of crime,
because of pollution, the richer people, the middle class, are
moving out, and poor people are moving in. Twenty years ago I
rode the subways. Now I don't. They don't work properly; and
you look at the faces of the passengers, and those faces are full
of agony and anguish."

After this surprisingly poetic flourish, Elish buckled down to
actual facts. "Look at the condition of the city now," he said.
"Look at the air pollution. It's caused, for one thing, by incinera-
tors inside houses or apartment blocks, oil burners and so forth.
Now the use of these has lessened, and in that sense the air
pollution is less. Now, however, the main source of air pollution
is the traffic. We have a plan that will lessen the air pollution
in midtown Manhattan, where it's worst. Fifty per cent of the
traffic there consists of taxis, and about half of these taxis are
cruising, looking for passengers. The slower a car travels, the more
exhaust it emanates and the more pollution there is. But if we

can stop taxis from cruising in midtown Manhattan, we'd eliminate 25 per cent of the pollution caused by traffic."

Something that every stranger to New York notices at once is how noisy it is. All day and most of the night in Manhattan, there is the grate and roar of traffic, and through it, with strange outcries like those of prehistoric beasts, moos and wails and rising shrieks, thunder official vehicles of one kind or another: fire trucks, police cars, ambulances. In addition to this, there seem to be drills at work in many parts of the city on every weekday. Manhattan Island is made of very hard rock, and since New York is a vertical city, and skyscrapers need deep foundations, it is necessary to drill very deep indeed into the rock for safety.

"Noise pollution, yes," said Elish, that's the worst for people. It has a social impact and causes anxiety. But then New York is an unnatural place to live. Part of the discourtesy of most New Yorkers, perhaps even the high crime rate, is due to the fact that they lead unnatural lives. Most of the time they live inside concrete boxes. And they don't see grass; they don't see trees, only skyscrapers and each other. Well, what other pollution problems are there? Water pollution—but I think too much money's spent on that. An important point is to clean up the beaches so that people can swim and relax. That would also help their psychological problems.

"We have created a situation here," said Elish, "where we don't understand what we've done or how to solve it. The poverty percentage is rising. A third of the people are unable to support themselves. The middle class are unable to understand why they should have to pay more taxes. Their anger disables them from looking at problems rationally." Elish shrugged briefly. "I'll tell you something else. We have the worst pollution problem yet coming up. I've already told you, we collect about 30,000 tons of garbage a day, and the growth of this garbage is from 4 to 5 per cent every year. Now, even granted that, we can probably handle the collection of it.

"The problem is the disposal. At present the garbage collected is dumped in landfills. We've calculated that the landfill space will run out by 1985. Then where do we put this stuff? We can't throw it in the Hudson River." He looked out of the window, somberly shook his head, and said, "We have to think of something." He added, "Also, you realize of course that the 30,000 tons we collect daily is collected only from private homes? Business firms, industries and so on have private people to collect their waste. It's a problem, isn't it?"

What seemed to me hopeful in the city was that the senior officials I met were mostly young, and they all seemed intelligent, involved in their work, and full of ideas. Herb Elish had been, and Dr. Joseph Cimino, the Health Commissioner of the city, was. The problems they are involved with, however, are so huge that it seems impossible that they can ever be solved. "What is happening in New York," he said, "is that we are starting to have problems here that used to be confined to the Third World. Population problems are on the increase in all the minority areas: Harlem, the South Bronx where the Puerto Ricans are, Brooklyn where there are communities of Hasidic Jews, Chinatown. In all these areas we have overcrowding. A study of Fort Greene Park in Brooklyn showed an average of six occupants per room. Wherever there is overcrowding there are problems of health.

"Diseases that endanger public health, like salmonella, venereal disease, chicken pox, or meningitis all have a correlation with overcrowding. There is a lack of plumbing facilities in most overcrowded areas, an absence of running water. Naturally this also causes disease. In the ghettos, nutrition is poor, not in terms of adequate calories but of a balanced diet. School programs provide adequate supplementation for the children, but not, of course, for the adults. A lot of children are anemic, and there are a lot of cases of lead poisoning among ghetto children." This struck me as distinctly odd, and I asked Dr. Cimino to amplify.

"Most slum houses were built before 1940. They used a paint on the walls then that contained lead acetate. This stopped after 1940. The paint in most ghetto rooms is peeling off the walls. And lead acetate has a sweet taste. The children pull flakes of paint off the walls and eat them. It may sound very curious, but I assure you it's a real problem. But there are problems everywhere. Take the case of Chinatown. The Chinese there were very peaceful, they had no crime, and they came to health care clinics. Now a lot of ruffians have arrived from Hong Kong, there's gang warfare, and the attendance at the health care clinics is down."

I didn't see the connection between the appearance of gangsters from Hong Kong and the disappearance of people from clinics. Dr. Cimino clarified his remark. "We have 39,000 hospital beds in New York," he said, "and 20,000 nursing home beds, as well as which we have outpatient services that cover 6 to 7 million people a year. This is not counting private doctors and small clinics. The city runs twenty-three health centers and eighty-five child health stations. Anyone who needs medical care can have it free, provided he knows where to go, that is, to one of the scattered welfare centers in the city. But most ghetto groups do not know about this.

"If they do hear about it, it's possible they may have difficulty getting there because of not speaking or understanding English. But to come back to Chinatown, all ghetto areas now have a very high crime rate. Chinatown is the latest. It is literally true that some women are physically afraid to walk alone through the area to the clinic. This is especially true if they work and can't get to the clinic until evening. That would mean that they would have to walk home through the ghetto at night. And that's pretty risky. What is more, the same applies to the doctors. They feel it's unsafe for them to work in the ghettos."

Much of the crime in New York (and there's an awful lot of it) is said to be committed by drug addicts who will do anything to obtain money for their next dose. I asked Dr. Cimino about the narcotics problem. "Narcotics in the absence of crime are a minor problem, but narcotics and crime, if you mix the two, are terrible. Most of the addicts in the city now are blacks and Puerto Ricans, the ghetto people who live in a state of anger and misery. Whites aren't so much drug users as drug abusers. They adopt a drug culture, they take LSD, and so on, and they stay out of statistical surveys because they can support their habit.

The city runs thirty methadone clinics, where addicts are weaned off the needle. One consequence of the clinics' starting was that in nearly every neighborhood where one was set up, the residents raised a wail of horror at the idea of hopped-up hippies flocking past their front doors. Some 30,000 people in New York City are on methadone. "There are 50,000 to 60,000 registered in the treatment programs," Dr. Cimino said, "but I would estimate that there are over 150,000 active drug addicts in this city."

There are 7 million people in New York: If his guess is correct, it means that one person in every forty-six residents is a drug addict.

The consequences of sex can be many and various. The demographers are not really worried about the natural consequence, that is the birth of babies, for the growth rate in the United States is under 1 per cent. But the doctors are worried about a less natural consequence, which is venereal disease. According to a recent study, it is more prevalent in North America than the common cold. Dr. Cimino smiled rather grimly when I asked him about its prevalence in the city. "Well, syphilis," he said. "Four thousand new cases were reported last year. In all there are about 10,000, with 6,000 in the latent stages. Possibly only one case in ten actually reported his illness.

"As for gonorrhea, there are about 50,000 reported cases. I would estimate that there may be about 400,000 in all. Some people are ashamed to report a venereal disease, and some don't know they have it. It's not an epidemic; it's endemic. It's only been investigated over the last two years. It may have existed always." I was doing rapid sums in my head and now said, "If your figures are correct, do you mean to tell me that one in every fourteen persons in New York has some kind of venereal disease?" "Yes," replied Dr. Cimino with a tight little smile. I was silent, not being able to think of anything to say. Dr. Cimino, however, continued.

"I think this has built up over a period of time. I think what we're seeing is the consequence of a relaxation of moral codes that started a while back. It isn't the prostitutes, as a rule, who have VD. They usually have a doctor and are checked regularly for any venereal infection. The people who have it are kids at school or college, ordinary housewives, middle-class men. We have clinics where they can be treated in absolute privacy. But, well, in these days . . . ," he looked disgusted, *"Women's Lib,"* he concluded obscurely, "and all that."

The season was turning: When I came out of his office into the street, a cold wind was abroad looking for autumn leaves to blow down. It couldn't find any.

Wherever I traveled in the Third World, people asked me awe-struck questions about New York. Was it as beautiful as it looked in pictures? How could they come to see it? They looked towards the great city as towards some kind of paradise in concrete. I was enigmatic in my answers, for I didn't think they'd believe me if I told them all about the city. There are good people in New York, as in any place where there *are* people, and good places— that was the way I saw it on my first visit, ten years ago. It seemed different then, or perhaps I am different now. To me today New York seems helpless and wounded: The problems that pile up in any large Western city seem to have accumulated to an extent that they have swamped it. Nowhere is paradise. In New York as in the Third World there were hurt and lost people.

Off the Bowery, I visited a care center where the alcoholics who inhabit the area are treated. A friendly doctor took me round the wards, where the patients, who could have been any age at all, lay still and skeletal under white sheets. "They mostly drink red wine," the doctor said. "It's very cheap. Two or three men may invest in a couple of gallons and share it, or one man will buy a bottle and drink it. They get money by doing odd jobs, and they spend it all on liquor. Some of them hire a room in a flop-house; others sleep on the street. They're all in pretty bad shape, usually filthy and infested with vermin, and some have malnu-trition."

Downstairs ragged men, some of whom had sores on their hands and faces, were seated on benches. "They're being en-tered," the doctor said. "That's what they look like when they come in. We clean them up, and let them rest, and make sure they eat properly. We offer them all the help we can, physical and mental. But in the end, when they leave, even if they make an effort to work and live properly, they often wind up back on the Bowery." His face was full of pity. The ragged men sat on the benches in silence, looking down at the floor. "It's in their minds," the doctor said. "Something has wounded them there. Things are simply too much for them.

"They have families, some of them, whom they have left. Some are fairly well educated. Maybe what has happened to them is a consequence of life in New York. In this city the psychological pressures on a man are tremendous, and they can break a man who has some kind of inner weakness. It's an unnatural place to live," he said, echoing Herb Elish. I said goodbye and went out into the bleak street. An old man was lurching down the sidewalk on the other side of the road, his hands in his pockets. His lips were moving: He seemed to be talking to himself. I was too far off to hear what he was saying, but from the expression on his face it can't have been anything very happy.

A friend of mine took me on a visit to his former school. It was an expensive school, the hall of which, when we arrived, was full of small noisy children being collected by solicitous but apparently rather tired mothers. "Don't worry," said my friend, when I looked at him in alarm, "these aren't the ones you're going to talk with. They range up to sixteen and seventeen." We climbed a flight of stairs and were met by a friendly lady, who put us into a kind of conference room. Presently a troop of boys and girls came in. The youngest was fourteen, the eldest seventeen. They arranged themselves around the table and looked at me with frank curiosity. They all looked intelligent.

Honestly speaking, what I wanted to find out was what they thought about various not entirely related topics. I asked them what they felt about Watergate and Nixon. They were all very vehement about it. Watergate had been all over the front pages and the television screen for weeks and obviously seemed real and immediate to them, but they were not so alive to other political matters. They agreed with one another that Vietnam had been a shame and it was marvelous that the war was over, but it was obviously not real to them in the sense that Watergate was.

There was, in fact, a curious unanimity in their political opinions, which puzzled me a little. This, however, my friend later told me, was a school where a number of what are known as liberal intellectuals sent their children: It may have been that what they said on political issues were echoes from their parents. The generation from which their parents came would nonetheless have been concerned with world affairs, which these children seemed not to be. Politically, they seemed interested only in the United States, and even in other matters their interests were wholly localized. A girl volunteered that her main interest was the prevention of pollution. I asked her whether she meant in the United States or all over the world. She said, "In New York," and I inquired why only in New York. "Because this is where I live," she replied, rather scornful of my stupidity. I changed the subject and asked how many children each of them would like to have. They seemed rather vague about this.

A tall boy with acne eventually said, "As many as I can afford." A second boy said, "Two." The rest either hadn't thought about it or didn't want to say. They had a sex education class and knew about contraceptives. They also knew there were centers where you could be cured of venereal disease in strict confidence. Finally, I asked what they thought the average age was at which pupils in this school had their first sexual experience. "At twelve or thirteen," said the boy with acne. I thought this very young, but all the rest said he was right. They disagreed whether anybody in the school had ever become pregnant. The boy on my left said he thought one had.

Their thoughts about population and family planning, like most of their other views, tended to be somewhat localized and personal. It was good not to be pregnant, so you ought to know about contraceptives. I talked about the problem of population increase in some parts of Asia, and the dangers and difficulties that this could cause. This intrigued them: Like young magpies, one after the other, they took fluttering hops at the problem, trying to find a solution. One boy, if I understood him correctly, said that there were a lot of old and useless people in the world and if they could be eliminated by some kind of euthanasia, everything would be fine.

I left a little later, thinking, in rather an elderly way, of how precocious children had become since I was a child. Back in the hotel, I read a study on the sexual activities of adolescents in the United States. In 1970 there were 9.4 million girls of between fifteen and nineteen years of age in the country. About 37 per cent, some of whom were or had been married, were sexually active. Half of these children did not use any forms of contraception, and in 1973 600,000 babies were born to mothers under twenty. A study conducted in New York City between July 1970 and March 1971 revealed that for every 1,000 babies actually born to adolescent mothers, there were 526 abortions. That is to say, two babies were born alive to each one aborted. Moreover, the babies who were born were often unusually small, and a number of them died before their first birthday. The actual birth was often more difficult and complicated for the mother than it would have been for an older woman. Apart from this, the mother often had to cut her education short. Pregnancy is the most frequent reason for young women leaving college in the United States. To conceive a child while you are yourself more or less a child would therefore seem to be undesirable on many levels, but the young in one another's arms cannot be expected to be reasonable.

Nevertheless, this is a real problem and becomes doubly so if one thinks of the high incidence of venereal disease in the United States. What can be done about it is another matter. The American sex instruction programs are very thorough, and they are taken to schools and colleges around the country, so it is hard to feel that young people are unaware of the possibilities of indiscriminate intercourse without any precautions. Possibly parents should provide their daughter with the pill from the time she reaches puberty; this would at least be a realistic course of action and rather less embarrassing than if she suddenly declares she is pregnant.

There are a number of organizations that provide not only advice but a certain amount of help—psychological and otherwise—to young people in trouble. I went to one such place in Greenwich Village. There was a huge room on the top floor, where a number of people were carving pieces of wood, making paper flowers, and indulging in other activities that seemed to me more or less pointless. I have honestly never been able to see what this type of therapy does for someone in mental trouble except restore him to the status of a child, which I really don't think is very desirable. I was taken down to the basement and introduced to a number of young people. Some were tensely talkative and excitable, others rather listless. They were a mixed lot and included a Dominican youth, a young black woman, and assorted white Americans.

The Dominican said that his people had a raw deal in New York and that this made him so sad that he had become a narcotics addict. The black girl said that the color of her skin and the reaction of other people depressed her so that her psy-

chology had changed for the worse; she had become belligerent
and aggressive and suffered mentally. A limp white girl said she
had run away from home after a quarrel with her mother and
promptly started to take drugs to alleviate her misery. In every
case, they said that everything had changed since they had first
visited the center.

Those on dope, according to them, had ceased to take it. Those
with mental difficulties were now calm and healed. They had long
friendly group discussions about their problems (it sounded a little like Moral Rearmament), and now all was well. All this may
have been true, but to be as deeply dependent on this center as
they were seemed to me a bit depressing. They looked on the
center as a substitute for home and on the staff as substitutes for
their fathers. What alarmed me a little was that so many young
people came here. Were they all dope addicts or mentally dis-
turbed? If this was the case, I thought, New York must be full of
such people. They demanded and deserved pity and help, and,
obviously, even if its methods were not to my taste, the center
had helped many. But what did this to them first of all?

Charles Kenyatta was once the bodyguard of Malcolm X and
ran a kind of private army called the Mau Mau. Those days are
behind him, and he is now a sort of personally appointed protec-
tor of the blacks. His latest activity, after the new hard-line narcotics law was announced, has been to move around Harlem
warning people of the severe penalties to which they were liable
if caught in possession of drugs. He had kindly agreed to take me
around Harlem, which is a place not many strangers visit, for
excellent reasons. Many of my white friends had told me that
there were two places where they never went: Times Square at
night and Harlem at any time.

Harlem was once a fashionable area where descendants of the
Dutch lived. As their properties deteriorated, they moved and sold
the houses to Jewish immigrants, who in turn left and let the
houses to black people, at the same time keeping a monopoly on
trade in the local shops. Blacks paid exorbitant rents and high
prices in the shops. Today, in Harlem, a white man who walks
around by himself can meet sudden and possibly hurtful trouble.

The same applies, in fact, to anyone not recognizably black. But I was with Charles Kenyatta, who is known and respected. He was greeted frequently by people who passed us. He gravely inclined his head in answer to each salutation. With his afro hair style and beard, he did actually look like some kind of patriarchal leader.

It was a Saturday. Harlem was full of people shopping. The younger people wore bright colors, African robes on occasion. The older people were more soberly dressed and more shabby. We came by an open market, the stalls heaped with fruit and vegetables. It could almost have been Africa. There was a prosperous look about the shops. We entered a bookshop called "Back to Africa," full of volumes on the continent and its culture. "You see," said Kenyatta, "once we were ashamed to be black. There were hairdressers that specialized in straightening a black person's hair. Those have disappeared. Now we wear Afros. And look at this shop."

He patted the piles of books about Africa. "We are proud of our past. We are proud of our culture." We left the shop. I asked, "Do people really want to return to Africa?" Kenyatta eyed me somberly. "Why not?" he said. "Those are our people. White men aren't our people." Beyond the market we suddenly started to see another aspect of Harlem: terribly dilapidated old houses, with shattered windows, obscenities chalked on the wall, refuse scattered on the steps and the sidewalks outside. A few young black men sat out on the steps; black women and children stared out of doorways. Kenyatta waved his hand around him with a baleful air.

"This is the way my people live," he said. "Those houses are full of rats as big as cats. The women don't dare leave their babies untended because they could be eaten by the rats. In some of those houses they've one latrine for fifty people, flush don't work neither, and no bath." The neighborhood was dotted with churches. Outside one, drinking from a can of beer, stood a very old man, who hailed Kenyatta. "This man," Kenyatta said, "he worked with Marcus Garvey, the black patriot." The old man nodded. " 'Twas a very long time ago," he said. "Garvey he been dead these fifty years now. He was a great man, sure he was. He was my friend, like my father."

I asked him about Garvey. He wrinkled his forehead, apparently making an effort to remember, and said, "He was a great man. He was my friend." We wandered around for a while, coming back through the open market and thence to Kenyatta's car.

As we drove out of Harlem, Kenyatta at first sat in silence. Then he said, "You saw it? Was it terrible? See, the people nice and friendly 'cept when a white man around. Friendly, even while they live the way they do." He dropped me back at my hotel and declined my offer of a drink. "I got to drive back to Harlem," he said. "Every Saturday afternoon I give my people a speech on the corner of West 125th. I'm going along there now to get ready for the meeting." He drove off and I went upstairs to Leela, who said, "How was it?" I said, "Interesting," and sat down to make notes about the morning. Like Kenyatta, she asked, "Was it terrible?"

I reflected. Had it been terrible? In a way, yes. I hadn't seen a white face in Harlem. It was a separate culture from the culture of midtown Manhattan. The whole city was a city of enclaves, race divided from race, color from color. The enclaves are filled with hatred and even if New York solves all its other problems, I do not see how the problem of racial tension can be solved. Certainly nobody seems to be making much of an effort to solve it, perhaps because most people think it is impossible.

And New York is not the only place that has social tensions caused by race. There is racial feeling in Britain, where colored laborers come from the West Indies and Pakistan. West Germany has brought in Italian, Yugoslav, and Turkish laborers, over a million and a half of them. A quarter of Switzerland's labor force comes from overseas. Algerians, Portuguese, and Arabs work in France. In all these countries there have already been signs of resentment from the local population, and a commencement of tension.

Obviously, it is an excellent idea for the richer European nations to provide work opportunities for the unemployed of other, poorer countries. But perhaps they should remember the example of New York, a city of immigrants who have formed separate racial blocs, hostile or indifferent to one another, a divided city, and be extremely careful in handling the potentially explosive situation at home.

Shortly before we left New York for Latin America, food prices rocketed, in particular the price of beef. It was said that they would soon rise more steeply still, and housewives with deep freezers bought up quantities of beef, so that there were chronic shortages. Many people replaced beef in their diets with tuna fish and soybeans as a source of protein, rather as, during World War II, the British ate an imitation lamb chop made largely of mashed potatoes. The growing shortage of food throughout the world was something most Americans had not realized, because not for many years had there been a food shortage in the United States.

In fact, America consumes a third of the world's natural resources, though its population is only 6 per cent of the total world population. But now, with the rivers and oceans of the world mostly polluted, the supply of fish has lessened; drought and the indiscriminate use of substances like DDT on crops have diminished supplies from the fields of the Third World. Every commodity in the world is becoming scarcer, except people. In the opinion of Lester Brown, a brilliant man who works for the Overseas Development Council in Washington, where I met him one rainy day, people all over the world will soon be forced to eat much less.

"It doesn't matter in America or in the rich European countries," he said. "People there eat far more than is healthy, anyway, and the standard of health will probably rise if they eat less. What's terribly worrying is what will happen to people in countries where they exist on a subsistence diet anyway." One answer to this, he felt, was a more equitable sharing of world resources. Another was an increased attention to ecology. Heavy deforestation in Asia had caused serious floods, animal species were dying out as their natural habitat was destroyed, and pollution caused disease as well as decreasing the world supply of fresh water.

There was gloom in New York as prices continued to rise. But what struck me at this period was that ordinary people—taxidrivers, waitresses, the man beside one in a bar—seemed to have been thinking seriously about the shortages and the rising costs, and for the first time to be relating them to the global situation.

They had started to think that there was something slightly odd and wrong everywhere, not merely in the United States. Anything that makes people think is a good thing, so perhaps the shortages were. But somehow the wounded quality of the city—of the minds of its inhabitants—remained unaltered.

One day, during a June thunderstorm, we took a taxi. As we traveled towards our destination, Leela asked the driver if this was normal for the month. The driver said tersely, "I don't know, lady. If you want to know about the weather, ask the guy who deals with weather reports. I'm a cabdriver." Leela, rather hurt, said that she had simply asked him a friendly question. "I don't want people to be friendly," the driver said. "I don't want friends. I don't want to talk to anyone." He had a frozen, terrified, and rather terrifying face. Nobody in Africa or Asia had behaved like this. Perhaps the population problem in the developed world is the worst problem of all.

CHAPTER TEN

"Theology now cannot work outside technology."

Bogotá sits high in the Andes, 8,000 feet above the sea; and higher than the city itself, on one of the hills around, Christ stands with his arms mutely outspread above the fine houses, the offices, the hotels, and the slums. The name of the city, however, isn't Christian. It came from the Chibcha Indians who lived in these mountains when the conquistadors came. They no longer exist. The spoor of the Spaniards has been imprinted in the names and faces of the Colombians of today. But once Bogotá was a Chibcha town, though—since the ancient Colombians, unlike the Indians of Mexico and Peru, built in wood—no relics remain, none, that is, apart from the gold worked by the Indians, now kept in a museum. This country was *El Dorado*.

El Dorado, "the Golden One," was a myth that the Spaniards chased, and that chased them, all over Latin America. They heard, wherever they went, of a land where gold was so plentiful that people went about clad in it. This was true, up to a point, in that the more decoratively minded of the Colombian Indian populace at the time of· the conquistadors wore golden breast-plates and armlets: Their children played with gold toys. For religious occasions gold masks were worn. One Spanish historian reported stories of a country where the people were made of gold, and it is interesting to speculate on what the conquistadors would have done had they come on such a race. Perhaps they would have melted them all down into their basic material.

In any event, Colombia, as the name suggests, was discovered for the Spaniards by Columbus, around 1503. After this, various quarrelsome conquistadors entered the country. Diego de Nicuesa settled a small area on the Atlantic Coast known as San Sebastián de Uraba. (The Indians killed some of his soldiers with arrows, as Saint Sebastian was killed.) Balboa founded the settlement of Santa María de Antigua. Pedro Arias, who cut Balboa's head off, created Panamá, at one time part of Colombia as the Spanish knew it. In 1525 Rodrigo de Bastidas founded Santa Marta on the Caribbean coast. This was the point from which Spanish influence fanned out over the country, and this was the town where the Asociación Latina Americana de Comunicadores Demográficos—ALACODE—seminar was held in July 1973.

Bogotá, the night we arrived, was cold, and both men and women wandered around the narrow clean windy streets in ponchos. I suffered from a violent attack of altitude sickness, but early next day we caught a plane to Santa Marta. It was less than a 2-hour flight away, but when we dropped down between the wrinkled hills and the wrinkled sea, there was a burning sun, and the earth was spiked with crucifixes of cacti. The hotel in which the seminar took place was a collection of pleasant chalets by the Caribbean, a hotel designed for holiday makers, which are what most conference delegates usually are, or at least wish to be. This seminar, however, was surprisingly serious, and sometimes, I thought, fairly lively.

Perhaps this was because, as Tarzie Vittachi, my friend who had come from New York to attend the conference, had told me, the meeting was to acquaint South American newspapermen with population problems, so that these could be knowledgeably understood. The delegates were therefore more or less linked by their common profession or vocation. At the same time, they had widely varying views. The most vocal opinions appeared to be those held by the revolutionaries who repeated endlessly, whether the topic under discussion was women's liberation, environmental pollution, or family health, that the revolution must come before anything else could take place. "These fellows," grumbled Tarzie at one session, "would wait for the revolution before they went to the lavatory."

Nevertheless, one word recurred in all the speeches: *machismo*, the male attitude of being the grumpy and privileged ruler of the family, the father who forbids his daughter to attend the university and choose her husband, the husband who beats his wife or makes her bear numerous babies and has a mistress on the side. Some said it was the worst problem in South America; some said it was dying out; and the revolutionaries, eyes flaming behind dark glasses, arms waving, blowing loud rhetorical trumpets in Spanish, said when the day had dawned the whole concept of *machismo* would depart. Myself, it seemed to me that *machismo* was not as unique to Latin America as all that: I have seen it in Bristol and Bombay. Maybe Spanish is the only language to have a name for it.

Meanwhile Leela swam in the Caribbean with Siti Vittachi, Tarzie's wife, and her little boy Imran; the sea wind made the palm trees sing at dusk; the crosstrees of the cacti appeared to await (hopefully) some new nailed burden; the bar filled every hour with refugees from the seminar; Alvaro García Peña, a splendid Colombian bear, ambled around talking to people between sessions; delegates sped off to town to buy last-minute presents for their wives and children or to the airport to catch quick metal birds to their own countries. In short, what usually happens at conferences happened.

On the final day, Rafael Salas, the executive director of the U.N. Fund for Population Activities, was present, a quiet, neat Filipino. He announced that UNFPA was prepared to fund ALACODE to spread the gospel of "development journalism." The delegates rose and cheered. Then one had another demonstration of the Latin American character. Everyone wanted to speak, to make flowery speeches of thanks. Even the revolutionaries said that they would publicize the problems of population, though the revolution had not yet come. Leela, Siti, and the interpreters came out of the sea like mermaids that night, and there was a party to celebrate the happy ending of it all. Then we left. Santa Marta forgot us all at once.

In Bogotá we looked at the Gold Museum. The museum is part of the national bank. I was told by a foreign expert, though most Colombians I met denied it, that the Indian gold in the museum, and even more so the Indian gold in the bank vaults, are what keep the peso of the country steady. Certainly, there were immense quantities of gold ornaments in the museum, and the display rooms were vaults in themselves, into which one was locked after one entered. The gold ornaments on display were both barbaric and civilized, like almost any human artifact, including television and the motor car: That is, they demonstrated a quality of humanity, which is civilization, and the barbaric quality that is what people do to a thing produced by civilization. The horrible look of some of the gold heads was unlike the quietness of some of the others.

The Chibchas who once lived in Bogotá had houses of wood and straw and bark clothes. They traded the salt they had for gold from the cannibal Panchas. They had a system of working gold without the use of high temperatures. They practiced human sacrifice like the Mexican Aztecs, tearing the heart out of each sacrifice, eating it. This accounts, possibly, for some of the more horrible golden figures. But the gentle figures, the toys, and some of the masks, demonstrate that these people had the quality of tenderness that any human community has. People are very strange animals—a truism: A woman will hold her own child in her arms, its shield and its sword, and not wince when her own husband showers the children of another nation with death. The gentle Spanish ladies who came after the colonization in 1550 watched unmoved while the Indians and their families were enslaved.

In 1819 the Republic of Colombia was founded. Simón Bolívar, who helped to release much of Latin America from the Spaniards, died, in fact, in Santa Marta, having helped in the work. In 1973 the Spanish and Indian blood was very mixed. You can now see Indian features in a person who has white skin. This was not entirely through equal and willing marriage, but because before their *señoras* came the Spanish needed women, and the only ones available were Indians who may or may not have wanted to couple with the conquistadors. Even after 1550 an Indian woman who was more or less a slave on a Spaniard's estates would have to do what her employers told her. There were probably cases the other way round as well.

Nowadays there are girls who come into the towns, as domestic servants, who rapidly become pregnant by their employers, or possibly by acquaintances outside the family for which they work, following, if they only knew it, an ancient tradition. The remedy

for it, since they can hardly return to families that expect the unmarried daughter in the city to support them, not vice versa, is
usually abortion—abortion performed by some unclean and unskilled woman. The result is usually complications, so that the
girl must be entered into a hospital for the infection to be cleared
up. Fifty per cent of maternal mortality, I was told, were caused
by the consequences of illegal abortions. In a hospital run by
nuns, 29,734 of the patients were being treated for these consequences.

Seventy per cent of these women were single, and 327 were
under the age of fifteen. The girls had had a rather wide range of
seducers: in seventy-three cases their own brothers, in ten cases
their fathers, and in three cases their grandfathers. The high incidence of these abortions is partly through ignorance of preventive methods and partly because, even when the woman has some
idea of contraceptive methods, she is also aware that the Church
forbids them. The Colombian Church, however, is a surprisingly
liberal body; at least, it has, over the years, become so. There was,
at first, tremendous opposition to family planning from the older
priests, but this seems to have died down or been stifled.

"Even before family planning methods were introduced into
Colombia," said Dr. Fernando Tamayo, one of the founders of
Profamilia and the doyen of the Colombian family planners,
"there were a lot of traditional contraceptives used. They had no
medical basis—like drinking water after intercourse, using lime
juice as a douche, and so on—but at least that proved that people
wanted family planning; they wanted to limit their families. Over
the last couple of years, the younger priests have seen this, and
they are very progressive now. They oppose abortion and sterilization, but otherwise they are for us.

"In the past ten years," Dr. Tamayo added, "the Colombian
Church has found it difficult to recruit priests. The number of
those who want to become priests has dropped by 50 per cent. A
lot of seminaries have closed down." He did not seem particularly
saddened by this. "The desired family size in Colombia," he said,
"as I wrote in a study I made, is about 2.4. From a thousand interviews in my study, I calculated that the actual family size is
about 4.8, that is, people are producing twice as many children as
they want. Colombia has 11 million people here, and the problem

isn't really one of population size. It's the speed of increase that is difficult to cope with, more than anything else."

He said, "We have 40 per cent of the population under fifteen; and with the life expectancy now fifty-six or fifty-seven, we also have a number of people over sixty. All these are dependent on the active part of the population. Every active person in Colombia has 2.5 people dependent on him. The average per capita income is $350, and so the quality of life suffers for both the provider and the dependents. You can see the desire of the people for some proper form of contraception in that there are about 200,000 illegal abortions each year. The health of the nation suffers from all this. The Church and the politicians have come to realize this. But for many years it was an uphill battle against tremendous odds."

Profamilia teaches women about contraception and supplies them with the pill and other devices. It is a tidy place with tired patients, some with infants in their arms, awaiting their turn for a consultation. Apart from the distribution of contraceptives, Profamilia detects cancer through pap smears.

"If we don't have any family planning," said Dr. Tamayo, "the population will double itself in eighteen years. If we do, it will take twenty-two years. Four years will provide us with a little breathing space and planning time. The birth rate is dropping with the improvement in educational facilities and the fact that more women are now taking up employment of some kind."

Isabella Carreras de Gómez, an active and articulate lady of middle age who runs a training program on family planning and is a sociologist, didn't entirely agree with this. "We had a study of middle-class families," she said, "and asked both the men and the women what number of children they desired. The men said one or two, the women three or four. This amazed me. *Machismo* is so powerful here, and I have always felt that a primary attribute of the *machisto* is to prove himself virile by begetting many children. We investigated the matter, and what we found was this. The women were largely uneducated and not equipped to take up employment. Therefore they had to stay at home.

"When they stay at home, they have to justify their existence to their husbands. They want to have many children, so that they can look after them and prove to their husbands that they are useful in the house. This is another aspect of *machismo*: You could call it a concealed aspect." Sra. Carreras is very heated on the subject of *machismo*. "Out of every 10,000 male students, she said, "30 finish up at university. Out of every 10,000 female students, 1 reaches university. Sometimes a bright girl in a poor family will cut her education short and go to work so that her unintelligent brother's studies can be paid for. I tell you," said Sra. Carreras furiously, "this *machismo*, it operates on every level.

"We have to change men, to offer them new values. Now they have only *machismo*, pride in the penis. A man here in Colombia may have three or four different women, to prove that he is *machisto*, and have children by all of them. In some areas of this country, 65 per cent of all children born are illegitimate. Our policy is to try and educate men to look at a woman as a human creature, not simply as a source of pleasure in bed and a cook and maid. I talked to a woman once who had had an abortion. She knew about contraception, and I asked why she hadn't practiced it. She told me that her husband said it spoiled his pleasure. When she became pregnant, he said 'Get out. Don't come back till you've got rid of the kid.'

"So there is this *machismo*, and another aspect of it is that a man is afraid to allow his wife to take contraceptives because he thinks she may be unfaithful. Then of course there are the religious women. It is a funny kind of attitude that they have. In 1968 the Pope came to Bogotá. Profamilia was astonished: Shortly before he arrived, all the women with IUDs came to have them removed. No patients went to Profamilia while the Pope was here. The day after he left, Profamilia was astonished again. All the women who had had their IUDs removed came back to have them replaced." Sra. Carreras laughed heartily. "It is not so funny," she said when she had finished laughing. "All these people must be educated."

Her organization has 622 social workers who have so far talked to 2 million people all over Colombia, collecting research material on family attitudes and structures and teaching people about family planning. "It will take ages," Sra. Carreras said. "Today the ambition of the village girl is to marry as soon as she can. They usually marry without love, and there is usually no kind of dialogue between husband and wife. When they procreate, it is the consequence of an unplanned act. Also, a poor woman may have many men in her life, and a child by each one. This can lead to terrible consequences, not only for the woman herself but for the children. It depends, of course, on the woman's character.

"There was a case we had—there are probably many other similar cases—of a woman who had eight children by different men. There was nothing to eat in the house. The eldest girl was fourteen. The mother looked her up and down and said, "You're ready. You can go." The girl put on her best dress and went and stood in the streets. She came back in the evening with a few pesos, enough to buy food for the family. She had found a profession. Was this not also caused by *machismo*—first the *machismo* of the men who used her mother, then the *machismo* of the men who used the child?" She sighed and went to her balcony and looked out over the red roofs, the churches, the white houses. "Still, Bogotá is beautiful," she said.

It was beautiful especially on Sundays, when the avenues were empty and the parks full and a multitude of churchbells sobbed for the sins of the people. What had puzzled me greatly about the prevalence of abortion in Colombia was that if the people did not practice any contraceptive method because they were Catholic and thought contraception a sin, why did they practice abortion, which was surely also a sin? An intelligent and comprehensive explanation was offered me by Raul Trejos, the director of the U.N. Information Center in Bogotá. "If you take the pill," he said, "or you have the IUD, this is a process that continues. You can't go to the priest and confess unless you stop the methods. Abortion is a single act. You can go and confess to an abortion and the priest will give you prayers to say and forgive you. I think this is why there are so many abortions in Latin America."

Dr. Guillermo López Escobar, one of the founders of the family planning movement in Colombia, told me that 2.4 hospital beds were available to every 1,000 people in Colombia. About one-third of these beds are taken up by women suffering from complications after abortions. There is also a shortage of doctors: 1 doctor to each 2,000 people. "In some areas," Dr. López said, "there is 1 doctor to every 10,000 people. What is more, there is only one trained nurse to every three doctors. The death rate is falling, that is true, but we still have terrible problems. There is malnutrition everywhere. Half the population is situated in rural areas where the disposal of excreta presents a sanitation problem.

"In addition to this, there is a shortage of potable water in these areas. Even in the south of Bogotá you will find places where the only water supply is from a public fountain. Partly because of this, there are a lot of people with intestinal parasitical infections. The incidence of tuberculosis here is also a little higher than in the rest of the Third World. If our population doubles in the next two decades, as it will do at the present growth rate, we will be in trouble in spite of our present economic growth. Even now, with this economic development, which is outstanding, it seems to me that the quality of life has decreased. One-third of our school-children are undernourished, and there is less food available today."

Dr. López is now the president of the Corporación Centro Regional de Población. "But such an organization did not exist ten years ago." It was in the 1960s that a few doctors in Bogotá started to become aware of the problems that affect population and the fact that they were bound up, in their country, with family planning. They were appalled at the numbers of abortions, at the ill health of the population, and at the rates of infant mortality, which are, even now, 120 per 1,000. Dr. López was one of these men, the others included Dr. Tamayo, whom I had met, Dr. Antonio Ordoñez, Dr. Bernardo Moreno, and, perhaps the most dynamic of them all, Dr. Hernán Mendoza, who is now dead. They met first in 1963 to discuss their views.

"We realized we knew nothing whatever about population problems," Dr. López said. But Hernán Mendoza started to read widely about them. Dr. López was lent books by a visiting economic adviser, who also pointed out to him that planning for a country was impossible if you did not know how many future citizens you were planning for, that some attention had to be paid to the keeping down of the population to a size that could be best served by the national economy. It was only thus, said the economist, that a country could hope to have people who were reasonably healthy and had clear minds, or at least minds as clear as any human mind can aspire to be. This took Dr. López further into Mendoza's crusade.

The medical schools started to study family planning. The Ford Foundation handed out money to help. At this point contraceptive services were only delivered through a few private doctors, the original band of musketeers. "When we worked in the hospitals," Dr. López said, "we saw the misery of those who were pregnant with a sixth or seventh child whom they didn't want. Tamayo and I started a center with a few IUDs, and Tamayo set up a private service in his own office. Then Hernán Mendoza tried to develop services in the government sector. Slowly, things started up. We held seminars, we opened clinics. We talked to the priests. It took a long time, but now, here we are."

One day, early in the morning, rain fell on Bogotá, and the rain in Colombia smells like an excellent after-shave lotion, and tantalizes the skin like one. Christ was hazy on the hills above the city, his vision obscured by lazy dripping clouds. I took a taxi into the rain, past ponchoed pedestrians, to the offices of the National Conference of Colombian Bishops. The driver leaped out and opened the door with a Latin flourish. Then he turned to the bleakly handsome, entirely secular building I was about to enter, and made the sign of the cross. I was mildly surprised. I was even more surprised when, before he re-entered his vehicle, he bowed deeply to me and said with a succulent sort of respect, "*Adiós, padre.*"

Upstairs, I met Father Francisco Escobar, the secretary of the conference. Father Escobar is a small, spry man, and though a friend of Dr. Guillermo López Escobar, he is no relation. He studied for a while in America and speaks English with a slight American accent. He is obviously a very intelligent man. "The relation between a man and woman here," he said, "is typically Hispanic. The man is the head of the family, so he is always right. He gives the woman money, so the woman has to—" Father Escobar paused for the properly Christian word, "receive him. So a man can pick up any girl and the children are forgiven him. Here there is male superiority everywhere. There is no correlation between sex, culture, and intelligence.

"We have to change the relationship," Father Escobar said. "It's very difficult, but we face danger if we don't. We have to introduce sex education, for example. We have to prepare teachers, and they will have to work against television, pop songs, and movies. Not because we think these things are immoral, but they contain the seeds of *machismo*. Much of our pop music comes from Mexico, and there is one very popular song that says, 'We are men, we are men, therefore we are always right.' It's a tremendous cultural problem. Love has to be present in sex. All the values of our people have to be changed. And this is so hard. Here couples need each other from an economic point of view as well as for sexual reasons."

The rain had stopped, and cars were swishing like snakes through the puddles it had left. A dim sun appeared and cleared the clouds away from Christ. "The presence of a woman is not economically important for the man, only sexually important. The presence of a man is economically important for the woman not sexually important. Abortion, as you know, is a viciously important factor here. In the past, people have practiced contraception secretly, if they knew about it. But even then it was a burden on their souls; it was a sin. Now it is all different. There are many courses for priests to tell them of the new horizons of the Church. Now we are working for values. We are no longer working for a system."

The gyrating clouds went somewhere else, and Christ stood in his pleading posture, clear on the hill. "What is important," said Father Escobar in his quiet voice, his eyes inexpressive behind his thick spectacles, "for us," he sipped his coffee, dark, sweet, and Colombian, "is love." He looked at me as though he thought I would laugh. I didn't. "We have to tell them that to plan your family is a sign of your love. We have to say that if the rhythm method doesn't suit you—the Church in the Philippines is fifteen years behind the times—you have the freedom to use other methods, and even if you adopt these other methods you are free to take Holy Communion without any sin upon your soul. You understand this?"

I said I had been born a Catholic, though admittedly I do not practice the religion, and I understood. Father Escobar said, "Within the Church there has been a change because we have a new approach, a human approach. Not only for the Church, but for all Western society, reproduction was the first purpose of marriage. Now love has its own fertility, in our view. Love has its operations at three levels. First there is the couple. Then there is the family, which is the couple and its children. Lastly, there is the family in connection with the society in which it lives. Catholic families must be aware of the problems of society. They may be aware of them on simple levels: in this country, the need for sanitation, etc.

"And now there is a new problem. Twenty years ago, when a child was born, there was a Colombian saying: 'He comes with bread under his arms,' that is, God will see that he is fed and looked after. With this mixture of irresponsibility and religion— though the saying came from local culture, not from the Church —procreation was said to be the will of God. Ten years ago the change came. Professors find it easy to say that the time has come when it is essential to space or limit our families according to how we can support them. But go to a priest in the mountains of Colombia who has been preaching for a quarter of a century that family planning is a sin. Go to his congregation. Try and explain all this.

"It may take years for these new ideas to penetrate their minds, and it is there, in the most backward areas, that the greatest need for change, and rapid change, exists. Our objection to Profamilia, for example, is because they simply offer medical services, not education. That isn't enough. You have to explain to the people. People have to suffer a real internal battle before they can change. You can change the structure of an economy by laws, but not the mind of a human person. This *machismo*, for example, this must change. The change is not to do with the Catholic Church but with society itself. You know, our Latin American women have a tremendous devotion to their families. It's important for our culture.

"But this in turn is a cause of *machismo*." He spread out his small neat hands in a despairing way. "It is a vicious circle. The women love their families. That is excellent, but they create *machismo* in turn. How do you destroy something good to destroy something bad?" He sat silent for a moment, confronted by one of the eternal problems of the human race. "We cannot play with people," he said after a while. "We have to respect them." He stopped once more, and the rain started, the sound I like best in the world, crackling in the hollows of the earth, richocheting from the stone that people inhabit. Up in the hills the old priests shouting hell fire would have their brows, possibly, cooled. Weather is so democratic; whether you are screaming during an abortion or sitting in the Tequendama Hotel drinking a martini, the same rain, I thought, makes the same sound and everyone hears it.

What people say is not like the rain, except that it is liquid and vanishes down the drains of the ear. "Abortion is against human life," said Father Escobar. "So the Church now opposes it. It's a technical viewpoint. We are now trying to study where human life starts. We thought it was at the moment of fertilization. Now we are making a study, both theologically and medically, as to when it actually does. Theology now cannot work outside technology. Now we have to look for answers. It is not a problem of sex but one of human life. Religion is a sociological fact. Look at Catholicism here. Christ is not important; the Virgin is, and some of the saints. It goes back to a time when the people were Indians.

"What the Colombian poor worship are the lesser saints and the Virgin; these intercede between God and mankind. The people need something that they think will intercede. If a man is a Hindu or a Jew or a Christian or a Muslim, the suffering of people is the same everywhere. The Conference of Bishops has prepared a letter, which is now with the Cardinal of Bogotá and will be submitted to the President, in which they have said that they are agreeable to every contraceptive method except for abortion and sterilization, because they feel this will alleviate the suffering of the people and help the nation as a whole. We are creating a structure that will help us to carry this program on to a useful conclusion.

"This is a sex education program that will be integrated into the national health program. When a young girl reaches puberty in our schools, a nun will talk to her about menstruation. No other person would dare do this, not even perhaps her mother. Now the intention is that the nun will advise her on sexual matters, and she will listen—she may listen." The idea that a nun, unless she is the kind of nun featured in pornographic volumes, would be able to teach a young girl how to conduct her sex life seemed a bit odd to me, but I felt a genuine respect for Father

Escobar, and, so peculiar is the Catholicism in Latin America, I thought it might even work. It was raining still: Father Escobar said he'd drop me.

On the way back to the Tequendama Hotel, at an intersection, we met a muscular man with a smile that was mostly gold. "He is a bullfighter," Father Escobar said when we had left him. "He is a good bullfighter, but now is not the season for bulls. He is my friend. I like to see the fight of bulls, you know?" And as he dropped me outside the Tequendama, he said a bit sadly, "You, you come from outside, you have no country. Travel is your work. For us, it is different. For us, this is our country. But from what you tell me, you are a stranger everywhere." I stood in the rain as he drove away, and I wondered, not happily, if it was true.

Dr. Jorge García Silva is a Chilean who works for the International Center of Development Research in Bogotá. He is a young man and when I met him he was dressed in an English tweed suit. Countries present new problems to his organization, which then funds them. The center has its headquarters in Ottawa and branches in Singapore, Dakar, and Bogotá. The policy of the institution is directed by a board of twenty members, 51 per cent of whom are from underdeveloped countries. "Malnutrition and abortion," he said, "are the two biggest problems in Colombia." It was another rainy, fragrant day, and because he had recently moved into a new office, heaped with uncompartmented files, the air smelled of damp paper as well as rain.

"The problems in Latin America vary from country to country," he said. "The fertility rate is high, and the mortality rate, because of improved health services, is falling. You know, South America is like Asia. Central America has the highest growth rate in the world, 3.8 per cent. There will be a doubling of population in most of these countries in the next decade. But family planning programs are badly received in Latin America. It's a very political problem here. The programs come from the United States, and people feel that this is an imperialist penetration, not for racial reasons, as the blacks in America feel, but for political reasons. In Colombia there are no proper leaders: They are all right wing.

"In other countries . . . ," Dr. Silva hesitated and added "like Chile, which is known for its family planning programs throughout South America, the leaders are from the Left and they have political influence, which they exercise in family planning programs. Industrial development is important as a cause of this. Colombia is an agricultural nation. Agricultural workers are different in their political thinking from industrial workers; inexperience of political realities is very important so far as this is concerned. Fifty per cent of maternal mortality in Colombia is caused by illegal abortions. Even now that the Church is changing its attitude, it opposes abortion, which could be legalized, as it is in other countries like Chile."

We wandered off into the rain, and later I went to Planaction, the planning commission of the Colombian Government. The family planning part of this is directly under the control of the President of the Republic, but the organizer and head, Dr. Luis Eduardo Rosas, a tall, crisp, youngish man, implements the various programs. He told me, as others had, of the drift from the countryside into urban areas, the same problem that appears to occur everywhere in the Third World. The reasons for this drift are very complex: Facilities in the cities of underdeveloped countries are obviously better in the sense that you have medical facilities, electricity, potable water (to some extent) and, the peasants feel, job opportunities.

It all reverses itself: Because of the influx of population into the cities, the number of job opportunities available lessens, the facilities available are strained to a point where they often crack dryly apart, and people who have lost a village tradition that once sustained them find themselves without roots. The young ones turn to delinquency and the old ones to despair. Dr. Rosas was not unhopeful, however. Construction is necessary in the urban areas of Colombia, he said, not only to house people but for the creation of new offices and factories. It was felt that the newcomers from the villages could be put to work on construction sites, for houses in which they could live and factories where they could work.

On yet another rainy day, Raul Trejos and I were taken by the inhabitants of a slum ironically called Vista Hermosa, "beautiful view," to where they lived. The slum sprawls out over a red hill in the city suburbs. You reach it up an unmade dirt road, which, when we were there, was runny with slush. In the intervals between showers small boys came out into the wind to fly home-made kites made of old newspapers. The houses on the hill were made of plywood or of brick, with broken slatted roofs. Some had glass windows, broken too. "These people came from the villages," said Luis Ortega, the son of the landowner on whose property the houses had been built. "Most of them came from the Boyacá area to the south."

Ortega was a young man, handsome, with the lengthy hair and deliberately casual clothing of the new kind of liberal. "This is an organization for poor people," he said, "and they pay the rent however they can. The rent monies are applied to organize facilities for the people, like improvements to the school and the health center here." The men of Vista Hermosa were mostly the construction workers Dr. Rosas had earlier spoken of. Their average income was about ten dollars a month. They had heard of the glories of the city over transistor radios, which even the Colombian peasantry now possess, and had come to partake in its splendor. "They earn about the same," Ortega said, "as they would at home."

"But the food here is not so good," he added. "At home they grew their crops; they had livestock. Here they do not have all this. Here you will find children of two or three years old who cannot walk because of vitamin deficiencies. The people can't return to the villages now, because they sold their land and property to be able to come here. The money they obtained from the sale has been spent to build their own houses here." Above the rugged red slopes of the slum the clouds looked down; hobbled burros grazed in the yellow unkempt grass. But on the walls of the tumbledown shacks there was a profusion of rusty cans that had once contained food, filled with flowers, the need of people for symbols of the life outside the one they were confined in. We saw the pink brick school; we saw the health center. We saw the people, ragged or covered in ponchos, collecting to welcome us.

It was not for some little while that we realized with some horror than they were under the impression that we had been sent by the United Nations to help them. A woman in a shawl came up to me, plodding through the melted red mud, and whispered furtively to me in Spanish. Someone translated. The woman had a daughter of fifteen who was very brilliant in school. The teachers felt she should continue to the university, and so far as I could understand she wanted to be a biochemist. The woman had an Indian face, with dignified lines that kept crumpling into involuntary tears. The rain had started up once more, dripping from the roofs of the battered shacks. She had no money, she said, to send her daughter to the university.

Feebly, unable to think what else, I suggested that scholarships might be available. She raised her head under its shawl and looked at me with eyes deeply sunk in the wrinkles of old tears. (I later realized she could not have been more than forty.) "Yes," she said, "but in the meantime the daughter had become pregnant." I could think of no possible consolation. "Many here have abortions," the woman said. "But they are not clean abortions. I want money from the Naciones Unidas for her to have a clean abortion, and then they must give me money so I can send her to the university. Do you think I want her to live the life I do, that my other children do? Should she not be able to live differently?"

I had a stunned sort of feeling. It had visited me often in the last few months, when I had talked to the poor, the helpless, the hopeless. It was always during these terrible and endless conversations that I felt, for the first time in my life, that to have a few million dollars to spend would be a desirable rather than a spiritually destructive thing. The daughter never appeared, but I could visualize, from the mother, the thing that, bereft of help, she might become. She may not have been as brilliant as her mother said she was, but she was obviously a person who looked beyond the shacks of her hillside home towards cloudy Bogotá and thought of an illimitable future where she would be able to work as something more than a prostitute or a maidservant. To be deprived of this hope would be her death as a person. And who was I, not myself capable of being a philanthropist, to supply her with her life? I stammered, and the mother looked at me with all the hope draining out of those dark, sealed, hopeful eyes. She shrugged her shoulders, and she turned away.

In some of the shacks, there were pictures of Pope John and pinups of various ethnic types. Goats hopped around on the hillsides, chickens cackled, and the children came to look at us with their bright, almost resonant eyes. The echo of a world outside could bounce from those eyes into their minds; the minds could, being already awakened, move and stride. But I could not implant any such echoes. Neither could Raul, though (a gentle, and diffident, intelligent man) he probably wished to, and we paddled on up the muddy slopes. We saw children drawing water from the well that served the village. It was the color of excrement, its surface indelibly afloat with insects and tiny brown crumbs of decay.

In the kitchen of a tin roofed house, from which the housewife had emerged to welcome us, a trough of some kind of cereal mixed with dried meat was cooking on a smoky fire. As I talked to the wife, I noticed that a dog, whose fur had dropped away around its haunches to reveal pink scales, had entered the kitchen, leaped up on the hearth, and buried its snout in the steaming bowl. I pointed this out, and the woman drove the dog away. "What an awful waste," I said and suddenly realized that I was talking like a fool. "It will not be wasted," Ortega said. "They will eat it, of course. They cannot afford to throw food away." Pigs snorted and scuffled down the narrow lanes, their excrement steaming as the pale sun rose to follow the last gust of rain. Ortega offered me a bottle of aguardiente. "You are not happy," he said. "This will make you happy, also it will keep out the cold."

I went into the shack of a woman called Georgina de Torres, a woman obviously of Indian blood, even to the fact that she wore pigtails and a sort of tunic. I took her to be about fifty. She turned out to be thirty-five, and she had had sixteen children, nine of whom had died. Ortega said, "The ones who died were killed by diarrhea and vomiting—most of them, that is. Some also died through pneumonia. The husband is a construction worker. He gives her money he earns; he drinks. She does not know how much he makes, because he does not tell her. But when he is drunk he beats her, and he beats the children, even the babies."

In the one room in which Sra. de Torres lived, the children who survived were sprawled about on mattresses, and one of them, who was two years old, had tiny, deformed legs like cigarette stubs and, his mother told me, couldn't walk. "She wakes up at five o'clock," Ortega translated, "and cooks maize porridge for breakfast. This porridge remains on the stove till lunchtime, and then the children eat it. She adds more maize in the afternoon, and then they have it for dinner. The husband usually does not return till very late and then he does not eat." He indicated the floor, on which a number of empty aguardiente bottles lay. "They have never talked," he said, "after the children were born. They never speak to each other at all. It is not because she does not want to speak to him. It is because he does not wish to speak to her. She says that if she had money now she would leave him, buy clothes and food for the children, and try and send them to school."

Sra. de Torres met her husband when she was a waitress and he a truck driver who used to eat in her cafe. He used to walk her home after work. "Then we married. After we had had three children, I said we cannot afford more. But *machismo* . . . so we have had sixteen." She had to walk a long way, daily, to bring water for the cooking and washing. Her oldest child, a boy of sixteen, has run away from home because his father beat him. "I only went to school for three months," she said. "But even I know that people should live better. How can you live better than animals," she asked me, the Indian eyes slanted and inward, "if you do not even know that you are able to be people?" Raul's face was tragic. On the red slopes the rain fell.

CHAPTER ELEVEN

"Its success is not because it motivates people,
but because people motivate themselves."

What I remember most about Costa Rica is the rain. The mornings in San José, the little capital, were usually blue and clear. Towards noon, like the eye of some predatory bird, the sky filmed over with cloud. The rain started to hiss down at lunchtime, frequently accompanied in a dramatic fashion by thunder and lightning. It usually poured down until nightfall, and next day the sun was usually up once more in a burnished and cloudless sky. What irritated me about the rain was its quality of inevitability. It was as though, daily, one had an unwanted appointment and had no means of putting it off. More or less punctually, every day at the same time, the rain came.

San José, however, is a pleasant little town, devoid of skyscrapers, with narrow pavements and white houses. It is green and has plenty of trees scattered about. It also has a national theater in which, when I was there, Dame Margot Fonteyn was performing. There were numbers of talkative young people to be seen around the town, in discotheques, boutiques, and snack bars. On the horizon were low hills, usually blurred with cloud. It was a provincial town of a type that I find rather sympathetic, and its inhabitants were unfailingly courteous, even though we didn't speak each other's language. Perhaps that was why there were so many tourists about.

Costa Rica is one of the five republics that compose what is officially known as Central America. People in the United States used to call them, rather scornfully, "banana republics," since their chief produce was bananas. Costa Rica also produces coffee. It is a tiny country: It occupies an area of 50,900 square kilometers, and its population in 1973 was 1.83 million. This gave a population density of 36 per square kilometer over the country as a whole, but since large parts of it are uninhabited, the population density rises to as much as 500 per square kilometer in the central plateau, where most people live. This constitutes a problem.

The problem was recognized early in Costa Rica. In 1960 the birth rate there was high, but the death rate was on the way down. The growth rate was therefore 3.8 per cent, one of the highest in the world. A family planning program was started, more or less on a private basis, and in 1969 the government adopted it as a policy. The death rate fell from 10.3 per 1,000 in 1958 to 6.5 per 1,000 in 1972. But the birth rate, at the same time, was brought from 48.2 per 1,000 in 1958 to 34.5 in 1972. The growth rate at present is therefore about 2.7 or 2.8 per cent. Costa Rica has one of the most successful family planning programs in the whole of Latin America.

This is one of the two most interesting aspects of the country, but the tourists who come there because it is cheap and has a pleasant climate, the rain apart, are usually not aware of either. The second aspect of Costa Rica that is of interest is that following a small revolution in 1948, the new President, José Figueroas, promptly abolished the armed forces. There may be other tiny countries in the world that have no army but, so far as I know, Costa Rica is the only country that had one and dismantled it. It is, in fact, an extremely progressive place, though it is still poor. Half the population have a per capita income of less than $400 a year.

When I first reached San José, a seminar was taking place in a suburb known as Alajuela. This was for young people from all over Latin America, and it was basically a seminar on population problems. I therefore hired a taxi and went out through blinding drifts of rain to Alajuela. The seminar was nearly over, but in the dining hall of the Methodist center where it was being held, a sprinkling of young men and women were consuming rice and chicken in a hungry way. They were eager to talk, and, indeed, once they had started it was hard to make them stop. They glowed with the opinionated incandescence of youth and kept interrupting one another. This didn't seem to be because they disagreed with one another—though they came from several different countries, they were all in agreement—but each one wanted to say his piece.

They all said that they felt the youth of Latin America would participate in the solution of population problems because that was a step towards development. "We had a general idea of the problems before this seminar," said a very nice girl with a heavy moustache, "but now our ideas are more concrete." She was interrupted by a Bolivian boy, also bewhiskered. The problems of population are essentially a part of underdevelopment," he said. "Look at France. There they planned for an increase in population by creating educational opportunities and a social balance." He was interrupted in his turn. I leaned back in my chair and let them carry on. It seemed of more interest to collect their views than to try and tell them mine. They, after all, were the future that the whole seminar had been dedicated to.

"Latin American politicians are very intelligent," said a boy, "but for their own benefit, not for that of the people. Illiteracy is very high in our countries. That is due to the politicians, because if people are educated they will ask for change. Family planning programs should include a literacy program." They all agreed on this. "But," the Bolivian boy said, "you must plan first, then have the revolution. If you don't work out a general plan first in which the people can participate, then you will fail, because the people will think all you have changed in the government are the faces." They were all very critical of the Church but said that their elders were much influenced by it. "There is inadequate information about sex," a girl said, "both at home and at school." She giggled nervously.

"The family structure in Latin America is very conservative," said the Bolivian. "I think today a girl—an educated girl or reasonably educated—is not very scared of what the priest will say if she takes contraceptives but of what her father will say. So if she becomes pregnant she will have an abortion. Abortion is illegal in Latin American countries. She will try and keep it quiet by going to some person who is unqualified, and maybe after the abortion she will become very sick. That is one of the worst problems in Latin America. Maybe first we should educate the parents and teach the children after that." Another boy said, "We should teach the landlords too. They have learned nothing about family planning. All they have learned is how to exploit the peasants on their land. That is why the peasants stay poor."

I drove back to San José in the rain, thinking about these young people. They had been unanimous in their opinions, and they were intelligent. Some of their ideas had interested me, though others had seemed rather confused. The point was that they were so alive, so full of excellent intentions, an untapped source of energy. As they grew older, the likelihood was that their ideas would become less confused and that they would understand themselves more clearly and formulate a clear philosophy. The trouble is, I think, that as this happens, most people lose the fire in their bellies. How best to use this fire before it is lost seems to me a problem. The older person may have ideas and beliefs, but in the end he works for himself and his family. The younger person may be confused, but he wants to work for the world.

At the moment, family planning in Costa Rica is run by a body called CONAPO, which consists of representatives from seven different organizations, all of which work as a united whole. CONAPO is the Consejo Nacional de Población, the National Population Council, and it meets twice a week. "It is an illegal organization," I was told by one Costa Rican family planner. "At least, it is not a legal organization." The difficulties of language! What I gather she meant by this is that it is not, in fact, sponsored by the government. On the other hand, the government does not oppose it and helps it in certain ways. It is also possibly true that the drop in the growth rate in Costa Rica is only due in a small way to what CONAPO and its component organizations do. There are many, including the officials of the Centro Latino-Americano de Demografía, CELADE, in San José, who are of this opinion, on the whole.

"Obviously," one CELADE official said to me, "family planning programs have helped to lower the birth rate. On the other hand, there was a sharp drop seen in the birth rate between 1966 and 1969, and it was only in 1969 that the clinics really got under way. I think the initial drop started not so much because of a birth control program as because of rising standards of education and improved living standards. It is true, I think, that the program of family planning here is one of the best and most successful, if not the best and most successful, in Latin America. At the same time, I feel it is a small program in a small country, and its success is not because it motivates people but because people motivate themselves. And this is due to education, I think, and to the higher life standards."

It may be that the standards of education and of life as a whole have improved in Costa Rica over the last decade: Certainly social services, for example, reach 55 per cent of the present population, a high figure in the Third World. According to a survey done by the American International Association for Economic and Social Development, the sample data show 9 per cent with no formal schooling, 77 per cent who received elementary education, that is up to the age of six, 9 per cent with some secondary schooling—this takes them up to eleven years of age— and 4 per cent who have been to college. At the same time, the literacy rate is comparatively high, and there are frequent radio programs about family planning and its close relation, in terms of health, to the development of an undeveloped country.

There are interesting things that come out of the study mentioned above. For example, the population being slightly less than 2 million, the sample study were asked how much they estimated it as. One quarter of the people studied did not know. The rest —this was about 63 per cent of the population—made guesses, ranging from a million to 2 million. Nearly 39 per cent thought that the ideal number of children for a Costa Rican family would be from four to five. A pregnancy before marriage was thought by 44.67 of the study sample to be bad, by 17.67 to be *very* bad. And then, I suppose as it does anywhere, it all varies wildly. I thought I had better travel to various places: to clinics in the city of San José, or to places in the country. I thought perhaps I ought to see how the Indians lived. Not many do now.

There were never a lot of Indians in Costa Rica, and the British brought in Jamaican blacks to the province called Limón, where they still live, expressing themselves in a kind of English.

I did not have the opportunity to go to Limón, since the roads were flooded and the bridges over the rivers impassable. I did, however, make a trip by car to an Indian village beyond the town of San Ysidro, about three hours' drive away. The Indians, I had been told, were not important in terms of the Costa Rican population. Maybe they aren't, statistically, but they were once the only race in Latin America, and whatever had happened to them seemed to me important.

The rain made vague threats of descent as we left San José. The clouds overhead dipped lower, and the palm trees rustled, but nothing beyond this happened. The emerald landscape with the hills beyond was studded with plantations of bananas and with trees of various kinds. Jeweled birds and occasional butterflies fluttered across the road. There were not many people to be seen, though a few villages occurred along the way. Most of the people one did see looked healthy enough, though they were scarcely clad in splendor. The children waved at us.

At San Ysidro, a town so small as to be virtually invisible, the rain started up. We stopped for coffee at a restaurant with a thatched roof supported on bamboo poles and shaggy walls. It was supposed to be an enlarged replica of an Indian hut. Apart from a couple of noisily yawning waiters who leaned on the bar and looked out at the rain, the place was empty. But there was a bandstand, though no band, and colored streamers fluttered from the bamboo poles of the roof. Today was apparently a national holiday. "By evening," the guide said, "this place will be packed. Costa Ricans like music; they like to drink. San Ysidro people will come here, and maybe people from outlying villages. There is very little in the way of entertainment for the people in areas like this. Today is an opportunity."

We took the road out of San Ysidro and presently branched off down a dirt track, mud under us after the rain, and dripping trees on either side. In small clearings in the forest by the track, there were thatched huts, the originals of the restaurant we had come from, and wisps of smoke went up from the cooking fires by which Indian women squatted. We bumped over a river on a newish bridge and presently had to stop and leave the car behind. As we walked down the slippery trail we passed a few huts. Some were thatched, others had tin roofs, but a common factor to all were that, apart for a woman or two, they were deserted.

"Perhaps," said the guide dubiously, "they are at work. Anyway, we will ask. They have a nun here, who looks after the school. Yes, they have a school. There it is." The school, directly in front of us in a large open space, was a stoutly built house with wooden floors. The walls were plastered with posters about health, what to eat and why, and the value of inoculations, all written in Spanish. However, apart from the posters and a couple of dogs who eyed us with the deepest suspicion, the whole place was empty. Behind the school was the house in which the nun lived. A gray mare was grazing in front of it. "Ah," said the guide, "her horse is here, so she must be here too." He rattled on the door, an action that produced nothing except a storm of noisy protest from the dogs.

We returned to the school and looked desultorily around it for a second time. Still nobody appeared. "Perhaps they're all in the forest," I suggested. The guide shrugged. "Perhaps," he said. "But there is a lot of forest, and I do not know where they are." It seemed a pity to abandon our mission after having come all this way, but I could not see what else to do. The school was empty, the nun had departed on some unknown errand, the dripping forest stood around us, and the rain had restarted. It was all very depressing. We sat on the damp steps of the school and looked up the muddy forest trail down which we had come. The guide philosophically rolled himself a cigarette and scraped mud from his boots with a twig. Then a young man appeared on the trail, walking slowly towards us.

He was short and dark, with long greasy black hair and a moustache. He wore a ragged shirt and trousers and in one hand carried a machete of exceedingly ominous appearance. It was obviously a surprise for him to see us, and when we greeted him he mumbled a shy answer and then stood with downturned eyes, wriggling his toes in the grass and mud. He looked different from the citizens of San José, and he had a different feel about him, a forest feel perhaps, or of something lost and not yet found again. Yes, he said, he lived in the village. He waved his arm at the forest around. The people were scattered about, he said, and the huts were scattered.

He spoke in Spanish, and I asked whether his people still spoke their original language. Some, he said, did: They spoke it to one another on occasion, more especially he added, when they were in the presence of Costa Ricans and didn't want the Costa Ricans to understand. I offered him a cigarette that he accepted in the manner of one handed a precious stone; he carefully lit it and sucked at it. Didn't he consider himself a Costa Rican, I inquired. He shrugged. During our entire conversation, I afterward recalled, he never once smiled. Yes, he eventually said, he was a Costa Rican. He was interested in national politics, but he felt that the Indians were not properly treated. At this point two women carrying bundles of leaves came down the trail and stopped to listen. They were much less introverted than the young man. One, who seemed to be about forty, pointed towards the schoolhouse. "We have a school; I studied there," she said. "It has been there since I was a child. All our children study there."

The young man agreed that the village had a school—he had been there himself—but what else did they have? They had had to plead for the bridge across the river before the government would allot funds for it. They had no gas, no electricity, no telephones, no doctor or nurse. The nun kept a few medicines, but if anyone was really sick, he or she had to be taken into San Ysidro. The women added that the children suffered a lot from worms and stomach trouble, and some from a sickness of the chest. They all now seemed prepared to talk, and as the rain had started to fall hard, we went back into the schoolhouse and sat on benches there. Presently two very young women, the daughters of a village family, arrived and also sat down. Neither could have been more than sixteen. They giggled shyly and kept their eyes on the floor.

Both the older women had lost children. One had three left, one four. They had heard of family planning, but it was up to their husbands to tell them what to do. It was rather difficult for me to ascertain how they had lost their children, or how many they had lost, but the children seemed to have died in infancy rather than during childbirth—from what exactly I could not find out. The two young girls who had followed us into the school were to be married soon. These were arranged marriages. Both girls had heard, in a vague way, about family planning, but neither had any real idea what it was, nor did either have any idea as to how many children they wanted to have. They said it would depend on their husbands and looked virtuous in the extreme. The young man, who answered that he would not marry till he could afford it (but did not know how much he needed to afford it) said he wanted two children, a boy and a girl. "If you had too many children," he muttered, "they died."

Apart from their language, little of their culture had been left to them. The older people were said to know some old songs and legends, but very few of the young people had learned any of these. They preferred the music they heard when the world breathed into their ears over transistor radios. But little of it can make real sense to them, who till their fields and chop wood and watch their infants die. The young man, for example, told me that he had been several times to San Ysidro during the twenty-four years of his life. But when I asked him how many times he had visited San José, he seemed amazed that I should ask. "Never," he said, "why should I have a reason to go there? But I would like to go. I would like to see the city." He looked wistful for a moment. Then he shrugged his shoulders and accepted another cigarette.

I noticed that a difference had taken place in the way that he received these cigarettes. We had been talking about an hour, during which time he had accepted six or seven. The grateful, tremulous care with which he had lit and smoked the first one had gradually disappeared; he plucked the latest one casually from the packet, lit it with a flourish, and blew out a cloud of smoke that any middle-sized dragon would have been proud of. If one were to take him out of rural life that he himself said was hard and miserable and drop him into the city he wanted to see, what would happen to him? In a few days he would accept its wonders with the same flourish with which he had come to accept my cigarettes. But once I left his village my cigarettes would leave with me. And once he came to really settle in the city, poverty would pull the city's wonders beyond him. I don't think it is a question of the young Indian or millions and millions like him, exchanging an innocent but miserable rural life for a less innocent but equally miserable urban life—whether they should or why they should. It is a question of seeing that life in either sector is made more bearable or less miserable for the masses of people.

My last sentence, now that I reread it, sounds like the remark of a simpleton, which it may well be. The thing is really to dis-cover ways and means of making life more bearable for the living. I think one obstacle to this is the fact that, however poor, desolate, and destitute they are, very few people actually find life unbear-able. They may find it difficult and sad, but they do not want to surrender the heartbeat they have to the endless silence of the infinite spaces. They are prepared to put up with a lot of hard-ship, so long as they do not actually die. If they were not prepared to do this, and if they asked themselves why this hardship existed and how it could be ended, every one of the population problems in the world would be more easily soluble, assuming that the governments and their bureaucrats were equipped to help.

Costa Rica is a tiny country, but it has done at least something towards solving its own population problem, though the Indians I met seemed very poor indeed, and I understand the same is true of the blacks in the province of Limón. In Limón, however, I gather that the blacks accept family planning as a means of health care, and the Indians, I think, would do so if they were told more about it, for nightly the radios—and the Indians I met listened to transistors—has a program on the desirability of fam-ily planning. But you need more than static caressed by a voice to tell you about it: You need a living man or woman, standing clothed in flesh, explaining it all to you, as one human person to another. I know that the Indians form a very small percentage of the Costa Rican population, but they remain people, dis-inherited people, but still people. They deserve to be taken better care of. They ask for it. I thought of them, that rainy afternoon after we left the village, all the way back to San José.

I wanted to see a clinic that catered to mother and child health, and a friend took me to one, some distance beyond the city, the day before I left. There are thousands of clinics all over the world, or the Third World, like the one I saw in the suburbs of San José. It was a little before noon when I arrived there, it was raining once more, and the prim plastered outer room was full of women, some pregnant, some not, some with children, some not. We were taken in to the doctor. Helped by a couple of nurses, he runs the clinic alone, and about forty women a day come in for contraceptives. He wore dark glasses and looked a bit tired, but he offered us coffee and biscuits and talked about his work. Because of the publicity in Costa Rica by the seven organizations that form CONAPO, because of the radio programs, because of the good social services offered, he said, women came to the various clinics, and the standard of health among mothers had risen.

Pills are apparently most popular amongst Costa Rican women, and the IUD is not much in demand. The clinic tells women what they can use and checks to see what will best suit them; this is done by all the other urban clinics. In the rural clinics, the doctor said, follow-ups are hard to do. About 30 per cent of the female population of fertile age use contraceptives, though the number of dropouts is difficult to confirm. This is within the national program whereby women, according to their incomes, buy contraceptives by coupons of different colors, the price varying according to the coupon color. There may also be a number of people outside the program who obtain their contraceptives privately. The doctor smiled, his nurse entered; he was obviously busy. We moved out.

But I asked to see two women—one with several children, and one with a few—and we were put into a private room, into which, presently, came a woman of thirty-six with a brown, dry, pitted face, wearing a neat flowered dress. "They put their best clothes on when they come here," said my friend. "She would not wear this kind of thing at home." The lady had seven living children, the oldest sixteen and already at work, the youngest two. She had lost three in infancy. She heard about family planning from a neighbor, then came to this particular clinic—"it serves very poor people," my friend said—and there the doctor explained. Now she uses the pill. Her husband is a laborer. She says he earns about twenty dollars a month. She cannot really afford to feed and clothe the children on that.

"But she is helped by her sixteen-year-old daughter who works as a servant," my friend went on, "and she can give all the children, and her husband, two meals a day of rice and beans. Sometimes her husband will buy a piece of meat. This may be once a week or once a fortnight. She cannot afford to send the children to anything above primary school, though she had the wish once that her sons would be engineers. This is not possible. She feels very tired all the time, and she wishes she had heard of family planning earlier. But her husband might not have liked it; at least not then. He does now. They can afford to survive now, but she wishes her sons could have been engineers."

I looked at the dark, lined face of the woman: Her bone structure was beautiful, and she must once have been beautiful—all that destroyed by hunger without anger at why this should happen to people. She said she spent about five dollars a week to feed the seven children, her husband, and herself, and her daughter's wages paid the rent. They lived in a 2-room house.

"Oh, very poor," said my friend. "Very poor indeed. Of course, there are people worse off, many. But what do you do with such people? They are not progressive like us." He was speaking in English, so I didn't feel too embarrassed, since the woman didn't know what he was saying. At the same time, I did feel embarrassed because he was saying it. I said in a rather rapid way, "Thank her very much and my best wishes and could we now see the other one." We shook hands with the first woman, and she was replaced by a second, also neatly dressed, but younger. She was twenty-six and had one child—a boy. Her husband, who worked on building sites, earned about thirty dollars a week. They wanted one more child, which she hoped would be a girl, but they wanted to space the children: The boy was four; in two years time she wanted the girl. She said, "I heard about family planning in this clinic. My husband agreed, so now I take the pill."

She thought her mother-in-law wouldn't approve of it, nor the neighbors, so nobody knew she took it except her husband and herself. "My husband and I eat rice and beans," she said "but for the child I buy what I can, fruit and milk and meat as the clinic tells me. The clinic also provides me with coupons to buy this cheap, and the boy is in fine health. I don't think I can make a mistake with the pill, because the clinic told me how to use it, and I went to school and so I know how to keep a record. But

I do not recommend the pill to any of my neighbors because then it would spread and people we do not want to hear about this would hear."

We shook hands and she left. We went out through the front room where all the women sat, awaiting the doctor, some with children in their laps. Other children ran about, squealing like piglets, between the ranked chairs. The children at least looked healthy. Most of the mothers looked starved, tired, but hopeful. The Costa Rican program may not be the most successful in the world, but it works because the people, in particular the women, seem to want it. The elder people may not want their children to want it, but their children do, for the welfare of their own children. I suppose, if the program works in the world, this is how it will eventually work. It will work through tormented fathers and tired mothers, but it will only work if they are told, as in Costa Rica, what they can do.

Next day the next plane, the usual torments: the strap of the shoulder bag biting happily at one's flesh, the handle of the typewriter, loved and known when it is stripped of its case and lies flat on the table, cutting into one's fingers, the delays, the tiredness, the anxiety about catching the connecting flight at the other end, and rapid checking with fingers in breast pocket (passports? traveler's checks? health certificates? letters to contacts?), the clambering up the ramp, the difficulty in not getting seated next to talkative strangers, the adjustment of one's legs over the shoulder bag and the typewriter on the floor in front, the not being able to smoke and being able to sweat, the roar of the engines at last, the bestial snout of the plane tilting, shedding another country as you rise. That's all over in Costa Rica. Now you wait for the next country.

CHAPTER TWELVE

"Are we to say to them that the conditions in which they
live are terrible, therefore they must not have children
and their people must die out?"

When I was a boy, I longed to visit Brazil. I thought of it as
one immense forest, through which the Amazon flowed thickly
and stickily, the forest packed with wild animals, Indians, and
lost explorers, the river full of caymans and piranhas. As a man,
this picture stayed in my mind. But when we actually reached
Brazil, I never saw so much as a patch of forest, let alone an
Indian with a blowpipe. I did see a museum where there were
blowpipes on display, but these were unaccompanied by their
original owners. It was a disappointment, except that the country
in itself is such an absolute phenomenon. In its own way, it is
unique.

Brazil was colonized by the Portuguese; hence, it is the only
Latin American country where Spanish is not the national language. But it is also the fifth largest country, in terms of area,
in the world, and it occupies an area of some 8 million square
kilometers, that is to say, slightly less than half the area of the
South American continent. Its population now is estimated at
about 100 million people. It also has one of the largest popula-
tions of animals in the world, not only the jaguars, tapirs, and
monkeys but pigs, sheep, goats—animals you eat, by and large,
not animals that eat you. There are, in fact, about 100 million
head of cattle, the same number as there are people, and beef
is important in the Brazilian economy.

In addition to this, Brazil produces more coffee than anyone else in the world. It produces more dry edible beans than anyone else (though these are consumed, on the whole, domestically and, I must say, are an acquired taste). It is the second-largest producer of corn in the world, the third-largest producer of cocoa, the fourth-largest producer of sugar, the largest Latin American producer of tobacco, and the largest Latin American producer of cotton. Having said all this, I think I should pause for breath and add that it is the richest of all Latin American countries.

We landed in Rio de Janeiro, having flown over São Paulo, the largest city in Brazil, a city spiked with skyscrapers, buzzing with traffic, a kind of emergent New York. Rio itself sprawled vastly by the sea. From our hotel room we looked over the Copacabana beach, at the huge rollers coming in to the beach, ten feet high, the glass body of the wave as it settled itself to rear, and rose, curving, the neck of a giant horse, foaming at the mouth, crashing down in runny splinters on the shore. Riding the neck of the wave there was always, fair weather or fine, some muscular young man on a surfboard who obviously had nothing better to do. Along the beach stood clusters of people, watching the glass horses of the waves and their riders. They also seemed to have nothing better to do.

But this was all in the city area. The taxidrivers, too, rode the wild horses of their machines, plunging and fighting their way past each other down the skyscrapered avenue at a considerable rate of miles per hour. Beyond the lush offices and the high-rise residential flats were what are known as the *favelas*: the tenements and slums, shabbily crowded together, where the families of the poor lived. Beyond the kicking swells of the sea was the Pan d'Azucar, Sugarloaf Hill, to which tourists daily rose like angels in a cable car, and, of course, the giant white Christ on another hill, looking at the skyscrapers and the *favelas* with the pitiless eye of one who is above all these things. The people from the *favelas* probably couldn't afford the cable car and could only afford Christ in church on Sundays, when the collection plate went around. The average gross national product per capita income in Brazil is assessed at about $400.

Of the 100 million people in Brazil today, 62 per cent are said to be white, 26 per cent are said to be mixed with black or Indian blood, and the rest are pure blacks and pure Indians. The Indians are at the bottom of the heap, since they are numerically very few and since they mainly hang out in unapproachable parts of the Amazon forest. It is true that in the last few years some new tribes have been found in the reaches of the Amazon including, allegedly, one of giants, but it is unlikely that there are many more Indians than there are estimated to be—about 1 per cent of the total population, and in any event they lead their own lives.

The history of any country plays an important role, I feel, in the problems of its population today. Attitudes are formed by history. The Portuguese arrived on the shores of what is now Brazil in the late fifteenth century. In the first year of the sixteenth century, Brazil was claimed as Portuguese territory. Considering that the interior of the country was unknown and visibly inhospitable, and the Portuguese had no idea whether it was occupied by anything between medieval dragons and forest nymphs, they were probably as brave (though probably also more greedy) as the tall, inarticulate astronauts who were so frequently on the moon in recent years.

There, anyway, on a shore of thick forest, the Atlantic swells pushing their ships in, were the Portuguese. They bustled in, found some Indians, not beautiful like Rousseau's noble savages, but by the Portuguese certainly damned, and put these lilliputian people into slavery, growing sugar for them. Sugar and the wood of exceptionally large forest trees were what the Portuguese exported for a while. Then, finding that the Indians, like the West African blacks, were dying of the diseases their conquerors had imported, they decided to import African labor. It was a country not unlike parts of Africa.

The blacks came, on the stained, patchwork ships, and lived on the coast, and were whipped, and worked. In the eighteenth century, at least the early part of it, the Brazilian population, apart from the Indians, who had taken refuge in the forest, numbered two-thirds black and one-third white people. Why the blacks didn't beat their masters down and establish themselves in new homes remains a mystery: Maybe it was because the Portuguese were confident masters, knowing they could wing their way back to the Iberian peninsula on their long ships at any sign of rebellion. Maybe it was because the blacks had no ships to take them to their own country, and they could not work compasses to point to those havens of family and known water and food. The only revolt there was came from the Muslims brought from the interior of Ghana by Arab slavers. Religion appears to have been a cohesive force amongst them. Groups of them fled into the forest around Baía, where they mostly were, and set up small encampments known as *kilombos*. The Portuguese sent out punitive forces to recapture these blacks, and the leaders customarily had their heads cut off.

The whole pattern of population in Brazil reversed itself in the eighteenth century. Hitherto, the Portuguese had used the country for sugar; they now discovered gold and precious stones. As a result, many more people came out from Portugal to try and make their fortunes. By the end of the eighteenth century the population stood at 3 million. That is to say, it had trebled over 100 years, and the whites now outnumbered the blacks, forming two-thirds of the total population. The Indians were not counted, at least not the inaccessible forest Indians, though there were others who were enslaved by the Portuguese and made to work on their plantations.

The nineteenth century brought a curious phenomenon to Brazil. It became the only country in South America ever to exist as a monarchy, when the French armies' of Napoleon entered the Iberian peninsula in 1807 and the court fled to Brazil. Rio became the capital, and eventually, in 1822, Brazil declared itself to be an empire independent of Portugal. The empire continued until 1889, when the emperor was deposed after a military coup and shipped off to Portugal. Into the new republic came a steady flow of immigrants from numerous European countries, England and France, Poland and even Russia.

In 1900 the population of Brazil stood at about 16 million. Thirty years later it had doubled to 33 million. By 1950 it stood at 51 million, an increase of 18 million over the past twenty years. But there was an increase of 19 million in the next ten years, bringing the population to 70 million in 1960. In 1970 it had reached 93 million, which meant it had leaped forward by 23 million in the previous ten years. The birth rate has remained fairly stable. It was 45 per 1,000 in 1960 and 43 per 1,000 in 1970.

But the death rate has fallen sharply in recent years, hence the growth rate has risen. The estimates of what it is vary somewhat, but CELADE says it is 2.8 per cent, and this seems the most widely accepted figure. This is a high growth rate, but most Brazilians do not take it to be a problem.

In Brasília, the new capital, which is positioned in what is considered to be the exact center of the country, I talked to Ambassador Miguel Ozorio Almeida. He is widely considered to be one of the most intelligent men in the country, and he is certainly very articulate. He sat on a sofa in a sunlit office and talked. "So far as family planning is concerned," he said, "we have never had an explicit policy. A committee, of which I am a member, has been formed to study the matter, and our findings will be made public later in 1973. But the Brazilian citizen is free to choose what he wishes for himself and his family. We have emphasized it.

"But what we resent is this. Certain organizations and countries tell us that people should not have children unless future generations are assured a good life. What about the Eskimos in the Arctic? Are we to say to them that the conditions in which they live are terrible, therefore they must not have children and their people must die out? Can you ethically make such assertions? What logically follows is that the Swedes, say, have a right to live and we haven't." He was indignant; he flourished his hands as he talked. Then he paused and delved into a heap of books on his desk. "Look at this."

It was a slim volume that appeared to be a textbook on how to learn English. The ambassador flicked through it till he found a page heavily marked in black ink. He read a sentence from it. "One of the great problems the world faces today is population. This is from a textbook, please note. It is brainwashing of the worst type. There are other sentences about the evils of population." He read them all. "This kind of thing," he said, "is what we resent." He was an impressive man. His commitment to what he said and his own conviction, were clear, but I felt that his zeal took him too quickly past certain aspects of the situation as a whole.

Most of the immense expanse of Brazil is either very sparsely inhabited or not inhabited at all. Some 93 per cent of the population occupy roughly a third of the whole country. Moreover, about 60 per cent live in urban areas. São Paulo, the largest city in Brazil, has about 6 million people, Rio about 5 million, so a tenth of the entire population lives in these two cities alone. Here because of the availability of medical services, the infant mortality and the death rates are comparatively low, but so is the standard of living in the *favelas*, and there is a good deal of both unemployment and underemployment. In the northeast of the country, where there is a high concentration of black population, the infant mortality is very high. In Recife, for example, it is quoted as 207 per 1,000.

One reason why so many Brazilian intellectuals are opposed to family planning is that there is so huge a quantity of untapped land available. Some feel that a growth in population is necessary for economic development; in other words, that there should be more people to populate and develop these empty areas. The military feel that these areas could be occupied by a neighbor that needed land for its own people and that there should therefore be a Brazilian population there. A question that occurred to me was, with so many people apparently flocking to urban areas, how could the government persuade them to turn back and become pioneers in virgin lands.

"I will answer all this point by point," said Ambassador Almeida. "You are right about the dangers of the drift to urban areas. Recently, there was a conference of mayors to discuss how they could filter people who had no employment. Even Brasília has its problems. It was planned for 500,000 people. Now the population is over 600,000. The city was not supposed to have an industrial area, but because of the unemployment that is starting, industries are being set up. We are going to formulate coherent steps towards the solution of this problem. What we may even do is set up barriers around the cities. Unqualified people would be redirected to new areas.

"They come to the city thinking they will be saved from poverty, but they suffer from the same poverty in a different environment. Where their salvation lies is in agricultural areas that we are planning. We are opening up the Amazon, over an area of 800,000 square kilometers, an area bigger than France. There is fertile soil there, and we have a new road that passes through. Our basis is that the agricultural areas will each be centered around an agroville, an urban center that will supply primary education, medical services, electricity, storage facilities, and simple mechanical help. Banks and legal advisers would be available there."

The ambassador had one of those husky voices that always have a hypnotic effect on me, and I had a peculiar feeling that I was in a kind of dream. Indeed, the idea of opening up the Amazon sounds like a dream. But the Brazilians have already accomplished a number of remarkable feats, and, with the highway system they have built in recent years, it is very likely that they can accomplish this. "You asked me about the northeast," the ambassador said. "It is the problem zone of Brazil. It has stagnated for years. It is plagued by a monoculture of sugar. Sugar cultivation is a highly seasonal activity, and it was one of the poorest areas in the world. We have a program to rehabilitate the northeast, but progress is slow. Now, however, it is no longer isolated, as it used to be, because of the new roads."

The ambassador smiled proudly and said, "In 1950 we had fewer paved roads than any Latin American country. Now we are building an average of 30,000 kilometers of road, and paving an average of 10,000 kilometers, every year. All this is due to our industrial expansion. Ten years ago we were one of the poorest countries in the area, after Paraguay and Haiti. The growth rate of our economy was about 6 per cent per year, which meant an increase of 3 per cent in per capita income. This year the growth rate of the economy reached 10 per cent. This means an increase of 7 per cent in the per capita income. We have reached a stage where, unless we make really fantastic mistakes, the per capita income of every Brazilian in the next seven years should average out at $1,000 a year."

"To come back to family planning," the ambassador said, "in the northeast most clinics have birth control services. If our commission recommends an explicit policy towards family planning, the government will not campaign for it. I think any doctor or organization will be free to publicize the availability of the service, but I don't think the government would spend the taxpayers' money on this kind of thing. It would be a health measure, part of the medical service, and the ordinary family would have to decide for themselves, once they knew it was available, whether or not they wanted it." He smiled and stood up. The interview was obviously over.

Brasília, like Canberra, is a federal capital, specially built to be a capital. It is a city that reminds one of a painting by Dali, but done entirely in white. It has wide avenues dotted at intervals with inexplicable and futuristic monuments, tall ministries set in impeccably exact lines, glass houses so neat that it is obvious nobody has ever dared throw a stone at one. Spinning towers of ocher dust occasionally build up on the plains beyond but never seem to mar the glass and marble of the ministries, in the pools and fountains of which stout and healthy goldfish swim. On the far side of a willowed lake is the residential sector, where many diplomats live. Hung with scented flowers, their houses at night look out over the lake at the fallen constellation of stars that are the lights of the capital.

Brazil is a rich country, and one has a sense of this in Brasília. But it is in many ways a peculiar country, in that, like the United States, or India, or Russia, it is not so much a country as a continent in itself. Because of its large unexplored areas, the Brazilians are still as much pioneers as the American settlers of the West. But at the same time, since industry in Brazil did not really start up until after World War II, they are in the middle of their own Industrial Revolution. Insofar as the bulk of the population is concerned, the wealth of Brazil is still a latent force. It does not yet, to any considerable extent, change the lives of the poor.

I talked in the Ministry of Health to Dr. Justinho Alves Pereira, the head of the staff. "There is no problem of population in Brazil," he said, "but there is a serious health problem." I would have thought a serious health problem to be a problem of population, but perhaps it was a question of language—our interpreter was himself not tremendously proficient in English. "In the northeast," said Dr. Justinho, "there are grave problems as regards malnutrition. The people have protein deficiencies, and they are short of vitamin A. The southern states of Brazil are rich, and they produce a lot, and here there is no problem. The death rate,

especially the infant mortality rate, is low there. One of our problems is to persuade doctors to enter the rural areas. They prefer
staying in the towns."

This seems a constant problem in the Third World, and I suppose a problem of human nature, in that a doctor earns money
in towns and can live in a house in comfort, and it would be
quite the opposite once he agreed to go into the field. It seems
a difficult problem to solve until the governments concerned offer high incentives to physicians willing to take off into rural
areas. "Also," Dr. Justinho explained, "it is difficult to train paramedics. But the government has programs under way, though
it's not easy to get funds to attack all the different problems in
the country. In the cities there is a pollution problem, particularly one of water pollution through sewage and so on. The government spends hundreds of millions per year on that alone. Eighty
million are spent on social security."

This social security is basically for salaried people. They pay
8 per cent of their salaries to the government, and the employer
pays 18 per cent. If a person is out of work, he must apply to one
of the charitable institutions, which are funded partially by private money and partially by the government itself. However, in
1970, a nationwide average of 1,800 people were dependent on
each doctor, and one hospital bed was available per 294 people
in 1967. With these depressing statistics, we left Dr. Justinho. Our
trip to Brasília was nearly over, and Leela and I debated our next
move. She thought we should go up to the northeast, which I
thought was an excellent idea, but it would be a long trip, and
we were now rather short of time. Eventually, we decided to
return to Rio and the white beaches and the waves.

The waves were taller and louder than ever, and there were
sudden falls of rain throughout the day. Through this rain we
went to see Dr. Ralph Zerkowski, a well-known statistician. Dr.
Zerkowski sat at a long trestle table entirely covered with books,
magazines, empty cups of coffee, and full ashtrays that he was
rapidly bringing to the overflow point. "I am worried," he said.
"I am worried. I have worked in various services to see how the
urban areas can absorb industrial manpower. There is a job shortage likely. We must increase agricultural facilities to slow down

migration, or the services in urban areas may prove inadequate. Family planning will show the average man he has an alternative to having too many children, but the government has no fixed policy, and there is no mass communication vehicle to deal with the problem." Dr. Zerkowski crushed out another cigarette. "The Movimento Brasileiro de Alfabetização, a literacy campaign, has helped a lot. The literacy rate is fairly low."

He seized a book and flipped through it to the page he wanted. "About 38 per cent of the population over five years old is illiterate. As literacy increases, knowledge will increase. The growth of the economy at present keeps pace with the growth rate, but there are gross inequalities of distribution. If by the end of the century we could achieve a growth rate of 1 per cent, that would be ideal." He paused, attempted to drink coffee from a cup that happened to be empty, frowned, put it down, and said, "I spoke earlier to you of agricultural facilities that would be offered to keep people from moving to the cities. This would be through land reform, but a new kind of land reform, not a distribution of land that is already owned, but a distribution of new land. We have plenty of land in Brazil.

"The problem in opening up the Amazon would be the high technological skill necessary, and the cost. People in the developed countries say that we are killing off our Indians like the U.S. pioneers did. That is nonsense. The Indians are dying out anyway; there are very few left. Amazonia is so thinly populated that there is no problem. If we open it up . . . well, Brazil, Canada, and Australia are the three countries of the future. We see the food shortage all over the world. Well, in the years to come, we will be able to feed the world." He then agreed that the diet of most poor Brazilians, especially in rural areas, was wholly inadequate, and that the improvement of their diet was an important health problem. "But it is bound to improve," he said impatiently, "with economic development." Perhaps it will.

At the moment, the poor farmers and the inhabitants of the *favelas* eat what is basically manioc flour, and manioc does not have a very high nutritive value. The flour can be eaten as it is, which isn't very palatable, or it can be mixed with water and eaten as a kind of porridge. Beans are often mixed with this porridge, and on good days dried meat or some fish may be added. Even the poor usually drink coffee and eat a kind of brick sugar. This is hardly a balanced diet, and it is a curious fact that many Brazilian peasants are averse to the consumption of fruit and vegetables. But the intake of calories, for most Brazilians, is higher than that for the people of most other Latin American countries—except in the northeast. That appears to be the disaster area of Brazil, not yet much touched.

According to Dr. Helena Levy, a sociologist at the Catholic University of Rio, many urban workers send their children to primary school, which is free. "It isn't only because they want them to be educated," Dr. Levy said. "Some want it, but I think nearly all of them send their children because they save a meal that way. At lunchtime the children are fed by the school. They are given milk or orange juice, which they probably wouldn't have at home; also a balanced meal, with meat, or cheese, or porridge. The parents find it difficult to send the children on to high school. This is because, though high schools are partly free, the parents then have to pay for uniforms, for books, for transportation. It costs quite a lot for one child. I would think the minimum would be $700 a year."

Outside, in the rain, the university sprawled amidst trees, an attractive place with neat buildings, little paths, and wooden bridges, full of handsome and happy children of both sexes who rushed busily about with armfuls of books, laughing on the way to their lectures, something I never did when I was a boy at Oxford. "Now, of course," Dr. Levy said, "particularly among our young people here, there is a certain amount of premarital sex, and they marry each other for love. Their fathers would have had premarital sex, but only with women of no reputation, and they would have chosen their wives carefully, making sure that the women could cook well or sew well. They would have had affairs outside the marriage, but the wife would have been made into an outcast if she did the same. It is *machismo*, you see, *machismo*.

"Sometimes the wife would know about the mistress, but as a rule, so long as her husband fulfilled his part of the marriage contract, kept a roof over her head and the heads of her children, fed them, clothed them, sent the children to school, she would feel there was no point in creating a fuss. This is less so today in the towns, but *machismo* is still powerful in the rural areas. There there is a patriarchal society and the man decides everything: the future of his children, the number of his children, the duties of his wife. . . . It's a peculiar business, this *machismo*. In rural areas the man still wants many children, as a labor force. Boys are better earners than girls, so he may prefer boys. You see this because in the migration to the cities, the eldest girls are sent first, before any of the boys. The boys will stay behind and work on the farms. The girl will come and enter domestic service, though now some work in industries. The likelihood is that she will become pregnant.

"Through whom?" said Dr. Levy with a little shrug. "Through her employer, her employer's son, her boyfriend. And then, since she can't return to the village pregnant or with an illegitimate child, she will have an abortion. People try and conceal the fact that there are so many abortions in Brazil, but it is true, and because abortion is illegal she will have it done privately and badly, and then she will have to be sent to hospital. You see, they don't know about contraception and since pills have to be paid for, they don't have the money, if they do know, to use them systematically. A private doctor may prescribe them for a rich woman; a poor woman has no chance. The Church plays no very important part here in the acceptance of contraception: That's because many Catholics here are not too rigid."

This would appear to be true. The blacks came from West Africa to Brazil with their own tribal beliefs. The Catholic faith was imposed upon them and became somewhat confused, in their minds, with their original religions. Obliging blacks still perform, for a small fee, the *macumba*, or voodoo rites, for the gullible tourist in Rio. However, as a friend told me, the real *macumba* is also performed in Rio, and more so in the province of Baía, though it would be highly chancy for the tourist to visit such a ceremony. Christian saints have been tied up in these rites and their names and statues used to bless activities for which they would certainly not have been canonized by the Church. Because of the amount of miscegenation that took place at the time of the first colonization (the 1970 census did not break the population down racially for demographic rather

than democratic reasons, because it was so difficult to determine
who had black blood and who didn't), a certain degree of
African belief has crept into the Catholicism of the country.
"Many people who are not visibly black," Dr. Levy said, "believe
in magic and witchcraft."

Dr. Isaac Kerstenetzky, the most respected demographer and
statistician in Brazil, received us in a large and sumptuous office
above one of the main streets of Rio. "You wish to talk to me,"
he said, "about population, hm?" and handed me a copy of the
1970 census, adding, "This will answer all your questions."
Though rather dismayed at this abrupt termination to an interview that had hitherto lasted a little less than a minute, I persisted
with my intentions, and presently he started to answer questions,
though we were frequently interrupted by his secretary leaping
in like a gazelle to inform him that he was wanted on the line
from Brasília. These calls he was always careful to take in an
adjacent chamber. I felt more and more like some kind of
international spy but crouched back next to Leela, always a
source of comfort, on a large sofa, and whenever Dr. Kerstenetzky
returned to the room, carried on. Another minor difficulty was
that my tongue constantly tripped over his name, and he had
clearly forgotten mine, so that we wound up by my addressing
him as "sir" and his addressing me, curtly, but very compre-
hensively, as "you."

Despite all this, he was very kind, and when he became interested in a question he answered it with the thoroughness and
efficiency of the professional. "You talk of migration to the
cities," he said. "An important fact is that we had a high rate of
economic growth in the 1950s, then a decline. Then towards the
end of the 1960s it rose once more, and there was a great demand
for labor. There was a negligible amount of open unemployment,
but it may be that the rate of disguised unemployment was high.
This is a developing country, and I am skeptical about statistics
under these conditions. Colleagues of mine in social sciences try
to tell me about the low standard of life in some areas. But I am
confident that if we maintain our economic growth rate, we
can provide for our people, in aggregate terms. The difficulty I

foresee is with education. I am of the opinion that qualitatively we are not doing as well as we should. Not all the teachers in the colleges are properly qualified.

"But I think this is changing also. The standards are slowly rising. The government is taking a much stricter stance as regards the qualifications of professors. There is no great brain drain in any of the professions, and we produce about 3,000 doctors, for example, every year. The trouble is, as you know, that the bulk of the doctors prefer to stay in urban areas. Our life expectancy is about sixty. Even in the northeast, infant mortality is declining. We have a project now to see how far infant mortality is actually connected with nutrition and how far with intestinal and pulmonary viruses. There isn't any acute problem now, as regards standards of nutrition in different areas, as to inadequacy of supply." I asked what would happen if the Amazon was opened up, as the government wants to do. Would this not lead to ecological disturbance, which in some ways might affect the entire world? I had been told by an ecologist that the still, rustling breath of the trees around the Amazon provided the world with 25 per cent of its oxygen. If the trees in an area larger than France were cut down, would this not have an extremely drastic effect?

"If you remove too much of the forest," Dr. Kerstenetzky said, "you would get, eventually, desert instead. But there is a lot of forest. Also it would depend on the type of development in the Amazon. What we plan to do is not on so huge a scale that it should cause the hysteria it does among the developed nations. They should concentrate on their own pollution problems—and all their other problems—before they start worrying about how we develop the Amazon area. The problem in the Amazon Valley is that of adequate development for human settlements, to move population into the area under conditions in which they can really live. That is what we are trying to do. It will take time, money, and a lot of technology, but eventually we shall solve it." He was a confident as well as a capable man. I liked him.

The impression one has of people in downtown Rio is that they are fairly prosperous. The wealthy Brazilian women who

step out of their cars to shop in the Copacabana area are the
most ornately dressed and adorned I have seen anywhere in the
world. Glittering necklaces hang round their necks, rings flash on
their slim fingers, their clothes are sleekly cut in peacock colors.
They are like gigantic dolls, and, indeed, they are toys for their
husbands, who like to dress them up. But the young couples
who drift hand in hand down the pavements or moon over each
other in sidewalk restaurants do not look poor. Even the scruffy
ones look as if they can afford to be scruffy, that is to say, as if
they have chosen their own appearance, not as if it has chosen
them. The large number of shops in the fashionable areas indi-
cate a certain amount of buying power amidst the population.
The bookshops and record shops are full of young people, also
the boutiques.

But one day, as Leela and I sat under an umbrella off Copacabana beach, with a vaporous sun falling rapidly into the sea
ahead, I felt a tugging at my feet, looked down, and saw a small,
black shoeshine boy attempting to dab polish on my shoes. I
tried to shoo him away, but he wouldn't take any notice. Within
minutes we were surrounded by a number of shoeshine boys, all
about ten or twelve years old, and mostly black, ragged, and
skinny. They crouched all around us, under the table and beside
our chairs, like a gang of little frogs, grabbing at our shoes and
hopping in pursuit when we moved our feet. They grinned at
my remonstrances; they had a kind of bitter gaiety about them
that was beyond their years, a gaiety that seemed born of despair.
Eventually, several waiters rallied and drove them off. I felt a
little guilty. These boys are apparently like the urchins in Saigon
in the war years: They not only pester you for tips and cigarettes but rob you if they can.

"They are, as a rule," a friend told me, "without parents or
homes," not even homes in the *favelas*, those swamps of desti-
tution outside the fashionable areas. Leela, one rather dull Sunday, thought we should take a tour around Rio and obtained a
number of tour itineraries from the hotel porter. As we looked
through them, I noticed that several brochures mentioned that
the tour would pass through the *favelas*, "where the poor people
live." The shanties of the slum towns seemed to me to bear a
sufficient resemblance to cages as they were, without hordes of

rich people arriving to stare at and take pictures of their inhabitants. I suppose being very poor takes away your capacity to be very angry. Anger does not solve the problem of hunger. It is for the government to enable people to be angry if they want to be, to enable them to protest against intrusions into their privacy.

Brazil has a population problem, as I see it. Here, a rarity in the Third World, is a country with an economy that appears to be flourishing. There is plenty of space available. But the economy flourishes in terms of GNP and so forth, terms that mean nothing to the poor, who reap none, or very few, of its benefits. It seemed to me that before Brazil increases its population and opens up the Amazon Valley, it should look after the shoeshine boy in Rio, the migrant in the *favela*, the black in the sugar plantations of the northeast. Otherwise, the inequalities of opportunity will remain exactly the same in twenty years, when the country may have become more rich and more powerful. It may be true, as Dr. Zerkowski suggested, that in a short while Brazil may be able to feed the world, but it ought first to feed its own people, and to feed not only their stomachs but their minds.

CHAPTER THIRTEEN

"You can blame it . . . on the nature of the people,
on geography. Maybe you can blame it on God."

The massed Andes lay beneath us as we flew towards Chile. At first they loomed up in wrinkled elephantine ridges, apparently, from the air, bereft of trees or people. They had a gritty look, and their slopes were of brown earth and rock. The ridges rolled on beneath us for hours, a prehistoric landscape. Then the mountains took on individual shapes, with jagged peaks thickly creamed over with snow, and below us we saw the immense icy blueness of Titicaca, the highest lake in the world. From thousands of feet above, we could see the shape of rocks through the clear snow water. When we landed at La Paz, the Bolivian capital, everyone became irritable and breathless. The city is 12,000 feet up.

We got to Santiago in a windy twilight. It was very cold, though by the calendar we were used to it was full summer, and in the airport lobby a small man was moving around in a purposeful manner, loudly shouting my name every minute or so. I had always thought this a welcome reserved for royalty, but it was not a welcome at all. The small man was the U.N. driver who had been sent to collect us. Pedro was eager and friendly and, though he spoke no English, carried on a commentary in Spanish on the landmarks we were driving past. Since it was very dark, it was rather difficult to see the architectural wonders that he appeared to be pointing out, but we were grateful for his efforts nonetheless. Once at the hotel, we went to bed.

Next day, drawing the bedroom curtains, I was astonished to see, all around us, high mountains thickly smothered in snow, and on one of the lower hills a tall statue of the Virgin Mary. Santiago certainly needed a little heavenly help. The Chilean currency, the escudo, had suffered a terrifying inflation. The official rate was 150 escudos to a U.S. dollar, but a dollar on the black market fetched 1,500 escudos. Foreign money was purchased from tourists by rich professional Chileans who want to leave their country. This was due to several reasons, not least of which was the unsettled political scene.

In the gray, dull streets the presence of the military was notable. Even more noticeable were the queues. There were lengthy and patient queues everywhere, waiting in silence in the cold to buy food, oil, even cigarettes. It was not so much that these were rationed, as that they were in short supply. Some housewives would start to queue at dawn for their meat. Another racket evolved around all this. People who have to attend offices and have no time to queue hire others to queue for them and buy food from them at twice or thrice the normal price. Many of those in the queues were not making their purchases for their own consumption but for black market sales.

It was a gloomy picture, and the dull chill in the air did not help. Santiago has some fine old houses and churches, but the bulk of the buildings seemed drab and scarred. The walls along the tumbling river carrying chipped yellow lumps of ice were covered with political graffiti in red and black paint. At the same time, the city center has a fairly prosperous look, and there are a number of very expensive shops there, including a large Gucci boutique. One explanation offered for this by a local official was that visitors who changed money on the black market obtained vast numbers of escudos, with which they were able to buy very expensive items for a small amount of their own foreign currencies.

My first look at the city depressed me deeply, but Pedro was very proud of it. He pointed out once more the landmarks we had missed in the dusk of the previous day. "*Muy bueno*," he kept repeating, "*muy bueno*." He may have had a point. The avenues by the river were lined with trees, now gaunt and gray, with cobwebs of leafless branches on their heads. Pedro assured me that in summer these trees would be ablaze with flowers. Perhaps if I had come to Santiago when the sun shone and the trees were in flower, my view of it would have been completely different. As it was now, with the gray sky above, the icy wind, the occasional falls of sad rain, it seemed a city surrendered after a long war.

In the sixteenth century, when the Spaniards arrived in Chile, they found about a million Indians there. There were Araucas in the south, but the central and northern areas were occupied by Inca tribes who had come down from Peru and who were naturally warlike. The Spanish conquest of the country was exceptionally ferocious, and not only was the population killed in considerable numbers by lead and steel but by diseases such as measles, which came with the conquistadors and to which the Indians had no resistance. Each conquistador was allotted an area of land, and the Indians previously resident in the area became his slaves who worked his fields. Black labor was also imported.

The whole Indian way of life was thus changed radically and drastically. Even their diet was affected. Prior to the conquest, the Indians had hunted and fished, but their staples had been a tuber, *papas*, and a plant called *quinoa*, also a sort of root, that had high nutritive value. This latter plant, which apparently had more calories than meat, disappeared when the Spaniards came. The Indians were made to cultivate maize and corn and later sugar cane and coffee. The tribes before the conquest had some primitive forms of population control: Continence was practiced while a child was still on the breast; also—a *very* primitive method—some tribes practiced infanticide.

With the coming of the Spaniards, and the conquest, however, the Indian population fell very sharply indeed. It was not merely that a number of men had been killed in battle or that smallpox, measles, and venereal disease had affected the health of the native population. It was also that the Indians had suffered a severe cultural shock, and, as a professor of history, Rolando Mellafe, told me in Santiago, they didn't *want* to have children who would be brought up as slaves. By the seventeenth century all their racial and cultural traditions were disappearing, and the Spaniards, since they had few of their own women with them, were intermarrying with Indians and also with blacks.

In the eighteenth century conversion was started in a really big way. Spain sent in its crowlike friars, and women. In 1810 Chile became independent, and by this time, though the Spaniards and their descendants, of various mixed or unmixed bloods, were thriving, the lot of the Indians was at its nadir. At the present time Chile has some 400,000 Indians of more or less pure stock. Its total population in an area of 750,000 square kilometers is 9.8 million. Of these people, no fewer than 68 per cent live in urban areas, the remainder in the countryside. The population of Santiago is 3.8 million. In the port of Valparaiso there are 90,000 people, and in Concepción there are 500,000.

"But," said Dr. María Luisa García, a slim woman in a leather coat, who sat at her desk in Santiago meditatively tapping her teeth with a pencil, "there is no population problem in Chile in the way of overpopulation. The whole thing is tied up with health and with economic development. The government has no declared population policy, but in the three years since Allende came to power the government has been trying by strong laws to split rural areas up, trying to develop small towns there and bring industry to them. You know," added Dr. García, striking a familiar note, "the great problem is abortion. The special situation here is the abortion of girls under twenty, and a contraception failure."

"The people in Chile are Catholic, but not so Catholic." I knew what she was trying to say. As the Catholics in Gabon still carry *gris gris*, so the Catholics in most parts of Latin America still tie their Catholicism up with old beliefs left in the blood. In Colombia and Chile Christ is not as important as the Virgin Mary, and a host of lesser saints are worshipped—saints whose supposed attributes in Chile would surprise the theologians in Rome. "Divorce is still illegal here," Dr. García said. "But the Church doesn't oppose family planning." The number of abortions, she said, was equally divided between married and unmarried women. The failure of contraceptives was through side effects.

Basically, it seemed to me after talking to several concerned people in Santiago, that the main problems were to cut down on abortion and encourage contraception. Dr. Hugo Behm, another

Chilean expert, told me that it was in 1968 that people became concerned about the problems of child care and abortion. A growing consensus of local doctors, in that year, declared that family planning was necessary. The rate of maternal mortality was very high, about 30 per 1,000, and 37 per cent of these deaths were accounted for by botched abortions. Even today, in Chile as in Colombia, a third of the hospital beds are taken up by women suffering from the effects of illegal and induced abortions.

Also, for every four babies born, there is one abortion, nearly always badly done and leading the bleeding mother to a hospital bed only in some fortunate cases. Others suffer alone, and survive, or die, mourned or unmourned. "The incidence of abortion has risen steadily," said Dr. Behm, "since the 1930s. It has nothing to do with Indian tribal customs; it is purely an urban development. Most abortions take place in urban areas. The people concerned are ignorant of contraceptives or afraid of them. If they obtain them, they do not know how to use them properly, hence the side effects. Maybe if abortion were to be legalized, a great health problem could be solved, at least for these poor women."

Despite the number of deaths through abortions, the life expectancy in Chile has risen, due to improved medical services, as in every other country in the world. In the 1930s, a Chilean could expect to live to thirty-eight. He can now expect to live to sixty-three. The death rate is 8.6 per 1,000; the birth rate, 28 per 1,000. I do not have a mathematical mind, and especially not when it comes to dealing with decimals. I was grateful when Dr. Behm told me that the growth rate per annum therefore came to 1.9, which is by no means high. "The incidence of infection and of parasitical disease is declining," he said but added in a rather gloomy way, "but the incidence of cirrhosis of the liver is rising." He frowned.

The mortality drop has been caused, to a considerable extent, by the lowering of infant mortality. In 1932, for example, the infant mortality was 172 per 1,000, which meant that rather fewer than 1 in every 5 babies died. By 1972, I was informed, it had dropped to 71 per 1,000, that is to say, very roughly, that 1 baby died in every 15 born. "Prenatal and antenatal care has been extended," Dr. Behm told me. "But malnutrition is still a problem, particularly in the rural areas. It isn't as high a cause of death as in India, but it is still a very considerable problem."

Dr. Behm did not tell me this, but from another scientist I gathered that perhaps the disappearance of the root called *quinoa*, when the Spaniards came, might have become a cause of malnutrition. Colonization by European nations of non-European countries may well have led, I think, to the malnutrition in the Third World over which so many descendants of the colonists wring their hands today, not out of guilt only, but out of pity. Maybe, in some cases, the guilt should be greater than the pity. I don't know.

"Once," Dr. Behm mentioned, "respiratory and pulmonary diseases and premature births caused death to a tremendous extent in Chile. In the 1930s 60 per cent of deaths were caused by these troubles. Now the main causes of death are cancer and accidents. It's a transitional situation now, and the causes of death here, apart from exceptions like, say, abortion, are like the causes of death in a developed country. Now, despite the fact of malnutrition, the people here, though short in height, are strong; they can work. Much more human labor is used in Chile than in most countries." I believed him. I am a little under six feet and had found it difficult to lift our large and heavy cases into the car on the night of our arrival. Pedro, who is about six inches shorter than I am, had done it capably, taking the cases from me, swinging them into the trunk with no loss of breath.

"Family planning in Chile," Dr. Behm said, "is for health reasons: the prevention of so many abortions, the care of mother and child." He is a quiet, sturdy, rather tired man. He rubbed his forehead with a square medical hand, blunt and efficient in the fingers, and said, "It is no part of the program to control population. It is only part of the program to look after the people. We were always set on that. There was only one problem, which was to bring the death rate down. We have done this. The growth rate here is rising only because people are more healthy. The death rate has fallen. But the birth rate is standing still. The subtraction of one from the other causes the growth rate, but that may stabilize."

Shortly after this I went to a Santiago hospital to meet Dr. Jaime Zipper, who claims to have perfected a new kind of IUD. Dr. Zipper is stocky and willing to talk about his new weapon against unwanted births, which he produced from his desk. It looked like the antennae of a Martian in a very bad science film: willowy plastic wands, above an apparatus that, by a great stretch of the imagination, could be taken to be a face. "This," he said, waving it before my own face, which was uncertain of what precise expression to assume, "is the T-form loop invented by Dr. Howard Tatum of the Rockefeller Foundation. I bound it in copper, and it is very successful." He caressed the antennae, smiling. "I think it works."

He then departed on some necessary errand, and my companion, a friendly and very bright Chilean reporter, said, apropos of nothing in particular, "When I was young I thought of nothing except parties and girls. Girls, girls, girls," he said, losing himself momentarily in a dream. "Now," he said, having recovered from his memories, "the Latin character is not like others. We are gay," he said, "in an irresponsible way. We are not, in Chile, like other nations that have known war and have suffered." But outside the door of Dr. Zipper's office were sad women, shabby, sometimes with lined Indian faces, headed towards the contraceptives in their neat shelves, the bed for abortion complications. They weren't gay.

As for being irresponsible, I wondered, who had been irresponsible? No sharp and brilliant young blades of the society world would have plunged themselves into this patient morass of exhaustion. And the tough, short, poor husband, suffering from malnutrition if what I had been told was correct, who plunged his own misery into hers—could he be called really irresponsible, or simply tired and in need of a consolation that she, in that brief thrash of bodies, might also take from him? They shambled past the glass doors, some with infants in their arms, bellies swollen already, facts lost in incomprehension. My journalist friend followed my look and said, "Yes. It is very sad, no? Ve-ry sad."

Dr. Zipper came back. He carried another of his inventions in his hand. "In 1968," he said, "it became clear that the plastic IUD was imperfect. There are side effects and intrinsic limita-

tions. The IUD idea is to introduce a foreign body into the body
of the woman. The bleeding increases with the size of the foreign
body. But if you minimize the mass of the foreign body, the
pregnancy possibility is higher. An active material will minimize
both the bleeding and the risk. Copper can be made into wire
with which the IUD is bound. With our studies over three years
we have proved that the life of the wire within the uterus is
five years. Thirty micrograms are dissolved every day

"The expansion rate of the uterus over tests made on 100
women in a year, is 6 per cent with plastic. But with copper wire
the expansion rate is 2 per cent. The pregnancy rate is one in
twenty, but though plastic IUDs can be naturally expelled, with
copper the rate of expulsion decreases. Eighty per cent of the
women in my clinic want IUDs, though the spread of the method
is hard to explain. Motivation here is better than in other clinics,
and if the woman has side effects and bleeds we can explain to
her that it won't last forever. We follow up closely, with pap
smears for cancer, and also check the address of the woman three
times to make sure she is not coming under a false name for
fear of her in-laws and husband.

Now we only have two spacing methods possible for birth
control: one the IUD and the other one the pill. In the use of
the normal loop . . . well . . ." He was a friendly man, like a
mole out of Beatrix Potter; he waved his loop in one stubby hand
and said, "Twelve out of every 100 women bleed so much that
the loop has to be removed. Twelve more expel it through natural processes. So 76 cases out of every 100 are successful." He
had white hair that he frequently caressed, sometimes, inadver-
tently, with the hand that held the IUD. "The promotion of the
IUD has been too strong and too unrealistic. You motivate, you
explain, then insert the loop. But if the woman bleeds, it fright-
ens her. She removes the loop, and next time she conceives she
has another abortion. But still we have had success. In 1968 we
had 6,000 abortion cases at this clinic, and in 1972 it had dropped
to 3,500. He handed me his loop, in a box. "Please study it with
care," he said, as though presenting me with some holy text.

In 1959, when Dr. Zipper first started to insert the IUD, his
impression had been that most women desired four or five children. He thought the number had now fallen and that women

wanted two or perhaps three. "Most women with four or more children who come to the clinic want to be sterilized," he said. "We do 4,000 sterilizations a year now. The people who come here are mostly poor, but a phenomenon has taken place in the last three years. Young unmarried women come here for the IUD. Also teachers, lawyers, professional people, the kind of women who ask for it in the developed world. In this particular respect, Chile differs from a number of other Latin American countries." He shook hands. We left.

The presidential palace dominates the large central square of Santiago. Within the huge wooden gateway, a number of sleepy soldiers lolled around. We climbed an unevenly carpeted staircase to an anteroom that was filled with chandeliers and portraits of former presidents, most of whom looked as though they had already been dead when the painter started work. We sat down, and after a while President Salvador Allende came out of an inner office and shook hands. He started out as a doctor, and was dressed like an English country GP in a tweed coat and rather battered trousers. He had black hair and a white moustache and also a somewhat distrait air that, considering the state of the nation, was understandable. He said, first of all, that he had himself been a doctor and that he was therefore much interested in family planning as it affected the health of the people.

"The main population problem in Chile is one of health. Living conditions here in our country are bad, and we must work to improve them. The shortage of potable water supplies and the shortage of efficient waste disposal systems are our worst problems." He paused, shaking his head. "Look at Santiago itself. There are so many tens of thousands, so many children, so many problems. I speak as a teacher of medical science. The problems are so wide and so complex, and they vary from area to area. Apart from the need for a proper water supply and waste disposal, another primary problem is housing. I suggest that you should speak to the ministers concerned." He was obviously short of time and had said all that he intended to say: He had conveyed his awareness of the population problems of Chile. We shook hands formally while photographers clicked their cameras, and left.

A couple of days later I called on the then Minister of Health, Dr. Gustavo Jirón, at a formidably large modern block of offices. A youngish and handsome man, dressed far more trimly than most of the other members of Allende's Cabinet I had seen, who seemed anxious to demonstrate their socialism by the quality of their attire, Dr. Jirón was seated at a broad conference table with one of his assistants, Dr. Patricio Arrayo. They both lit cigarettes and looked expectant. I asked about the part played by family planning in mother and child health care. Dr. Jirón answered in careful but rather imperfect English. "Our growth rate, 1.9 per cent, does not present any problem," he said, "but the mother and child health care has top priority in our health service. There are many difficulties. Infant mortality in the first year is a terrible problem, with a variety of causes.

"Malnutrition is a primary cause, but there are also intestinal and pulmonary diseases that kill the children." He blew a careful plume of smoke across the desk. "As to maternal mortality, there is, first of all, the tension of pregnancy, during which gynecological care is required, and the most common diseases that might affect the pregnancy should be diagnosed. But as yet our services are poor, and large numbers of pregnancies take place without any medical control at all. We are trying to change this situation, and we've started the Programa de Extensión de Servicios Materno-Infantiles y de Bien Estar Familiar. This program is in charge of distributing contraceptives to help couples to space their children, but it has many other aspects. For example, malnutrition is not as much of a problem now as it was two or three years ago. This isn't only for health reasons. Due to the President's scheme of redistribution of salaries, the social and economic levels of the workers have risen sharply." I thought of the endless queues on the streets, fighting to obtain the bare necessities of life but said nothing.

"We have organized a scheme of milk distribution," Dr. Jirón said. "Powdered milk is distributed to schoolchildren daily. Supplies of milk are available at all workers' centers and at all hospitals and polyclinics, for children only, of course. We continue this milk supply until the child is six years old. It is a tremendously costly affair. Each year we spend $50 million on it. We import the milk powder. But we are planning new variations. We are trying to combine the milk with other products: for example, a mixture of milk and wheat to form a sort of porridge. I would say about 80 per cent of all children under six receive a free daily milk supply from the government."

Dr. Arrayo, who until this point had been sitting still and peacefully puffing cigarettes, now entered the conversation. "Our plans also provide free medical service to each worker. Of course there are two types of medical service, the government medical service and the private type. The private doctors are used only by a few who can afford it." The government service, which is free to workers, is used by most people. The definition of a worker, however, as put to me by Dr. Jirón, seemed to be a little narrow. A worker, he said, was an employed person who was paid a salary. A farmer, however hard he worked, worked only for himself and was therefore not classified as a worker and not entitled to free medicine.

"But a great difficulty here," said Dr. Jirón, "is the shortage of doctors. We have more than 6,000 doctors, about 1 to every 107 people, but this isn't a totally accurate figure. The distribution of doctors is scattered. Most prefer to work in the cities, so there are some rural areas with 1 doctor per 30,000 people. All doctors, when they obtain their degrees, have to work for the government for between three and five years, and they are sent to rural areas. We produce about 350 doctors a year." I inquired if, as from other Third World nations, there was an exodus of doctors and other professional people to more prosperous countries. Dr. Jirón and Dr. Arrayo looked at each other in a very thoughtful way.

Then Dr. Jirón said, a little reluctantly, "We estimate that about one medical doctor every day emigrates to the United States or Canada." It seemed an astonishing statistic. "If 350 doctors are produced every year," I said, "and 365 leave, it means that you are losing more doctors every year than you're able to produce." Dr. Jirón admitted that this was so. "We are trying to stop this brain drain," he said, "but the political system is a factor. Many doctors do not like the political system, and that is why they leave. So we have been trying to bring doctors from

other countries into Chile. But here there are more problems.
The local medical colleges do not want us to bring doctors from
abroad. They are preventing it."

Dr. Arrayo sighed and looked sadly at the carpet. Dr. Jirón
said, "But we badly need doctors, so the government is improving their salaries, allowing government doctors to have private
practices, and so on, as an inducement for them to stay here.
The situation is not as desperate as it may sound. We are able
now to inoculate all children, and we are planning to produce
the necessary medicines and vaccines in this country. Our hospital system is fairly widespread. Each province has a main hospital and that, in turn, operates smaller hospitals and clinics. Nearly
all of them are run by the government, but in Santiago there are
a few private clinics. Ten per cent of the national budget is used
for health. It is quite a large sum. But then it is a large problem.
We hope to have a comprehensive health service all over the
country and also to increase private practice.

"What we must do is to increase the number of graduates from
the medical colleges, the number of nurses, and increase the medical service for workers and the care of mothers and children." It
seemed a very noble mission, but Dr. Jirón did not really say
with any clarity how the government proposed to carry it out.
With the shortage of doctors and nurses, and the irregular distribution of what doctors there were, Chile faced a typical Third
World problem, and to solve it would clearly take immense
amounts of money. The growth rate is no problem at the moment, true enough, but the quality of life for the people is. Time
is needed to raise it, and time is a commodity that Chile, again
in common with other Third World countries, is pitifully short
of. Its complex internal troubles eat away, every day, what time
there is.

The migration from the villages to Santiago is of two kinds.
One is an influx of young women from the rural areas who come
to the city in search of domestic employment of some kind or
other, though a Chilean friend complained bitterly that these
days nobody can afford maidservants except foreign diplomats.
He alleged that this is because the diplomats can pay the maids
what in their own currency is a pittance, whereupon the maids,

by selling the deutschemarks, dollars, or whatever on the black market, can obtain a princely sum in escudos. The other is an influx of men who are looking for work as unskilled laborers. There is a 5 per cent unemployment rate in Santiago.

Some of the men who come arrive with their families, which indicates a desire to settle down. Others arrive by themselves. This does not necessarily mean that they will return to their villages, even if they have left wives and children there. A number of men, I am told, collect new wives in the cities. The Chilean land reforms under Allende have not had much effect on reducing the drift from the countryside. According to Marshall Wolfe, an expert from the Comisión Económica para America Latina, the rural population remains fairly stable, because the natural increase is balanced by the movement to the cities. The growth rate is higher in urban areas. It is here that things may get out of proper control.

The Chilean per capita income is said to be about $500, this being estimated at the official rate of exchange of 150 escudos to a dollar. The redistribution of salaries carried out under Allende may have improved the nutritional intake of the population to some extent by enabling them to buy more meat, milk, and so on than before, but this is cited by some observers as the reason for the long queues: More people are buying such items, and they are consequently more difficult to obtain. Chile imports beef in large quantities. It also imports wheat.

There is copper in the northern deserts beyond the snowpeaks. This forms about 65 per cent of Chilean exports. Lumber, vegetables, and fruit are also exported, as well as Chilean wine, which is of moderate quality but better, in my opinion, than other South American wines. Central Chile is widely but inefficiently cultivated, and with the move of the peasants from rural areas, the cultivation is likely to become even more inadequate. Nevertheless, even if the population of the country were to double, Chile would probably maintain it, if all its resources were employed and deployed sensibly. It will take so much time to amend the present political chaos there, however, that it's unlikely anyone will be able to do this for some while. Moreover, there are certain physical difficulties that are endemic to the geographical shape and situation of Chile.

Chile is a sliver of land on the coast. It is a fairly large sliver, but because of its shape, narrow rather than wide, it has a longer seacoast than the whole of Brazil. "The transport costs," a Brazilian sociologist told me, "are very high, and this comes from the length of the seacoast, the scarcity of proper ports, and so forth. Moreover, people in Chile tell you that there is plenty of cultivation inexpertly done, the fact is that the cultivation done is done on the only available arable land. Because of the inexpertness of the methods of cultivation, it will take time to redeem this land and make it capable of maximum yield. I will tell you one thing," he said, cocking his eyes solemnly at me over his spectacles and looking rather like a bald cockatoo, "Chile as a country has never been viable, and it will never be viable. You can blame it on Allende, on the nature of the people, on geography. Maybe you can blame it on God."

Dr. María Luisa García, the slight lady in a leather coat whom I had met earlier, spoke to me once more. She is in charge of a government program for health and population and spoke partly in English and partly, to Leela, in French. She was a good deal more optimistic about the future of Chile than other people I had spoken to. "I," she said, "and other professional people find it difficult to relate ourselves to the general demographic situation in a country. But I would say that here in Chile, we do not see so much of the kind of life that the Indians lead. We do not see the kind of utter misery that exists among the Indians in Bolivia. Maybe our conditions are not ideal, but they are much better than those that prevail in Bolivia, or in the north of Brazil. The level of education is higher here, and there is less *machismo* prevalent than in other places."

She admitted that 15 per cent of the people were illiterate. For every twelve illiterate men, there were eighteen illiterate women. Education was important for family planning, yes, she said, in the sense that not only did women who were educated tend to accept the idea of contraception more easily but the degree of education affected the type of contraceptive employed. An educated woman —that is to say, an educated rather than a literate woman—would usually take pills, because she would know how to take them. A literate but not highly educated woman would have an IUD, because she would not have to bother herself about the days and times involved with pills; her IUD would stay with her, absolving her of worry. "But," said Dr. García, "family planning in Chile is purely a matter of health, purely a matter of avoiding abortions and of caring for the mother and the child."

In point of fact the growth rate in Chile has dropped, from 2.38 in 1960 to the present 1.9. What this is due to, nobody is entirely certain. The high number of abortions may have contributed to it, but the number of abortions has fallen in recent years. The use of contraception may also have been a contributory factor. Another possibility is that the urban migration may have reduced the birth rate: first because men come without women, to a large extent, and girls without husbands; second because the fact of living in a city, with limited accommodations and no natural resources such as the family crops to fall back on for food, may have led people, for reasons of health and finance, to cut down on the dance of the beast with two backs, or at least to bridle the beast with whatever means were available and possible. Dr. García thinks the growth rate will fall further.

"We've increased education," she said. "We have got more women working outside their homes. This is especially so in rural areas where the fertility is normally higher. Now women can get contraceptives very easily. Even if the government doesn't want it," she shrugged and made question marks of her eyebrows, "the growth rate will fall." But, she added, 45 per cent of the population of Chile is dependent on the other 55 per cent, that is, 45 per cent of the population is under fifteen or over sixty. "I think it will be a problem, this interference with life expectancy," Dr. García said. "Look at Sweden, where the expectancy now is eighty-five, and terrible dependency problems are caused. But the Soviet Academy of Science has written an article predicting that by the year 3000 old people will also be able to perform some useful work. Who knows how fast technology will have changed by then?"

The government, Dr. García added, had established a minimum salary of 4,000 escudos per month. This sounded splendid; at the official rate of exchange when we were there, it came to nearly thirty dollars. At the black market rate, however, it came to three dollars. This was on a subsistence level basis. A woman,

Dr. García said, was entitled to a sum paid by the government of 300 escudos two months before the birth of the child, and 300 escudos per month are paid for each child. "They can buy more food," she said. "In the rural areas a family will subsist on vegetables, like peas, greens, and potatoes, and they get some real vegetable proteins. It is quite different, as you have seen, in the cities.

"There they have a more varied diet. They eat meat and fish if they can afford it. It is a more varied diet than people have in most Latin American countries. But now there will be a tremendous concentration of people pouring into the cities. The big question is who will grow produce in the rural areas. It is true that more women than men migrate to cities. Formerly they only came as domestic servants, but now they work in factories too. Still, there will be a problem. We have set up research groups to study the various factors involved." Dr. García made a little switch and said, "Alcoholism is a problem in Chile. We make wine here, and it is cheap. We have no problem of drugs like coca as in some South American countries where there is a predominantly Indian population. Young people have started to take marijuana." She obviously did not approve of this at all.

I came back to what the research groups studying the depopulation of the countryside had discovered. "The studies made," Dr. García said, "were on future problems with an emphasis on continued urbanization in terms of natural resources. An economist, a demographer, and a sociologist have been studying all these problems, comparing them with similar problems in Brazil, Colombia, and Venezuela." The pencil between her fingers tapped delicately on the desk. "Yes," I said, "that's fascinating, but what did they find out?" The rain toppled clumsily down over Santiago and its queues and churches and the Gucci shop and the office in which we sat. Dr. García smiled, her pencil tapped the desk, she looked out at the rain, now being shunted by the mountain winds, and she didn't answer.

"You know," a foreign expert told me, "color feeling tends to be hidden here. There was no really tremendous import of black slaves, so you don't often see a black man here. Unless you travel out of Santiago, you seldom see an Indian; there aren't many

anyway. The upper-class population is mainly Spanish—they say
they're pure Spanish, but how the hell can you tell?—and Europeans, particularly Germans. During the last war the Germans
here formed a peculiar kind of SS regiment, with the idea that
if Hitler won in Europe they would rise up in Chile, capture it,
and hand it over to the Reich. It's only in the poor people that
you see the Indian blood clearly—small brown people with broad
faces—and they are pretty well despised by the Europeans. The
Chileans of the upper class think of themselves as purely European. Anybody with fair hair and blue eyes, even if he's the son
of a German pauper who was once a corporal in the SS, is accepted as upper class. If you happen to be squat and stocky and
have an olive sort of color about your skin, why then, man, you're
lower class." And there was not much, even in a socialist state,
you could do.

Our driver, Pedro, was squat and had black hair and black
eyes and a friendly and obliging look in his eyes. He had broad
cheekbones and a low but intelligent forehead, and despite the
difficulties of language that lay like a plywood barrier between us,
we were able to communicate. He was a man of kindness and
dignity, far more so than most of the "white" Chileans we met,
and was married and had children, whose photographs he very
shyly showed us. The day before we were due to leave, I tipped
him, not excessively, and the next day, before he took us to the
airport, he handed Leela a small parcel, wrapped in Christmas
paper and bound with ribbons, that contained a small, black,
clay ashtray. It was beautiful, and real; it had obviously been
used in Pedro's house, because there were traces of ash, not quite
erased, in the bottom of it.

But it had an Indian shape to it, though I don't suppose the
Araucas or the Incas used ashtrays, and it had been made by
somebody's hands, worked by somebody's fingers, in a last, linger-
ing, nearly lost tradition. I often wondered in Latin America how
much those tiny, hazy people in the forest and on the plains,
their towns stormed and wrecked by large pink men on absurd
horses, carrying swords and torches that were far from absurd,
influenced the Chileans one saw in the hotels and restaurants,
babbling about business and the misdeeds of Allende. The kind-

ness that sometimes flashed from the dark eyes of strangers asked for directions in the street seemed Indian, not Spanish.

A few days before we left, Pedro took us for a drive around Santiago. We bumped round a dirt road behind the hotel and drove a long way, past stately residences and clubs with pools, golf courses, restaurants, each one earmarked for Germans, Jews, yachtsmen, and other denizens of this wilderness of a world, and eventually passed a field full of shattered shacks, with tin roofs, walls built of bits of packing cases, the cracks stuffed with newspaper. There were a lot of them. Pedro pointed to one and said, so far as I could understand, that his mother inhabited this place. Where he himself lived I never found out, but it was probably in some such shack.

What did a man like Pedro, a kind man, sensitive, and with ambitions, feel, I often wondered, when he picked us up outside a luxury hotel, or when, on various errands, he came into the room and saw the leather cases marked with travel tags, the bottles of Scotch standing around, the books, and the typewriter? This was surely the problem, the whole problem. I don't believe that all men are equal, except in certain animal acts that they perform—defecation, copulation, urination—and in the fallibility of their bodies. I don't believe that I am equal to William Shakespeare, or E. M. Forster, or Einstein, and Pedro certainly wasn't, but apart from Shakespeare, who seems to have led a faintly uncomfortable life, I do not see—I'm really not trying to be sentimental—why Pedro should not have led as comfortable a life, physically, as Morgan Forster, or Einstein, or even me.

You think or you don't think; you are or you aren't. Not every human person thinks, but each one is. A physical equality, at least, should be not the consequence of opportunity but a consequence of society.

At the airport at Santiago the plane was two hours late. The gloss of snow on the mountains was shivered by winds that hurled themselves down into the city. We looked at the snow on the mountains and the wind at its arduous work in the pools of water on the runway. Time passed. It was warm in the departure lounge, and there was a bar. Eventually the flight was called. We emerged into the sunlight and the glitter off the mountains. On the roof of the building from which people wave goodbye were Pedro and Sonia Becquer, a kind lady from the United Nations. They had been waiting in the cold all that time, to say good-by.

We waved all the way into the plane. It shrieked and rose. Below us I could see on a cold hill the statue of Mary with no child in her outspread, asking, horrified arms.

Index